A Text Book of

INTERIOR DECORATION

A Text Book of
INTERIOR DECORATION

Authors :

P. Parimalam

A. Andal

M. R. Premalatha

Home Science College and Research Institute
Tamil Nadu Agricultural University
Madurai - 625 104

SSPH

SATISH SERIAL PUBLISHING HOUSE

403, Express Tower, Commercial Complex, Azadpur, Delhi-110033 (India)
Phone : 011-27672469, 27672852, Fax : 91-11-27672046
E-mail :info@satishserial.com, hkjain1975@yahoo.com
Website : www.satishserial.com

Published by :

SATISH SERIAL PUBLISHING HOUSE

403, Express Tower, Commercial Complex, Azadpur, Delhi-110033 (INDIA)
Phone : 011-27672852 Fax : 91-11-27672046
E-mail : info@satishserial.com, hkjain1975@yahoo.com

Print Again : 2023

ISBN : 81-89304-50-X

Composed, Designed & Printed in India

Foreword

Interior design is a multifaceted profession in which creative and technical solutions are applied within a structure to achieve a beautiful interior environment. These solutions are functional, enhance the quality of life and culture of the occupants and are aesthetically attractive.

There is a great scope for a trained interior designer both in India and abroad. Designers are involved in planning the interior spaces of almost all buildings - offices, airport terminals, theatres, shopping malls, restaurants, hotels, schools, hospitals and residences. An interior designer should have knowledge about the materials and the products that will be used to create and furnish the space, and how texture, colour, lighting and other factors combine and interact to make a space livable.

The book covers topics related to all these aspects of interior designing and decoration. This book will cater to the needs of the student community, architects and interior designers and those in other related fields. The authors have taken meticulous care in bringing out the latest in designing with relevant visuals to enhance easy understandability. I wish to complement the authors for their commendable effort in bring out this book which meets the demand of professionals involved in interior decoration.

C. RAMASAMY
Vice Chancellor

Acknowledgement

The authors wish to place on record their indebtedness to Professor Dr. C. Ramasamy, Vice-Chancellor, Tamil Nadu Agricultural University, Coimbatore for the opportunity, encouragement and suggestions in brining out this book.

The authors acknowledge with gratitude the expert advice, suggestions and timely help offered by Dr. K. Vanangamudi, Dean (Agri), Agricultural College and Research Institute, Tamil Nadu Agricultural University, Coimbatore.

Sincere thanks are due to the Deputy Director General (Edn), Indian Council of Agricultural Research, New Delhi for providing us the financial support for publication of the text book under ICAR Development Grant Funding.

The authors wish to express their sincere thanks to Dr. K. Sheela, Former Dean, Home Science College and Research Institute, Madurai for her encouragement and moral support offered during the various stages of the literature collection and compilation. The authors also wish to express their sincere thanks to Dr. A. Andal, Dean, Home Science College and Research Institute, Madurai, and who is also one of the authors, for her encouragement and support offered during the process of bringing out this book.

The authors place on record their heartfelt thanks to their family members for their untiring cooperation and encouragement extended during every stage of accomplishing the task. They also wish to acknowledge the help received from friends and colleagues either directly or indirectly in completing this text book.

Preface

Interior decoration is a field of expanding vocational opportunities creating an increasing demand for its graduates. Its importance lies in the fact that the interior use of room is changing frequently due to the fast changing lifestyle. In the process, many schools of interior design are started and they offer diplomas and degrees. This book is planned for students of interior decoration and also for Home Science students. Though there are a number of books on this subject from the Western world, the authors felt the need for a book to suit Indian situation.

This book covers aspects such as elements and principles of design, colour, furniture and furnishing, windows and window treatments, accessories, flower arrangements and floor and wall finishes. Though interior designing and decoration is a vast area, we have confined to the basics of these concepts.

Our approach to this book has been finally eclectic and also pragmatic at the same time. We have tried to incorporate the latest information available on each area aspect of the subject. To have easy understandability, certain designs and concepts have been illustrated in a simple and lucid manner. We are sure that this book will meet the long felt needs of students of interior decoration. We hope that this book greatly facilitates the teaching / learning process of interior decoration.

However, inspite of the time and toil the authors have devoted to the completion of this work, they have no illusion about its comprehensiveness. It is hoped that some critical and alert reader may naturally discover some lapses in this arduous task and we welcome suggestions for improvement of this textbook.

Authors

List of Illustrations

Contents

CHAPTER 1

Elements of Design

1.1. Introduction

Man has a strong urge to express his creative and aesthetic instincts in visual form. Since his home is the centre of all his activities, and his way of life thoughts spring from within this protective shelter. Man from the earliest times appears to have begun at first to paint and draw simple pictures on the walls and floors of his dwellings. This has helped him to satisfy his inner creative artistic impulse – the love of the beautiful. The inherent instinct for decoration, therefore, seems to have closely bound up with the structure of the home or other objects he produced or came into contact with, in all forms and shapes. Thus man has devised many designs to decorate his living space. These designs keep on changing from time to time. However the main source of design has been nature.

All visual designs may be reduced to elements, factors or dimensions. The elements are line, direction, shape, size, texture, value and colour. These elements are the building blocks of art structure. Artists use these elements as a "visual alphabet" to produce all kinds of art forms. The art elements serve as tools in conveying fundamental ideas in painting and in sculpture and also in creating objects which meet the material needs of mankind, architectural, commercial and related arts.

1.2. Line

For many art students as well as professional artists, line seems to be one of the important elements of art. Imagine creating a painting, sculpture or design without drawing lines to divide the paper or canvas into recognizable shapes and forms. Think about how important a role line plays in the creation process. Lines can communicate an idea or express a feeling. They can appear static or active. Lines define objects. We will take a look at how artists use lines expressively.

Fig. 1.1. Look at this simple, yet powerful mask. The artisan who created this mask added an echoing pattern of lines to embellish the mask. What does this do to the visual quality of the mask? Curved lines follow the rounded contour of the cheeks and forehead. Straight lines follow the contour of the nose and mouth. The artist selected types of lines that would enhance specific areas of his mask. If the mask was left unadorned, would it appear as powerful?.

Line is the most basic element of art; a continuous mark made on a surface can vary in appearance (length, width, texture, direction, curve). Lines may be used to create harmony or contrast as the need may be. They compel our eyes to follow them. Five varieties of lines: vertical, horizontal. diagonal, curved, zigzag are mostly used to create a design. Each of these lines have specific characteristics.

1.2.1. Vertical lines

These are masculine in effect. They are severe, strong, direct, disciplined and militaristic which suggest life, activity and dignity. Vertical lines create a feeling of height. Some of the examples where vertical lines dominate are the doorways, full length draperies, wall cupboards etc.

Fig. 1.2. Use of vertical lines in interior gives an illusion of height

1.2.2. Horizontal lines

These suggest rest or repose. They have an effect to nullify the illusion caused by vertical line. Low lying table, sofa, bookshelves etc. have the horizontal lines more emphatic than other lines.

Fig. 1.3. Horizontal lines are generally used in designing of low back seats and in sofas.

1.2.3. Diagonal lines

These suggest movement and force. They disturb the discipline of vertical lines and the solidity of horizontal lines. Forward slanting lines, suggest push and backward suggest

Fig. 1.4. Diagonal lines effectively used in interiors

pull. In nature, they remind one of the windy days when trees bent towards the earth. In architecture, diagonal lines form the slant on roofs. In the home, they appear in staircase and in the diagonal plaids of fabrics or wall papers.

1.2.4. Curved lines

They give a graceful effect when applied on anything. These lines are feminine in effect and are graceful, subtle, carefree, youthful and gay. There are varied degrees of

Fig. 1.5. Use of curved lines in interiors provides an elegant appearance

curved lines. These lines are found in tie back curtains, graceful carvings of furniture, table lamps, etc. In nature, curved lines are suggestive of clouds, apple, trees, rose petals and winding streams. In architecture, curved lines are found in Taj Mahal –the gem of Indian architecture, renaissance cathedrals etc.

1.2.5. Zig zag lines

A wide variety of lines are used to create different effects. These lines are forceful and also sometimes disturbing.

1.3. Direction

A line has a direction. The four primary directions are - Horizontal (H), Vertical (V), Left oblique (L) and Right oblique (R). Adjacent lines such as V and VR or H and HL are similar or harmonious. Directions at right angles to each other such as H and V or LV and RH are complimentary, being in opposition or contrast.

1.4. Shape and form

Shape and form are also a basic element of design and is sometimes referred to as area, mass or shape. Shape is two dimensional and form is three dimensional. Three dimensional forms are solids. Two dimensional forms with length and width are flat forms. Forms are closely related with lines. A sculptor uses form three-dimensionally. However a painter or illustrator has to create the 'illusion' of Form in their works. Forms unite with lines to achieve certain effects in the overall design of a room. A long, rectangular table or sofa, helps in creating a line of unity in the room. A combination of horizontal and vertical lines produces rectangular and square forms. Combinations of vertical or horizontal and diagonal lines produce triangular forms. A predominance of square and oblong forms are best suited for masculine rooms and a predominance of oval and circular forms are best for feminine rooms. Form in furnishings should suit its function and it should be influenced by the material from which it is made.

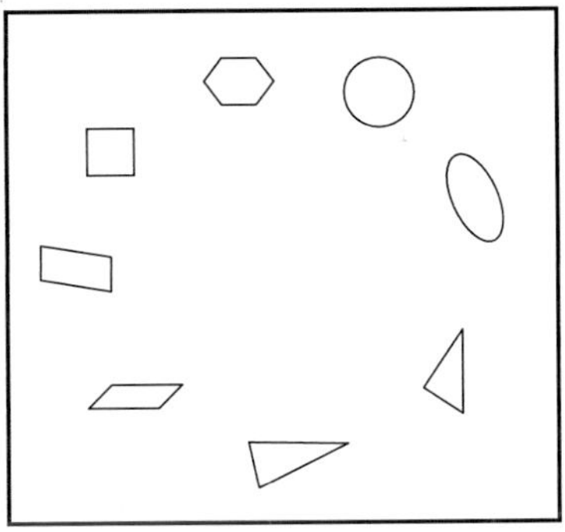

Fig. 1.6. Different shapes used in designing of art objects

Large objects regardless of shape tend to fill our field of vision and always speak for strength and power. Their importance is given by their bulk. It is divided into small, medium and big. Small and medium, medium and big will go each other in size. But small and big can be used together for the sake of contrast.

Fig. 1.7. Cushion cover designed with appliqué work uses a motif in same size and different colours

1.5. Texture

It refers to the surface quality or "feel" of an object - smooth, rough, soft, etc. Textures may be actual (felt with touch - tactile) or implied (suggested by the way an artist has created the work of art -visual). Visual texture is the illusion of a three-dimensional surface. We use our hands to feel real texture. Think about what you feel when you run your hands over the bark of a tree. Now think about what the surface of a piece of sandpaper feels like. These objects have real texture, texture you can feel as well as see. Artists strive very hard to imitate the look and feel of real texture in works of art. Perhaps an artist can't "make" the bark of a tree in his landscape "feel" like real bark, but the viewer will "see" the texture and be able to associate it with the rough feel of actual bark. Artists are masters of deception. In some works, the viewer is tempted to actually reach out and touch a work of art because it looks like it has a texture. They are surprised to feel only brushstrokes or a flat surface. The eye is tricked into seeing a "real" texture. Other artist purposefully adds a "felt" texture to the surface of their work. This allows the viewer to see actual texture and appreciate the interest texture gives to a piece of art.

Fig. 1.8. An area rug with geometric pattern indicates the texture

Textural surfaces range from smooth to rough; so a careful balance is needed in a room. The rough texture absorbs more light, and smooth surface reflects light. In small and dark rooms smoother textures should be used to reflect more light. Large rooms with many windows can show rough texture gracefully. Textures in homes may refer to wall finish, rugs, wood work, an oil painting, a ceramic urn or wood used for furniture. Some of the textures which create interest among the home planners and decorators are listed below.

Airy	Feathery	Lumpy	Shiny
Fine	Marbled	Silky	Coarse
Firm	Metallic	Smooth	Foamy
Perforated	Solid	Crackled	Polished
Spongy	Creepy	Powdery	Stiff
Crisp	Glossy	Rigid	Tough
Crystalline	Granular	Rocky	Uneven
Grooved	Rough	Velvety	Delicate
Hairy	Rubbery	Wavy	Dense
Harsh	Sandy	Waxy	Dull
Lacy	Satiny	Woody	Dusty
Leathery	Scaly	Wooly	Curly

1.6. Colour

Colour is produced when light strikes on an object and reflects back in your eyes. Of all the elements which go in to make the beautiful home, nothing stirs up enthusiasm and controversy as colour. The qualities of colour are dealt in detail in a separate chapter in this book. This element of art has three properties:

Hue -the name of a colour (e.g. - red, yellow, blue)

Intensity -the purity and strength of a colour (e.g. - bright red or dull red)

Value -the lightness or darkness of a colour

1.7. Value

Value refers to the lightness or darkness of a colour. The benefits of knowing how to manage value are very important to artists who work on two-dimensional striving to make their subjects, or the objects in their work, "look" three-dimensional. Light affects a true three-dimensional object in unique ways. Artists work hard to reproduce these light effects in their works, even though the drawing or painting is actually flat, two-dimensional. How many times have you been tempted to reach into a painting to grab an apple from the still life that looks so real you would think it was actually there. The mastery of representing or imitating true value has been one element of art that many artists devote years of study. Young artists who apprenticed with the great artists of Europe, spent months and years learning how to control value.

1.8. Design

Design is the backbone of graphic arts like metre and rhyme to a poetry. It aids one's aesthetic appreciation of subjects. Design, which is a part of art actually becomes a part of our life and personality and influences the enjoyment of everything we do, and of everything we select.

In the field of art, the term design can be interpreted broadly in a number of ways. Design may be a noun referring to a particular organization of elements for a special object of an art. Thus the structural design may be the organization of parts of an object itself – a vase, a chair etc. or it may be decorative pattern that results from the way it is organized – arrangement of bricks for the design on the wall.

A good design shows an orderly arrangement of the material used and in addition enhances the beauty and charm of the finished product.

Design may be classified as – structural and decorative design. Any object designed should have functionalism and beauty. Functionalism refers to satisfying the purpose for which the object has been designed and it should also have beauty.

1.8.1. Structural Design

Structural design is the design made by size, form, colour and texture of an object, whether it be object itself in space or a drawing of that object worked out on a paper. Structural design is more important than decorative design because it is essential to every object while decoration is the "Luxury" of the design. The criterion closely related to structural design is Functionalism.

Design is defined as any arrangement of line, form, colour, space, value and texture of an object in space, or a drawing of it on a piece of paper. It involves the proper choice of forms and colours and arranging them aesthetically and tastefully.

Requirement of a good structural design

If an object is intended for use, the requirements of its structural design are of four fold.

1. That in addition to being beautiful it be suited to its purpose.
2. That it be simple.
3. That it be well-proportioned.
4. That it be suited to the purpose for which it is made and to the processes which will be followed in making it.

In short, structural design must fulfill the quality of what we call today as "Form follows function".

1.8.2. Decorative Design

It is the surface enrichment of the structural design. Any lines, colours or materials that have been applied to a structural design for the purpose of adding a richer quality to it constitute its decorative design.

Fig. 1.9. A good structural design provides comfort and convenience to the user

Requirement of good decorative design

1. The decoration should be used in moderation.
2. The decoration should be placed at structural points, and it should strengthen the shape of an object.
3. There should be enough background space to give an effect of simplicity and dignity to a design.
4. Surface pattern should cover the surface quietly.
5. The background shapes should be carefully studied and as beautiful as the pattern placed against them.
6. The decoration should be suitable for the material and for the service it must give.

A person who makes an intelligent selection of any object needs to have a judgment of structural and decorative designs. Furniture, for example must be useful and comfortable and constructed if it is to serve its purpose well and it should depend for its beauty more upon good structural design than upon decoration. The relationship of utility and beauty has been emphasized for the permanent enjoyment of object one purchases. In general, the shape of an object should first of all confirm to its purpose and the decoration should not interfere with its functions.

Fig. 1.10. This beautifully decorated lamp shade exhibits the designers imagination

1.9. Types of decorative design

1.9.1. Naturalistic design

When the motifs are selected from nature and reproduced exactly it is called naturalistic decorative design. A realistic painting of a bouquet of flowers, leaves, naturalistic landscapes expressed in photographic paint are more or less the exact expression of something we see in nature. When these designs are used on fabrics, wall papers, the colours used are related to those found in nature. The applications of naturalistic design in interiors may be in pictures, wall papers, fabrics, paintings etc.

1.9.2. Conventional design / stylized design

When a motif from nature is adopted to suit the purpose of an object, the motif ceases to be naturalistic and it is conventionalized. Simplified flower or stenciled

Fig. 1.11. Naturalistic designs always have served as motifs for artists and designers

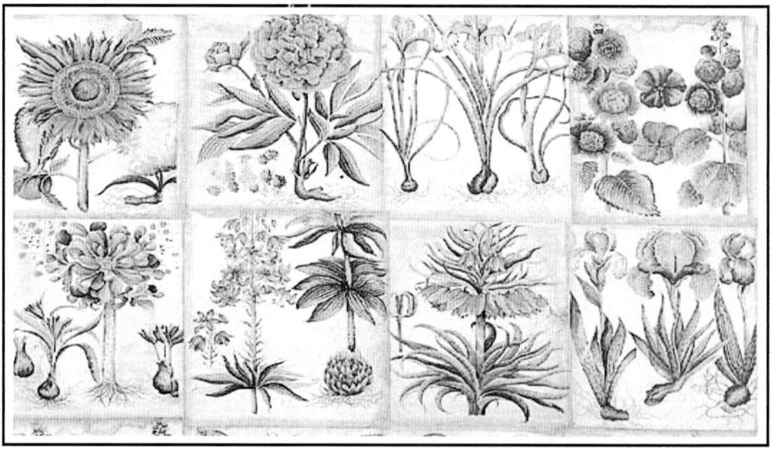

Fig. 1.12. A stylized design created by an artist finds wide range of applications in interiors

designed on wall papers, fabrics, rugs illustrates a conventionalised approach to decorative design. In this forms of leaves, flowers, animals, fruits are used but they are no longer used in recongnisable form. They are either simplified, exaggerated, rearranged or even distorted to achieve the purpose of the design. Applications of stylized designs include floor finishes, carpets, furnishing materials, wall papers, pictures etc.

1.9.3. Abstract design

Other motifs which do not have nature as their source but combination of lines, stripes etc. are classified as abstracts. Plaids, dots, stripes, checks and geometric pattern in textiles are examples of abstract design. In modern art, the application of abstract design is widely used. Abstract designs are widely used by artist to highlight some ideas or concepts. These designs may be flat design or it may express depth.

Fig. 1.13. Abstract designs are used to express ideas/views of the artists

1.9.4. Geometric design

Shapes such as square, rectangle, triangle, circle, parallelogram, cube, cylinder are often used in designing. Their beauty is derived from either elegance of proportions or their arrangement in relation to other shapes in a composition. Geometric designs are widely used in crockeries, floor coverings, wall papers, furnishing items etc.

Fig. 1.14. Geometric designs can be easily designed by any individual and can be used in furnishings

1.9.5. Historic design

Historic designs depict the events that had happened in the past and generally they are widely used to narrate the past events. It can also symbolize some happenings and find application mostly in the wall coverings which are used in places of worships - temples, mosques and churches. They are also used in furnishing materials.

Fig. 1.15. A historic design depicting a story

1.9.6. Biomorphic design

These designs have patterns of melting wax or of wavy nature. The artists may start with a basic geometric shape and gradually change it to a free, irregular one. We may round the corners or a square or dip in the sides in an irregular manner making it a less precise but more intriguing shape. These forms are referred to as biomorphic designs.

1.10. Summary

Interior decoration is a creative art. All designs can be reduced to the basic elements such as line, direction, shape, form, size, texture, colour, value etc. Design refers to arrangement of lines, forms, shapes and colours with two aims namely order and beauty. The types of designs such as structural and decorative design are used to create art.

Many types of decorations can be done using the naturalistic design, stylized design, abstract design, geometric design and biomorphic design. Thus this chapter gives the basics of art which enables the reader to have information related to these elements.

Fig. 1.16. Biomorphic design

Exercise

Student Project / Assignment

1. Develop suitable designs using any of the motifs - naturalistic, stylized or geometric for the following objects

   a. Furniture

   b. Curtain / Drapery material

   c. Wall paper

   d. Mirror

   e. Wardrobe

2. Evaluate any five of the art objects in the market and prepare a report indicating their functionality in interiors.

Choose the correct answer

1. Horizontal line suggest

   a. Illusion of height   b. Restful effect   c. Increase in space

2. A design that has an idea

   a. Abstract design   b. Conventional design   c. Stylized design

3. A design in which an idea is conceived from nature and modified by artist is

   a. Conventional   b. Naturalistic   c. Geometric

4. Illusion of height is obtained by

   a. Curved line   b. Diagonal line   c. Vertical line

5. A good structural design should be

   a. Well proportioned   b. Simple and attractive   c. Both 'a' and 'b'

6. Naturalistic design can also be termed as

   a. Realistic   b. Stylized   c. Abstract

7. Conventional design can be applied on

   a. Painting   b. Art objects   c. Any kind of material

8. Designs which depict the history of a place or event is known as

   a. Biomorphic   b. Historical   c. Geometrical

9. Primary colours according to an artist is

   a. Y, R, B   b. Y, R, G   c. B, R, G.

10. Lightness or darkness of a colour is known as

    a. Hue b. Value c. Intensity

Fill in the blanks

1. The feel of an object sensed by the touch is known as .... quality (tactile/visual).
2. A design inspired from the nature and modified by the artist is .... (conventional/naturalistic).
3. Graceful effects in interiors can be obtained by use of .... lines (diagonal/curved).
4. A study room chair should have a good .... design (structural/decorative).
5. .... and expressiveness are the primary characteristics of any objects (aesthetics/functionality).
6. There are .... elements of design (seven/eleven).
7. Use of light colours tends to create .... (illusion of space/illusion of height).
8. A design which has a definite theme is .... design (realistic/abstract).
9. .... designs can be easily created (geometric/stylized).
10. Surface enrichment of an object is known as .... design (structural/decorative).

State True or False

1. Lines tend to divide space and create movement.
2. The basic element of any design is the point.
3. All good decorative designs will also be a good structural design.

4. The latest designs in fabrics makes use of biomorphic design to a large extent.
5. Pattern and texture are the elements of art.
6. Use of suitable lighting tends to create illusions in space.
7. Indian artists use biomorphic motifs to create traditional designs.
8. Form follows function.
9. Value represents the intensity of a colour.
10. According to an artist there are four primary colours.

Match the following

1. Good decorative design	a Intermediate
2. Red orange	b Three dimensional
3. Visual appearance	c Paintings in caves
4. Form	d Brightness or dullness of colour
5. Historic designs	e Good background space
6. Intensity	f Suitability to the purpose
7. Functionalism	g Texture
8. Curved lines	h Naturalistic design
9. Floral patterns	i Arched door ways
10. Secondary colour	j Purple

Short answers

1. List the elements of design.
2. What is a value?
3. Define design.

4. What is a biomorphic design?
5. Differentiate a stylized design from naturalistic design.
6. Write a short note on application of lines in interiors.
7. What are the requirements of a good structural design?

Long answers

1. Classify design and write a note on the types of decorative design.
2. Elaborate on the applications of elements of design.
3. Explain with an illustration the qualities of a good structural design.
4. What are the characteristics of a good decorative design?

❑❑❑

CHAPTER 2

Principles of Design

2.1. *Introduction*

The principles of design refer to the organization of a work of art. Each principle interprets how artists uses the elements of art, composition and design to express their feelings and ideas. These principles of design are not formulas for creating beauty, but they do help in determining why an object is artistically good or poor. Harmony, balance, rhythm, proportion and emphasis are the major principles of design. These principles of art can be thought of as the yardsticks with which we are able to asses a design or an object. These are the basis for judging a good design. By studying these, our own work will become more sophisticated as we will begin to apply this new knowledge to our own works of art.

2.2. *Harmony*

The principles of harmony and unity are very important to works of art. Harmony in music results in pleasing tones to the ears. Harmony in art results from a combination of related elements of art creating a pleasing work for the eye. "Unity" infers that the work of art is presented as a "whole". When a work of art has "Unity", the viewer sees the work as a whole, not in separate sections. It is the fundamental requirement in any piece of work in which appearance as well as use has to be considered. Artists use certain elements of art again and again to create a sense of harmony. Using related colours, repeating lines and shapes and themes will also make the work appear harmonious. When you look at a work and sense that the piece is complete, you can appreciate the importance of unity.

The elements or components must blend to present a unified effect and each must contribute to the theme or the need of the design. One enjoys a certain amount of variation of the scale of interest, but for the sake of harmony this variation must always stop just short of absolute contradiction in any important matter.

Harmony is the art principle, which produces an impression of unity through the selection and arrangement of consistent objects.

When all the elements of design are harmonious we are aware of an integral work that is more than nearly a sum of the part. This relationship of various parts is responsible for the unity of the design and one component which does not fit into the design can destroy the totality of effect. Harmonious effect can be got by the use of line, shape, size, texture, idea and colour.

2.2.1. Harmony of line

Line and shape are the basic elements of design. Line can be static and dead, represented by a line lying in a horizontal position. A line can cause rhythmic movement and unity by vertical position. Curved lines look gracious and flexible. Diagonal lines are dynamic and create restlessness. It is possible to reduce the types of line in a composition to 3 main groups. They are

i. When a set of lines is drawn within a corner following the lines of the corner, repetition occurs.

ii. When a horizontal and vertical line come together as in a right angle or a corner, these lines are in opposition to each other and form contrast.

iii. Any line that cuts across a corner from one opposition line to another is a transitional line, but when a straight lines drawn across a corner is so sudden and sharp a contrast that it cuts off corner harshly is called contradiction.

Transitional line in its best sense is an easy, graceful line which leads from one line or shape to another, giving harmony instead of contradictions. If a curved line was drawn across the corner, the sharpness of the opposite of horizontal and vertical lines would be modified and that effect is transitional.

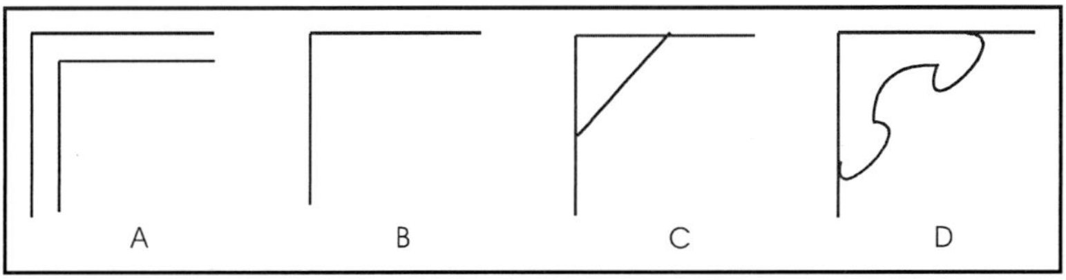

Fig. 2.1. Harmony of line

A Repetition B & C Contrast D Transitional

2.2.2. Harmony of shape

A combination of lines results in shapes. It can be obtained by grouping objects of same shape so as to create harmony. The harmonious shape that can be put into a rectangle is another rectangle of the same shape, and a circle makes a close harmony with another circle. Lines that oppose or contradict each other form contrasts in shapes and are the opposite of harmony. Some examples of these contradicting shapes are triangles and diamond shapes within squares, oblongs and circles. Transitional lines have a graceful, softening effect and have the power to bring together shapes which might in themselves be inharmonious.

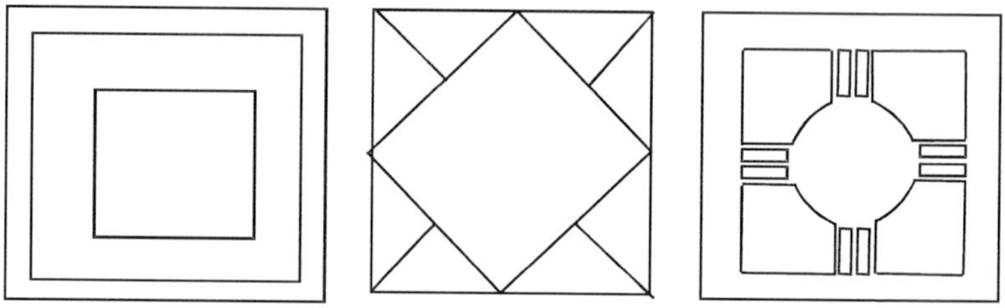

Fig. 2.2. Harmony of shape

2.2.3. Harmony of size

It will be seen that when sizes which are too different are used together they are inconsistent. Harmony of sizes refers to arrangements of furniture in the house in correct proportion or consistency in size, which is essential in interior design and in furniture design. This will be dealt in detail in proportion.

2.2.4. Harmony of texture

Textural surfaces range from smooth to rough, so a careful balance is needed in a room. The rough texture absorbs more light and smooth surface reflects light. In small and dark rooms smoothed textures should be used to reflect more light. Large room with many windows can show rough textures gracefully.

Fig. 2.3. Harmony of texture can bring in the desired mood in interiors

The interest in texture has become an important consideration to the manufacturing of objects made from the new plastics as well as from the traditional materials. Perhaps no people have developed aesthetic appreciation through the sense of touch more than the people of old China. For example, the coarse texture of oak suggests sturdiness, and one may use flax rugs, denim, homespun, crash or similar coarse textures with oak furniture; or working up to the middle group there are the finer textured fabrics, cretonnes, printed linens and some chintzes. On the other hand, the thin, fine silks, lustrous rayons, velvets, satins, taffetas and highly glazed chintzes, especially those with delicate designs, are textures which are out of harmony with oak but go well with walnut, mahogany and enameled furniture, because of the fine, satin like grain of these woods and their smooth surface. An example of poor texture combination sometimes seen in the shops is cane furniture upholstered in lustrous rayon. These textures are entirely unsuited to each other.

Fig. 2.4. A harmonious effect in interiors could be achieved by a good choice of upholstery material, carpets and window shades

2.2.5. Harmony of ideas

It is not enough that sizes, shapes, colours and textures should have something in common, but there must be harmony in the ideas presented together. There must be harmony and sincerity in the ideas suggested by the finishing of the house. Things that might appear well in a mansion would be distinctly out of place in a cottage. Rich period furniture need a formal setting and it is incongruous to try to introduce the Italian or French Renaissance into a small informal house.

2.3. *Proportion*

The word "proportion" means one part in relation to another. All people have a sense of proportion concerning themselves as compared to others. "My nose is too long for my face". "She has long legs". "His eyes are wide set." All of these comments reinforce the idea that we see and have opinions about the relationships between one thing compared to another. Artists use their sense of proportion to make statements or express a particular feeling about a subject in a work of art.

Proportion is defined as the relation between parts of the same thing or between different things of the same kind.

The principle of proportion is sometimes called the "*law of relationships*". It deals with relationship in size, shape, colour, texture and pattern. Its most prominent application in interior decoration is the relationship of spaces or organization of spaces. In other words, proportion and scale refers to the relationships of various parts of the design to one another and to the whole. The ability to recognize fine proportion is an invaluable asset to the homemaker. The house selection and arrangement of every article of home furnishing involve the power of judging proportion.

Greeks, after centuries of striving for beauty, arrived at a point where nearly everything they made exhibited good spacing. The oblong which they used as a basis of their space divisions is sometimes called the "*golden oblong*" and is a recognized standard for space relationships. *This Greek oblong measured approximately two units on the short side and three on the long*. Most people find this more beautiful than a square, because the equal sides make a square more obvious. The Greek oblong has more beauty than a very long, narrow oblong, in which the breadth and the length vary so greatly that they all seem to be related.

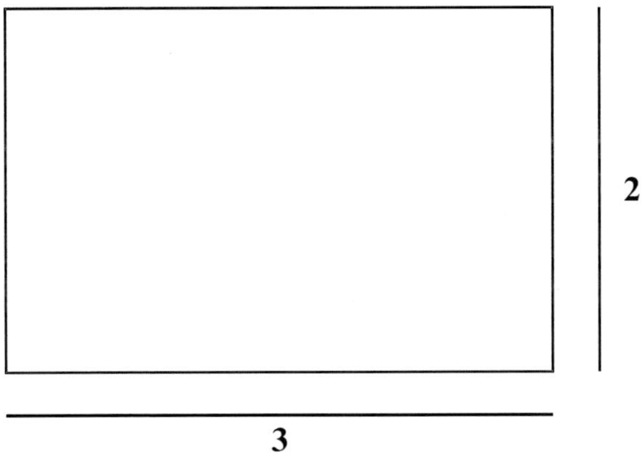

Fig. 2.5. The Greek oblong, which is a standard of good proportion. The sides are in the relation of two parts to three

The oblong, which they used as a basis of their space divisions, is sometimes called the golden oblong. Mathematicians sought the perfect proportional measurement. It became to be known as the "*Golden Mean*" or "*Golden Rectangle*". Today many artists feel that there is not necessarily one perfect means of proportion. Artists learned that distorting or exaggerating proportion could alter the effect of a work on the viewer. The same beautiful ratio is carried out in the smallest detail of a building. While the ratio of about 2:3 or 3:5 is the relationship used by the Greeks for their flat surfaces, their standard for solids is a ratio of about 5:7:11.

2.3.1. Division of space

One of the most important problems faced by the designer is that of organizing the total areas into five space relations. Pleasing proportions usually have some quality of strangeness. It may be evident that the space may be divided into two equal halves or two thirds or quarters. On the other hand, the divisions should not be so unusual that they are difficult to understand and appreciate.

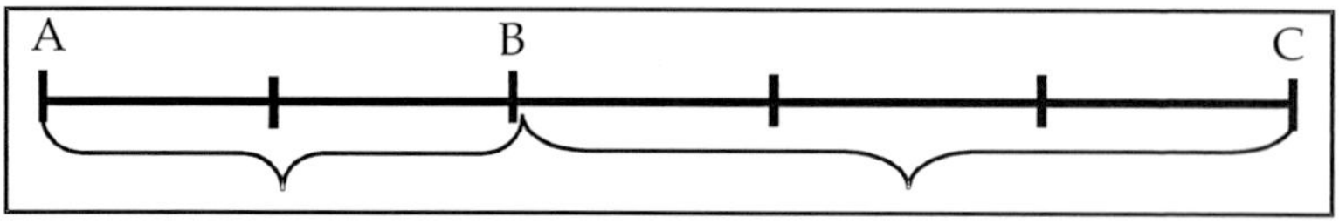

Fig. 2.6. Placing objects in the B would help in bringing interesting changes

Perhaps, no art problem occurs so often as the one in which a space has to be divided into two or more parts: example, when a garment is to be designed, when a name is to be written, division of wall space or in countless other situations where the same principle is called into play. If a particular space is to be made into two parts, the most satisfying result is achieved when the object / dividing line is placed at B which is little less than two-thirds the distance from one end or the other. However, this point should not be located mechanically, and these proportions are only approximate. Any position within the limits is potentially pleasing, and there is no necessity for a stereotyped choice.

According to Goldstein, dividing a space into more than two parts by means of lines or objects present three possibilities.

1. *All spaces may differ:* In the figure 2.7 (A) all the stripes and spaces between them are different. This gives the greatest variety obtainable. This spacing is excellent for relatively small areas or for a few spaces, but there is a possibility that the effect may appear confused

and inharmonious if a great many of these must be seen and compared at one time.

2. *All spaces are alike:* In the diagram (B) every stripe is the same width as the space. If carried too far, this kind of repetition makes monotony. If such a plan is used, it would be well to introduce sufficient variation in the colour or textures which supply the interest that is lacking in the spacing.

3. There may be variation in some of the spaces and repetition in others. In the diagram C and D a stripe is repeated at intervals alternating with a space from which it differs in width. C and D achieve harmony through the repetition of the same unit, but without sacrificing the agreeable element of variation.

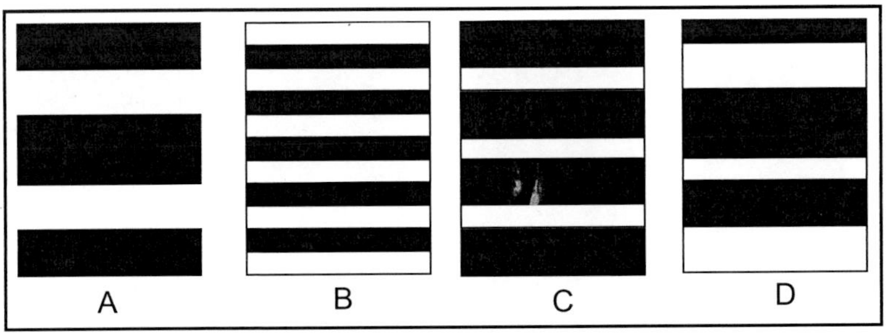

Fig. 2.7. Interesting variety of monotony is gained through spacing. (A) shows variety throughout. There is no repetition in its lines or in the spaces between them. (B) shows monotony in its repetition because all the lines and spaces are alike. In (C) the spaces differ from the lines, while (D) the spaces are different from the lines and from each other.

When arranging objects on a shelf, one should attempt to secure interest in their heights and in the spaces between them. Frequently one has to arrange groups of objects within a larger group. Perhaps it is desired to assemble several pictures so that they will harmonize with a particular wall space. If objects are to be seen as a group, the spaces between them should be smaller than the size of the objects. If this group is to be related to another near it, the space between the two should be smaller than the space occupied by either.

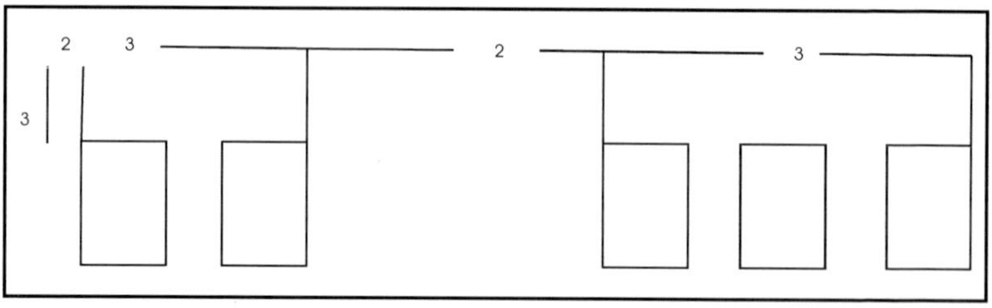

Fig 2.8. This shows a plan which may be followed in arranging objects so that they will group well. Think of each one of these blocks as a picture, a button, or a bolt of fabric – in fact, anything you wish to arrange in a group. Each group is seen as a unit because there is less space between the objects than the width of the object. The two groups are easily seen together because there is less space between them than the area of each group. Note that all spaces follow Greek proportion.

2.3.2. Creating optical illusions

To suggest a change in appearance of an area by means of proportion might involve the lengthening or broadening effects of vertical and horizontal lines. In general, we usually say that lines running in a vertical direction tend to slenderize and make an object appear taller, whereas lines running in a horizontal direction would make an object appear shorter and broader.

Figure 2.9. shows two rectangles of exactly the same size. In one horizontal line has been drawn and in the other a vertical line. Where the eye is carried across, the rectangle, it looks shorter and wider and where it is carried up and down, the effect is that apparently increasing the height and decreasing the width. It is often said that horizontal lines add width and vertical lines add height. While this is true, a second effect may be produced which must also be taken into account. Vertical lines can be so arranged that they will carry the eye from one line to the next, and while they still add height to an object they will also add width.

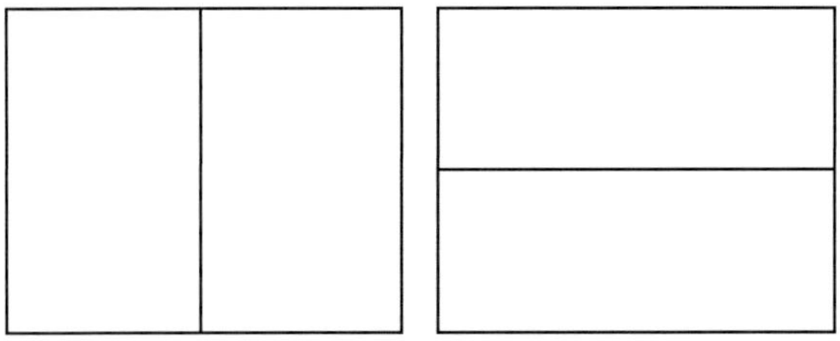

Fig. 2.9. Two oblongs of the same size showing that when the eye is carried up and down the height seems increased and the width decreased, while carrying the eye across tends to add width and decrease height

2.3.3. Scale

The third aspect of proportion is called *scale.* Scale, is the capacity to select objects and arrange them so that they look well together. Under the general heading of proportion, scale is the proper turn when considering relative sizes without regard for shapes. The design principle of scale is related to proportion. Both proportion and scale deal with the relative sizes of things. If there is a difference, proportion pertains to the relationship between the parts of a composition, while scale refers specially to the size of something, relative to some known standard or recognized constant. Scale, in this sense means,

- that the sizes of all the elements making up the structure have a consistent, pleasing relationship to the structure and to each other, and
- that the size of the structure is in good proportion to the different objects combined with it

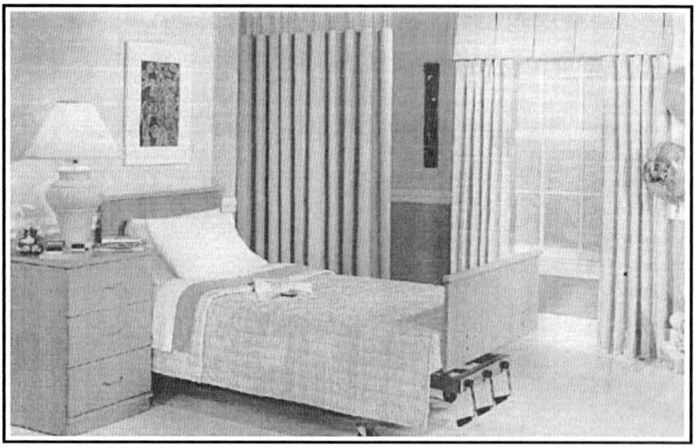

Fig. 2.10. A simple and well designed furniture, which is intermediate in scale is suited to the room of average size

A very small object will never look so small as when it is placed near a very large one. That is because the two sizes are not consistent. They accentuate each other by contrast, and are said to be out *of scale.* By following a consistent scale, it is possible to create *illusion* that cause astonishment when the actual sizes of objects are realized. An illusion to this effect can be stated from witnessing a well-staged puppet play. The puppeteer whose stage properties were in perfect scale with the puppets, could give his audience the ever-increasing impression of watching normal, people and objects. Similarly, an architect, while preparing a model of his building project, makes them according to a particular scale, gives the viewer the impression of viewing the actual building because everything in that model are in perfect scale.

2.4. *Rhythm*

Rhythm is a very important art principle. According to E.J. Beitler and B. Lockhart, 'a sense of order, a quality of gracefulness, a feeling of easy movement' - all lead to a principle of design; which we may call "rhythm".

Rhythm is related movement or the sense of leading the eye easily from one part of a design to another in an easy, flowing manner. We say that a certain design shows rhythm, but it is not in individual shapes, but in the change from one line to another, from one dimension to another, from one colour to another, one value to another. In music, it isn't that each sound is rhythmical but rather it is the change from one sound to another with the proper amount of time lapse between each note, or the change in pitch of each note that creates the rhythm. Sounds like a drum beat can become rhythmical when the beats are rapid at times and slow at others, arranged in a semblance of order or a "certain time". On the other hand, the notes might be all timed the same, but they may vary in pitch.

Rhythm is organized movement in continuity. It occurs in regular, repeated movement and also in variable transitional movement.

Regular measured rhythm is the simplest and oldest way of producing harmony and order. It is the basic element in music, dance and poetry, and it is important in architecture and interior design. Variable rhythm is found in the regular intervals of dissimilar parts. This rhythm may carry the eye along smoothly flowing lines or it may force the attention abruptly here and there in order to convey the desired emotional effect. This type of rhythm is employed to attract the eye throughout a painting until it is seen as a whole. Such rhythm unites all the articles in a group of furniture and also connects each group with adjoining group of furniture. Variable rhythm dominates in natural landscaping and in flower arrangements of the curvilinear or diagonal types.

According to Goldstein H. and Goldstein V., 'Rhythm may be defined as a form of movement. It must be recognized that not all movement in design is rhythmic'. Sometimes movement is distracting. Rhythm means an easy, connected path, along which the eye may travel in any arrangement of lines, forms or colours. In perfectly plain space, there is no movement, there is simply a restful place and the eye remains quiet at any point where it happens to fall. The moment that a pattern is placed upon that plain space and an object is placed against it, the eye will begin to travel along line suggested by the object or the pattern and at that moment, movement is created. This movement may be organized and easy and thus rhythmic, or it may be very restless, distracting and lacking in rhythm.

Rhythmic movements can be achieved through

1. Repetition of shapes.
2. Progression of sizes.
3. Continuous line movement.
4. Radiation
5. Gradation

2.4.1. Rhythm through repetition

When a shape is regularly repeated at proper intervals, a movement is created which carries the eye from one unit to the next in such a way that one is not conscious of separate units, but of a rhythmic advancement making it easy for the eye to pass along the entire length of the space. The greatest enjoyment of rhythmic sequence is to be found in nature forms.

According to Beitler, "A feeling of rhythm may be expressed by repetition of lines, colours and shapes, but in so doing we must also keep in mind the principles of proportion that deal with unity, with a certain amount of variety to add interest. Shapes that are all the same size and shape with the same spacing between each would give us an example of repetition, but it might be very monotonous. In securing rhythm through repetition, one must be careful to avoid monotony in spacing, for good proportion is a necessary accompaniment to repetition if beauty is to result. Moreover, when intervals are too far apart the movement will lack rhythm".

Fig. 2.11. Rhythm through repetition can be observed in carpets and in furniture

There are number of practical applications of this principle of rhythmic repetition. Combined with good spacing, it makes for pleasing effects. For example, stitching rows of braids or tucks on a dress, placing groups of buttons, repeating dots, circles, squares or any shape of spot in embroidery, or putting out rows of objects in a store display. It is interesting to remember that repeating a shape a number of times gives an effect of repose and sometimes a shape which is difficult to use as a single unit in design, will be successful when it is repeated at close intervals. A rhythmic effect is achieved in a costume when a succession of the tucks or braid on the skirt is repeated in the waist or a note of colour is carried from the part of an ensemble to another.

Exact repetition of a unit has a strongly integrated, clear and emphatic effect. In the space arts, exact repetition is used in wall papers, rugs, textiles, architectural ornaments and advertising photography.

2.4.2. Rhythm through progression of sizes and gradation

The second way of obtaining rhythm is through a progression of sizes. While a regular progression of sizes may be satisfying enough for scallops on lace and embroidery, one enjoys a more varied, progression when large objects are involved. Progressing sizes create a rapid movement of the eye, and they are often badly used. The example of this misuse is seen in the arrangement of pictures or other objects against a wall in a series of steps that carry the eye up toward the ceiling, and hence away from the part of the room around which one would like to have the interest centered. While a series of steps is undesirable because it leads the eye to the wrong place in the room, a group of objects in which there is no variation in height may be monotonous. In order to avoid both extremes, one should use a series of varied heights.

A gradual change in the length or thickness of lines may give variety says Beitler. But if it is so obvious that one is striving for gradation or progression, it too, become monotonous. Besides a gradual change in length or thickness of lines, one may seek variety in a change in spacing between lines or shapes, change in hue, value or intensity, change in amounts overlapped in a composition, change in texture from smooth to rough, shiny to dull.

Gradation is a sequence in which the contrasting extremes are bridged by a series of similar or harmonious steps. Gradation therefore, is a particular combination of contrast and harmony. Gradation is clearly illustrated by the value scale; in which black and white, the contrasting extremes, are connected by a continuous sequence in which the adjoining grays are similar or harmonious. All scales are various forms of gradation, because any scale consists of succession of graded steps. The word 'scale' derives from the Latin word 'Scala' which means steps, stairs or a ladder.

'Scala' in turn, is a kin to the still more ancient Sanskrit 'Skand', meaning to mount, rise or ascend. Gradation and scale are therefore, synonymous.

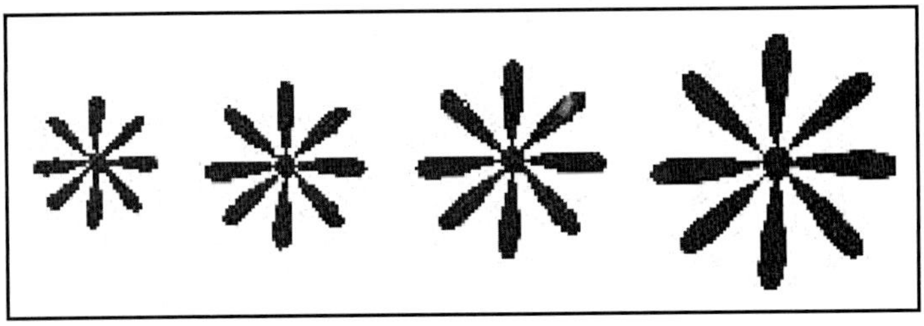

Fig. 2.12. Rhythm through progression of size

Gradation is a common and basic form of natural order. It exists in the ascending crescendo of sunrise and in the falling diminuendo of twilight slightly blending into darkness. The rising arch of a clear sky is a gradation of hue, value and chroma that progresses from the pale, warm-green horizon haze to the dark, cold blue zenith. All natural cycles, the waxing and waning moon, the ebbing and flowing tides, the slow measured passage of the season- all illustrate gradation in various forms. Gradation characterizes the flowing pattern of plant and animal life in all its successive, transitory stages from birth to death.

Fig. 2.13. Rhythm through gradation of colours

2.4.3. Rhythm through continuous line movement

Composition that shows rhythm through continued line are likely to be made up of very largely by curves say Goldstein sisters in their 'Art in everyday life'. This enlargement of the spiral of a shell brings out the beauty in the sequence of its line movement and in the rhythmical gradations of its spaces. One finds many fine examples of this type of rhythm in Greek sculpture and in Japanese prints.

In some designs it is not evident that any elements are repeated or that there is a progressive change from one part of the design to another and yet we have a sense of easy movement throughout the design. The related movement may be literally having breaks in the line but spaces that are small enough so the eye still moves over to the next section of the line in the rhythmical manner.

Fig. 2.14. Rhythm through continuous line movement

2.4.4. Rhythm through radiation

Radiation is a method of obtaining organized movement. It is a type of movement that grows out of a central point or axis. It may be observed in the diverging lines which form the pattern of snow crystals and some leaves. Radiation is used very commonly in designs for store display. According to Stepat-de-Van, 'diverging lines do not tend to carry the eye smoothly from one part of a design to another, they are sometimes useful in creating a particular effect'. Radiation is frequently employed as a basis of design in lighting fixtures, structural elements and many decorative objects. According to Beitler and Lockhart, 'Radiation means lines or parts of a design growing out of or extending from, a line or a point'. Frequently, one finds an arrangement in all the kinds of rhythmic movement used; such as room arrangements, exterior and interior of the house, embroidery and other handicrafts.

The principle of rhythmic line movement comes into frequent use in the design of a house. Perhaps it can be recognized more easily if one starts from a point where there is no apparent movement. In the outline of a square house the horizontal and vertical lines are of equal force, and so they balance each other. Use of rhythmic lines is always seen in arrangement of furniture, small articles in the showcase, curtains, draperies, etc. One place in house design where lack of rhythm is most frequently seen is the arrangement of doors and windows on the side of the house. In working out a house plan one usually begins with the arrangement of the rooms and places the doors and windows in order to secure best light and air and wall space for furniture. Unfortunately these openings do not always look well in relation to each other after the house is built.

Rhythm is found in designs of floor tiles, wall papers, furnishings like curtains etc. When the amount of desirable movement for walls and carpets has been decided, it is free to think of the design of the furnishings. In a room with quiet walls, the figured pattern of a drapery material may display a greater degree of movement than would be pleasant for walls and rugs.

Rhythm through continuous line movement can be observed in the selection and arrangement of small accessories in the showcase, arrangement of furniture pieces, use of wall hangings or wall frames on the walls, suitable

Fig. 2.15. This piece of art object clearly illustrates rhythm through radiation

design on the curtain, way of hanging curtains etc. All these should be kept or arranged in such a way that the eye travels from one corner to the other corner of that particular room easily or rhythmically. Restful effect can be gained through proper use of all these decorative things. When a person selects furniture he prefers to have it suggest stability rather than movement and so he chooses either straight lines or restrained curves. It must be remembered that too much straight line will result in monotony and this becomes noticeable if many straight line pieces are used together, opine Goldstein S. and Goldstein V.

Rhythm plays an important role in window display, and advertising. Various objects on sale are arranged beautifully in a series or in such a form that it will create interest in the minds of the people. In some displays there is such lack of organization that the eye is not drawn to any particular point.

2.5. *Emphasis*

The dictionary meaning of the word "Emphasis" is "to stress, to give importance or significance". The word itself is self-explanatory. It is true that every design needs some note of interest that catches the eye or arrests the attention. This quality may be referred to as the center of interest, point of emphasis or dominant area.

"Emphasis is the art principle by which the eye is carried first to the most important thing in any arrangement and from that point to every other detail in the order of its importance".

Whenever any object is selected or arranged with reference to its appearance, the principle emphasis is used, and the success of the result depends upon a knowledge of:

- What to emphasize.
- How to emphasize.
- How much to emphasize.
- Where to place emphasis.

2.5.1. What to emphasize

We need to be aware of the many possibilities of what to emphasize. In order that there may be an impression of clarity in any arrangement, whether it is in a room, a house design, exterior of the house, a picture, drawing room or any other room accessories, or a costume, the designer would find it helpful to form a rather definite plan. In making the plan, he would classify his material and arrange it according to what he considers the most important and what the least. In each field of decoration the most important feature may vary but the one that should have the least emphasis is likely to be the same, it is the balance against which objects are to be seen. From this observation we may draw one of the most important concepts in art: *Backgrounds should be less conspicuous than the objects to be seen against them.*

What you choose to emphasize as the focal point of an arrangement depends on the type and purpose of the room. Occasionally, some structural feature of the room will almost automatically become a center of interest-for example, a fireplace or a large window. When this is not built in center of attention, it is a simple matter to create one. Your focal point could be a particular furniture grouping or even one piece of furniture. In a bedroom for example, the bed is often the center of interest with all the other furnishings subordinate. In a living room, the point of emphasis may be the conversation or sitting area. However, a large pattern might provide a center of interest. A beautiful carpet or any rug with outstanding pattern or design may become a focal point. A sculpture or a mural, big painting might serve the same purpose. In exterior of the house main gate, landscape design, design of compound wall or front elevation of the house, lawn or garden with statue, pond etc. might be the center of attraction.

2.5.2. How to emphasize

On deciding what to emphasize the next step is how to give emphasis to that particular thing. How it should be done? How to place an emphasis? There are several ways by which one may create emphasis.

1. By the grouping or placing of objects.
2. By the use of contrast of colour.
3. By using decoration.
4. By having sufficient plain background space around objects.
5. By unusual lines, shapes or sizes.

Grouping or placing of objects

Grouping or placing of objects can be achieved by grouping objects which are similar in usage, materials, idea, size, etc. while arranging a particular area. For example, pots and pebbles have been used to create emphasis in a flower arrangement. Usage of focus light to create an emphatic effect can also be thought about in arranging a picture or any other items on the wall.

Emphasis through contrast of colour

An eye is quickly attracted by strong contrasts of light and dark or by contrasting colour. One of the most striking means of calling attention to any object is to place it against a background with which it contrasts. A striking contrasts of light and dark are to be used in any decorative scheme of a considerable size. This can be done by combining with them a large amount of intermediate values somewhere between these two extremes. The arrangement that shows equal amounts of light and dark would be as confusing as two equal centers of interest in a picture. The final effect of a good composition should be that of a dark scheme accented with lights or a light scheme made interesting through its dark notes.

Emphasis through the use of decoration

Structural as well as decorative design should be so beautiful that it will enhance the beauty of the house or any composition of art. Before decoration is considered fine structure should be outlined. When a satisfactory form is obtained, the worker may decorate it in such a way that the beauty of the structure will be enhanced.

A surface pattern that is good for a background has two main characteristics, first the design covers the surface rather closely, and second there is very little contrast between the lights and the dark. Care should be taken while selecting table linen, dress fabrics, wall papers, rugs and upholstery materials that has surface pattern. The two things of greatest importance in selecting surface patterns for backgrounds are value contrast and the amount of plain space around each figure.

By having plain background space

Psychological experiments show that an individual has the capacity to enjoy only a limited number of things at a time, and that if this amount has been exceeded he actually sees less rather than more. There are two important things about the principle of emphasis. First, an object gains importance when it is separated from the things around it and is given enough plain space for a background. Second, when objects are placed close together they are seen as a group and not as individual units.

By unusual lines, shapes or sizes

Emphasis can be gained by means of contrasts or unusual lines and colours. In interior decoration, while making use of different lines like straight or curve, unusual lines are used to create emphasis.

2.5.3. How much to emphasize

Emphasis may be regarded as a graded scale, and the greatest amount of force that can be used with good taste for each of these types will come at a different point on this imaginary scales. The best general answer to the question How much emphasis will it be well to use? is to "keep it simple".

2.5.4. Where to emphasize

If an object on a horizontal plane is to be seen from all sides it should be placed in the center of the space, with borders of equal width on all sides. This is agreeable because the object then looks the same from any direction. The placing of a cover and a bowl of flowers on the table is an application of this plan.

When a design is to be seen in a vertical position, Figure 2.16. suggests an appropriate placing for the center of interest. In this case the lowest margin is wider than any of

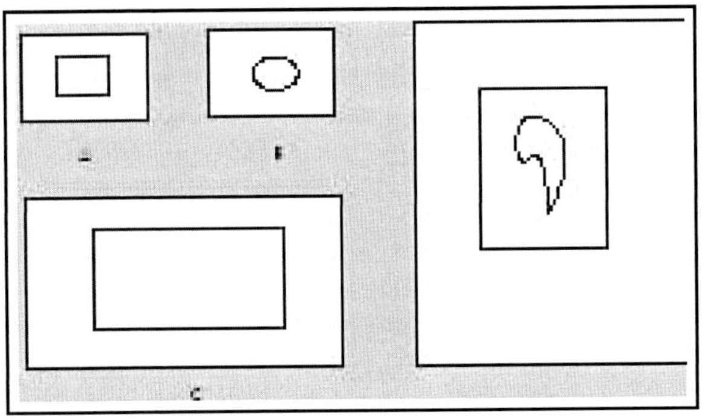

Fig. 2.16. (A, B & C) Objects on a horizontal plane and (D) object on a vertical plane

the others in order to overcome the optical illusion which makes objects in this position appear to drop in space. Application of this kind of placing are used in designing or mounting compositions, or planning a page of written or printed matter. The size of the margins would vary according to the emphasis of the object being used. A sheet of written or printed matter would follow the same relative proportions; but the margins would be smaller. When planning compositions it should be remembered that the greater the emphasis of the object the larger the plain space around it.

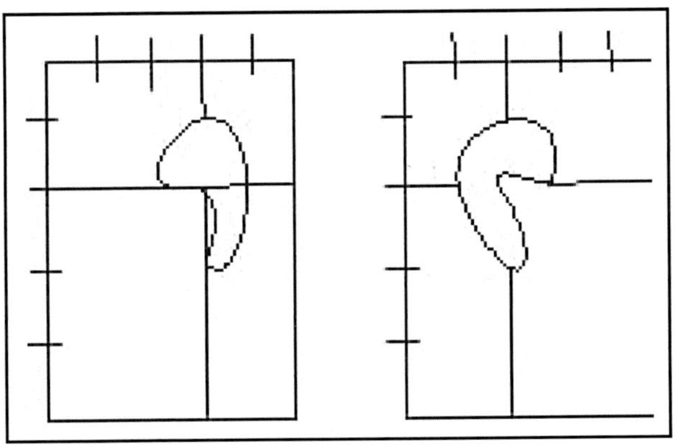

Fig. 2.17. Center of interest

Fig. 2.17. suggests positions for centers of interest where the lines of the object carry the eye off toward the right and toward the left. The position for these centers of interest were determined in the following manner; The top one side of the mount were divided into five equal parts, because the relation of two parts to three results in beautiful spacing, lines drawn through points 2 and 3 made interesting divisions in the rectangle, the points where these lines cross each other give four points on which centers of interest could be placed. The center of interest should be above or below the mechanical center and to the left or right, depending upon the direction in which the lines of the composition carry the eye. It is not necessary actually to measure these spaces, an approximate division will be as pleasing as an accurate one.

Levels of emphasis

- Emphatic
- Dominance
- Subdominance
- Subordinate

The same principle may be followed in emphasizing wall picture or in placing beautiful mirror on the wall; or only one mural on the drawing room wall.

Fig. 2.18. Emphasis in a bedroom is achieved by placing bed as the emphatic object followed by other objects in the room as dominance, subdominance and walls as subordinate

2.6. *Balance*

Balance in design is so natural that one is not even aware of it when it is present, but when it is violated there is a sense of discomfort or annoyance. We use balance as a way of controlling gravity. When we walk, our body changes our weight from foot to foot. If we were to loose our balance, what would happen? Stated briefly, balance is rest or repose. This restful effect is obtained by grouping shapes and colours around a center in such a way that there are equal attractions on each side of that center.

The youngest schoolboy can balance objects if he is told that balance works on the same principle as the seesaw. Equal weights will balance when they are the same distance from the center. If unequal, the heavier weight must be moved toward the center and the lighter weight away from it before balance is obtained.

2.6.1. Formal balance

It has been seen that the center of the space under consideration is the point around which all attractions must be adjusted. If objects are alike or are equally forceful in

Fig. 2.19. Bisymmetrical balance

appearance, they will attract the same amount of attention, and therefore should be equidistant from the center. This kind of balance is known as formal balance. Formal balance is called *bisymmetrical* balance when the objects on each side of the center are identical, and *obvious* balance when the objects are not alike but are equal in their power of attraction. Formal balance is quiet, dignified and gives a sense of precision.

2.6.2. Informal balance

If, however, objects do not attract the same amount of attention, they must be placed at different distances from the center. This second type of balance is called informal, or occult, or asymmetric balance. Informal balance is more subtle than formal balance and affords greater opportunity for variety in arrangements. Its success depends upon training the eye to recognize a restful composition.

The characteristic designs of the classifiable period are formal, whereas the art of Japan is informal. Japanese artists understood the art of occult balance, and they acquired such expertness that their painting, prints, and stencils are remarkable for their subtlety and spontaneity.

Fig. 2.20. Informal balance in interiors can create emphasis

2.6.3. Balance in exterior design

Whether one uses formal or informal balance depends largely upon the following conditions.

1. The spirit of the age in which one lives.
2. The use to which the building is to be put.
3. The type of people for whom the building is planned.
4. One's own personality.

If a line were to be drawn through the center of the house then it would be found that everything on one side is repeated on the other side, and so this house is bisymmetrical, or formally balanced.

In balancing objects one will make some interesting discoveries. For example, it will be found that an empty space is often more emphatic than a full one, just as a sudden silence in the midst of a long loud piece of music seems even more striking than the music. A large space left around an object will lend it so much more emphasis that it will be as important an attraction as a much larger one. By moving the articles forward and back, and to the right and left, one will soon discover just how much empty space a small unit needs between it and a larger one in order to secure balance. An object that is very striking or peculiar in shape or colour will have the same power of attraction as a larger one that is simple and inconspicuous; two such objects then would balance each other at equal distances from the center, even though there is a great difference in their appearance. Until a worker has trained his eye so that balance becomes instinctive, he should remember always to judge the whole display rather than to concentrate his attention on any of its parts.

In placing the furnishings of a room, the architectural openings must be taken into consideration. Very often balance is secured by having a large piece of furniture on

Fig. 2.21. Formal balance in exteriors

one wall of a room as a balance to an opening on an opposite wall. The large pieces of furniture should be placed first, with regard to balancing centers of interest in the room. The smaller movable objects would then be arranged so that they will make convenient groups as well as balanced units. After the furniture has been arranged the attention is turned to the balance within each group. A well-balanced wall will have the same amount of attraction on both sides of its center line. A well-balanced room will have approximately the same amount of attraction on opposite walls and, although the two side walls may be somewhat heavier than the end walls, there should be the feeling that the attractions are about equally distributed around the room.

Anyone interested in the meaning of designs will find that the kind of balance used in the arrangement of furniture and decorative objects helps to give an individual quality to a group. It also influences the character of the room. Bisymmetrical arrangements convey a feeling of formality, but it can be formality with the simplicity and charm of colonial days. However, if formal balance is carried to an extreme it may result in effects that are cold or stereotyped.

In working for a balanced room, one should continuously test both halves to see that one half does not present much greater attraction to the eye than the other. In arranging the room the four walls, with everything seen against them, must balance. If one side seems too heavy, it is necessary to add a brighter colour, a more striking shape, or simply more material to the weaker side, and to keep adjusting the attractions until the whole room looks restful.

2.7. *Summary*

To create a beautiful designs, certain guiding principles such as harmony, proportion, rhythm, emphasis and balance can be effectively made use. The art principles serve not only as formulas for creating a beautiful design, but also reason out why a design part / object is good or bad. Harmony - as the term implies refers to unity. Harmony can be obtained by lines, shapes, sizes, colour and texture. Proportion, otherwise called as law of relationship, deals with the division of space. Rhythm denotes easy movement of the eye on a design/ object / arrangement. Rhythm in interiors can be achieved by use of repeated designs, progression of sizes, and shape, continuous line movement, and radiation. Emphasis is an art principle that deals with centre of interest in any arrangement. The four levels of emphasis include emphatic, dominance, sub-dominance and subordinate. Emphasis in an arrangement can be created by use of plain background, contrast colours, decoration, unusual lines and shapes. The fifth principle is balance – that relates to equal attraction on both sides of the centre. Formal and informal balance can be obtained in both interiors and exteriors of the building.

Exercise

Student Project / Assignment

1. Discuss in detail about the applications of principles of design in planning the exteriors and interiors of commercial and residential spaces or complexes.
2. Analyze the recently constructed architectural buildings (hotels, residential and commercial complexes, schools) in your towns with reference to the principles of design.
3. Prepare an attractive advertisement for a consumer product taking into consideration the principles of design.

Choose the correct answer

1. The principle which refers to unity is

   a. Balance   b. Harmony   c. Proportion

2. A principle that deals with domination and subordination of objects is known as

   a. Harmony   b. Emphasis   c. Proportion

3. Greek oblong is related to

   a. Balance   b. Proportion   c. Harmony

4. A principle that deals with equilibrium is

   a. Emphasis   b. Harmony   c. Balance

5. Emphasis can be obtained by
   a. Placing of objects close to each other
   b. Using continuous line movement
   c. Arranging them in gradation

6. Occult balance is

   a. Symmetrical balance b. Radial balance c. Asymmetrical balance

7. A mirror image of one side of arrangement can be seen in

   a. Informal balance b. Asymmetrical balance c.Bisymmetrical balance

8. The first level of emphasis is

   a. Dominance b. Subdominance c. Emphatic

9. Use of decoration is one way of

   a. Emphasis b.Harmony c. Emphatic

10. Division of space for a flat surface is

    a. 2:3 b. 3:7 c. 7:9

Fill in the blanks

1. The principle of proportion can be termed as__________ (law of areas/law of relationship).
2. Golden rectangle is also referred to as (proportion/ harmony).
3. Centre of interest in any arrangement can be best indicated by ________ (harmony, emphasis).
4. ________ balance is easy to achieve in any arrangement (asymmetrical/symmetrical).
5. The most attractive place in any arrangement can be called as__________ (emphatic/dominance).
6. Rhythmic movement in interiors can be obtained by _______ (decoration/continuous line movement).
7. Harmony refers to __________ (lack of interest/ unity).

8. There are ________ levels of emphasis (four/five).
9. ___________ balance is one in which objects are not alike but have equal attraction (occult/obvious).
10. There are ________ principles of design (five/four).

State True or False

1. Interiors arranged as per the scale will always have a beautiful appearance.
2. The ratio of proportion should be observed in all aspects of interior designing.
3. Arrangement of inconsistent objects results in emphasis.
4. Creation of more than one centre of interest results in distortion of an arrangement.
5. Rhythm through repetition tends to create a monotonous effect.
6. Balance can be obtained by placing objects around a centre.
7. Harmony refers to the effect or impression of unity created in a design.
8. Informal balance provides more attraction when arranged in a skillful way.
9. A good design must satisfy all principles of design.
10. Objects placed against patterned background creates interest/attraction.

Short and long answers

1. Define the following

   a. Rhythm b. Balance c. Harmony
   d. Emphasis e. Proportion

2. List the ways of achieving rhythm in interiors.
3. Differentiate formal and informal balance.
4. What do you understand by proportion?
5. Write a short note on the following
   a. Scale b. Informal balance c. Law of relationship
6. Explain with an illustration the types of balance.
7. How will you achieve harmony in interiors?
8. Suggest ways of achieving balance in interiors.
9. Define Rhythm. How is rhythm obtained through progression of sizes?
10. What is emphasis? Explain the levels of emphasis with an example.

❑❑❑

CHAPTER

3

Colours

3.1. *Introduction*

Colour plays a profound role in our lives. Colours used in a planned controlled arrangement can produce moods, can reduce or increase tensions, cause excitement or sooth a tired person. Colours may be used to create illusions of space, luxury, warmth or coolness. Since colour is a source of pleasure to almost everyone, all homemakers should try to have beautiful colours in their homes.

Let us first understand what colour is. When light is passed through a prism, the white rays of sunlight are separated into the colours of the rainbow- violet, indigo, blue, green, yellow, orange and red. In other words white light is a combination of these colours. An object that appears to be green to our eyes is one that absorbs all the colours present in white light and reflects only the green rays. Black is seen when all the rays are absorbed completely.

There are different approaches to colour. Each of them may study colour from their own perspective. A physiologist studies colour from the way it is received by the eye. He wants to study the effect of colour on nerves. He is concerned with the way in which the eye receives the sensations of colour. Factory employers have performed fatigue experiments among workers and tried to reduce the fatigue level by change of colour. A psychologist studies colour and its effect on person's emotions. Most individuals have colour likes and dislikes and are affected emotionally by their hues. Colours that appeal to children may garnish to adults. A physicst studies wavelengths and intensities of light. He is interested in wavelength of light and their mechanical behaviour through prism and other media. A chemist studies the chemical properties of the natural and artificial colouring material used for the manufacture of dyes and paints. He knows that pigments mix differently and produce different hues from mixtures of coloured lights.

3.2. Colour Quantification system

Several artists and theorists have explored the potential of colours and studied colours, to the extent that they could compile their research into comprehensive colour theories. Fig.3.1. indicates the different colour theories. There are many colour theories that a visual artist can use, among which the more popular and widely accepted ones are those devised by Munsell, Ostwald, Chevreul, Rood and Prang. Here we would describe the Prang colour system and Munsell's colour system, because it is most widely used.

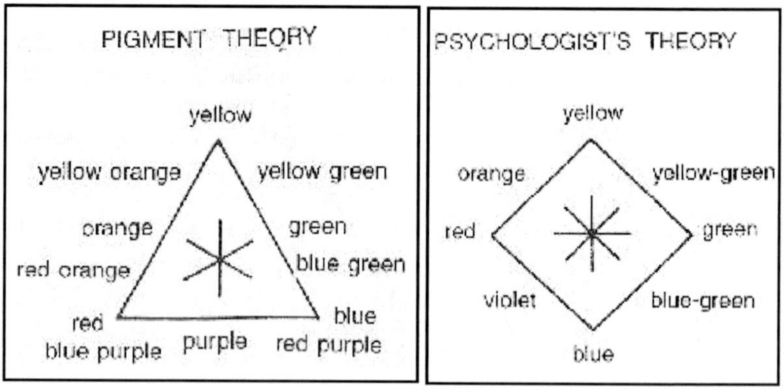

Fig. 3.1. Theories of Colours *contd...*

contd...

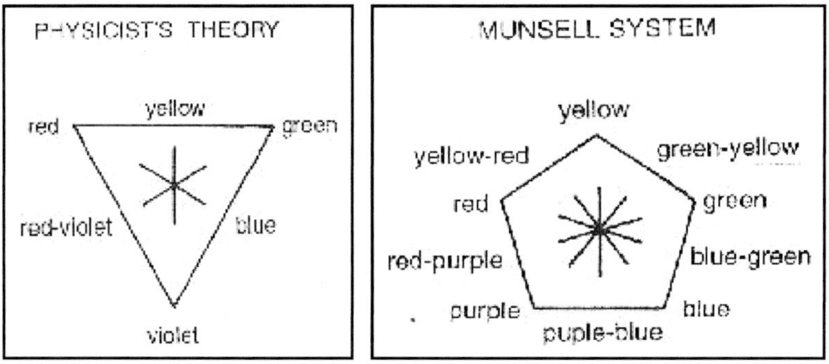

Fig. 3.1. Theories of Colours

3.3. *Prang colour system*

The Prang colour system was developed by David Breweser based on three primary colours. This is the system taught in most schools, and often a student does not even know about any other system, unless he chooses to study art or design, or related professions. It is popular because of its simplicity, and its failings can be easily overlooked for school-level art education.

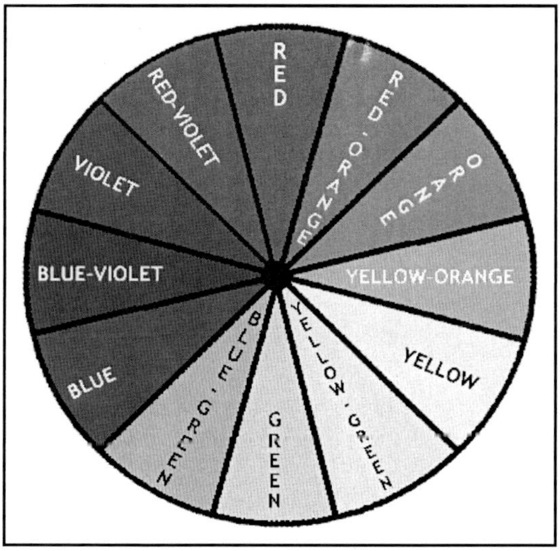

Fig. 3.2. Prang Colour System

The three dimensions of colour are as distinct as length, breadth and thickness and are referred to as hue, value and intensity. These terms are referred to synonymously as properties, qualities or dimensions of colour.

3.3.1. Hue

This represents the name of the colour. It is also referred to as warmthness or coolness of a particular colour. Hue is the attribute of a colour by which we distinguish red from green, blue from yellow, etc. Hue is the most important when viewing colour because our eye is more sensitive to hue than to brightness or saturation.

Primary colours

Colours such as red (R), yellow (Y) and blue (B) are the fundamental colours which cannot be obtained by mixing any other colours. All colours may be obtained by mixing these three fundamental hues in various proportions.

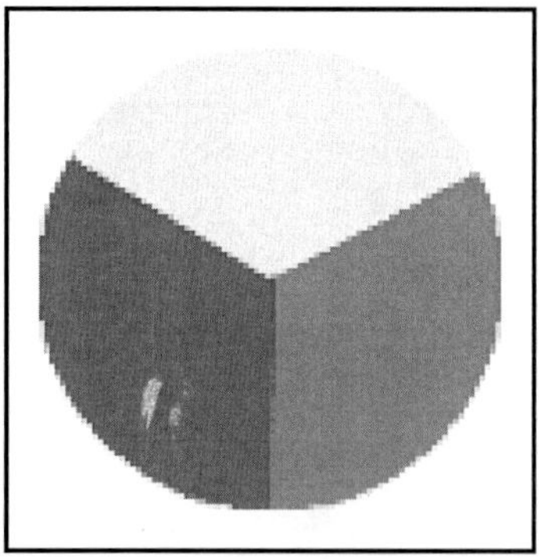

Fig. 3.3. Primary colours

Secondary / Binary colours

When two primary colours are mixed in equal amounts a different hue will result. This new hue is called a binary or secondary colour. There are three of these binary colours – purple (P) made by mixing red and blue; green (G) by mixing yellow and blue, and orange (O) from red and yellow.

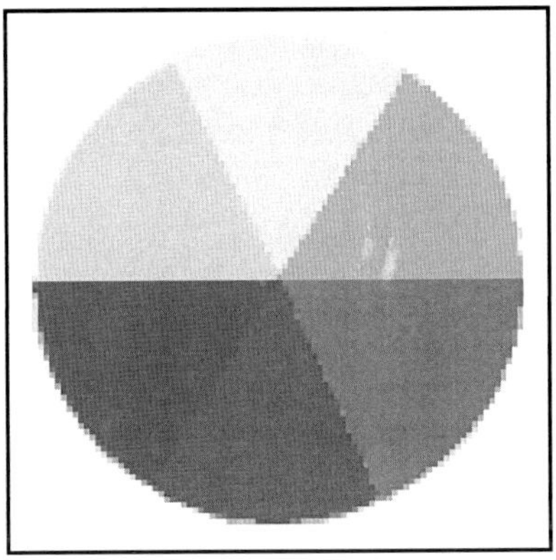

Fig. 3.4. Secondary colours

Secondary colours

Primary colours				Secondary colours
Yellow	+	Red	=	Orange
Red	+	Blue	=	Purple / Violet
Blue	+	Yellow	=	Green

Intermediate colours

It is made by mixing a primary with its adjoining secondary colour. The colours (3 primary and 3 secondary) are called as standard six colours.

Primary colours		Secondary colours		Intermediate colours
Yellow	+	Green	=	Yellow green
Red	+	Purple	=	Red purple
Green	+	Blue	=	Blue green
Red	+	Orange	=	Red orange
Blue	+	Purple	=	Blue purple
Yellow	+	Orange	=	Yellow orange

Tertiary colours

It is a combination of two binary colours. The resulting colour is a tertiary colour.

Secondary colours					Tertiary colours
Orange	+	Green	=		Tertiary yellow (T_Y)
Purple	+	Orange	=		Tertiary red (T_R)
Green	+	Purple	=		Tertiary blue (T_B)

Quaternary colours

It is obtained by mixing two tertiary colours.

Tertiary Colours	Quaternary Colours
Tertiary yellow + Tertiary red	Quarternary orange (Q_O)
Tertiary red + Tertiary blue	Quarternary purple (Q_P)
Tertiary blue + Tertiary yellow	Quaternary green (Q_G)

Warm and cool colours

Colours that lie right of the line near the blues are termed as cool colours (hues) and that on the red side are termed as warm hues. Red and orange are the warmest of all the colours and they are the most conspicuous. Blue and blue violet are the coldest hues and are quite inconspicuous. Green is between heat and cold but gets warmer nearer the yellow zone and cooler near the bluer zone.

Warmthness and coolness is the most important thing about hues. Among the warm colours there is a harmony quite as among cool colours although warm and cool colours are strangers to each other. But just as white complements black, warm colours too complement cool colours. These colours have the advancing and receding effects too. The warm advancing hues will make objects appear big or large and nearer to the observer, while the cool receding colours will appear to reduce size. Generally warm colours are cheerful and also exciting if in large proportion, while cool colours are calm, restful and depressing if used in largest proportion.

3.3.2. Value

This describes the lightness or darkness of a colour. There are many degree of light and dark ranging from black to white but Dr. Dennman W. Ross gives typical steps of value. White is the highest value, while black is the lowest in value. Midway of these two colours is the middle value.

The value of any hue may be named by comparing it with one of the steps in the value scale of neutral greys. If the colour chart is observed, we find the hues, gradually changing in value with the highest at the top, and the darkest at the bottom.

Tints and Shades

A value that is lighter than the normal colour is called a tint and the one that is darker than the normal is called a shade.

How to change values

Values are changed by adding white or water to lighten them and by adding more pigment or black to darken them.

Effect of different values

A colour may look darker against white, paler against black and against a grey with just the same value as its own, it blends and becomes very inconspicuous. Light values seem to increase the size of an object. Small rooms may be made to appear larger if they are decorated in light colours. White and other very light values reflect colour and seem to intensify the colour of the objects seen against them.

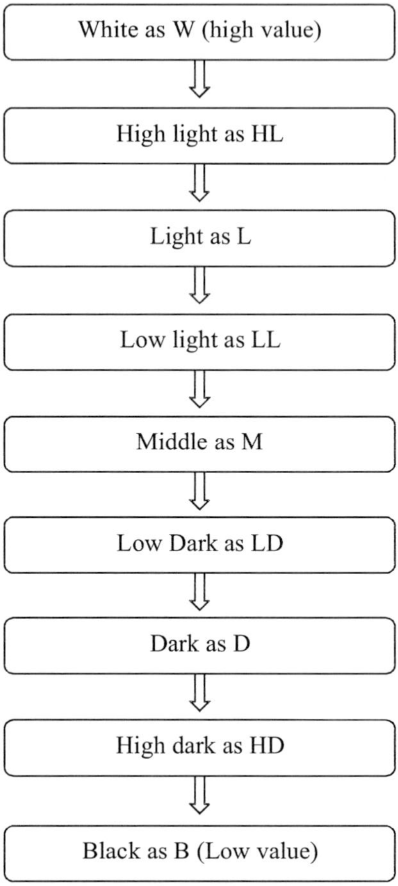

Fig. 3.5. Value scale

Black and dark values seem to decrease the size of an object. So dark colours would be a poor choice for a background of a small room, and a good choice for clothing for big made. White suggest distance and dark colours suggest foreground or nearness. Black also has the power to unify and help to bring harmony.

Close values are those which are very much alike. They are subtle and very quiet in their effect. When close values are used in larger proportions to an extreme, the result may be monotonous. In house furnishing, close values are agreeable. If many colours may add interest to a room, sometimes, entity is lost. This can be remedied by keeping the colour values similar enough to give reserve to the arrangement. Objects contrasting strongly in value with the background become silhouetted and call sharp attention to their shape. Therefore objects which are beautiful in shape may be used against a background of very different value. If an object is not beautiful or clumsy or too long, it should be placed against a background which is very near to its own value.

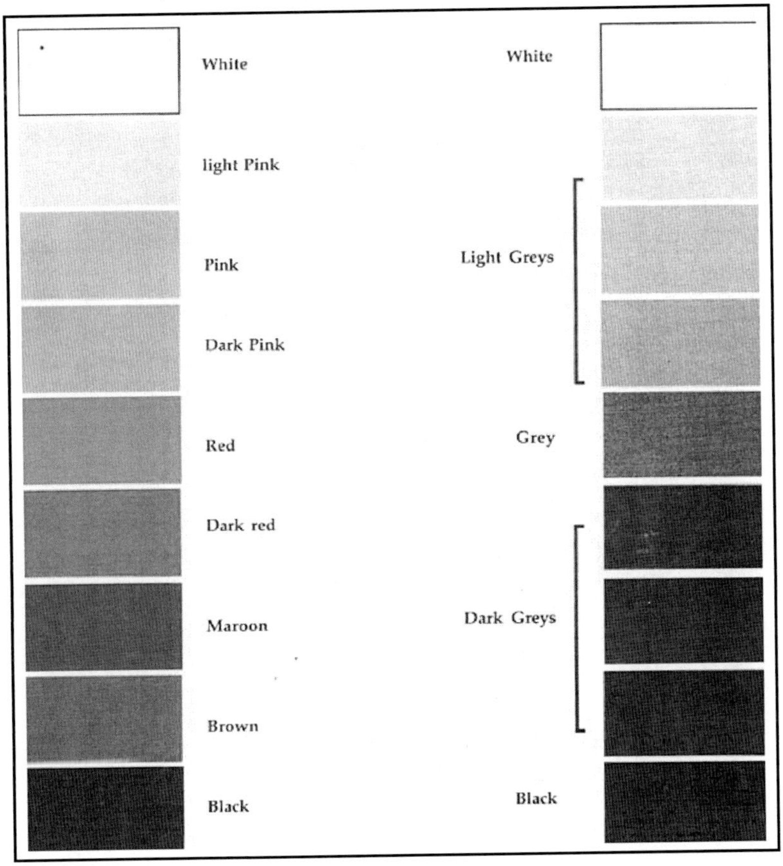

Value Scale

As close values produce quiet effects and strong contrast have opposite results, it will be found that where many objects are to be used together, they will appear more harmonized, when they are similar in value, than when they show sharp contrasts.

3.3.3. Intensity

Intensity or chroma is another dimension that tells the brightness or dullness of a colour. In other words it denotes the strength and weakness of a colour or it is the property that tells about the distance of the colour from grey or neutrality. It is the quality of the colour that makes it possible for a certain hue-say red-to whisper, to shout or to speak in a gentle manly tone.

The colours at full intensity are very striking and form brilliant and interesting effects when they are used with discretion. The colours in the lower intensities are more subtle and for general purposes they are enjoyed in large areas with the colours of full intensity used for accents.

In the colour chart those on the outer circle are said to be of full intensity as they are as bright as each colour can be. As the colours go down in brightness and toward the neutral grey, they are said to be of low intensity or chroma.

Changes in the intensity of a colour may be got through the admixture of its complement which lies opposite in the colour chart. When complementary colours are mixed they neutralize each other, when mixed in certain proportions they completely destroy each other and produce grey or neutrality.

Variations in intensity

When a colour has had enough of its complement mixed with it to make it half as bright as it can be, it is said to be one-half neutralized (½ N) or one-half intense (½ I). The inner circle of the chart shows six standard colours one-half neutralized. There are, of course, many steps in the intensity of each hue, between full spectrum of intensity and neutrality.

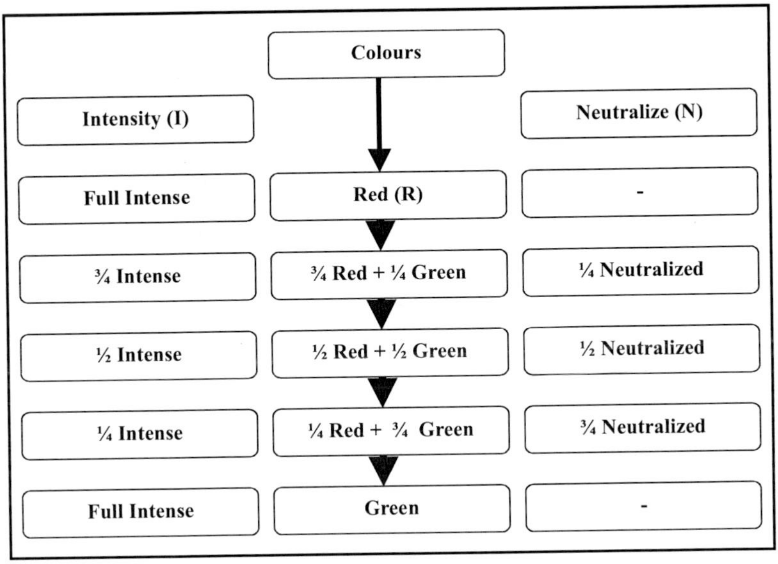

Fig. 3.6. Intensity chart

How to neutralize

1. In order to neutralize a primary, the binaries got from the other two primaries must be used.
2. To neutralize a binary, it is necessary to add the primary colour that does not enter into its composition.
3. The complement of an intermediate is a mixture of the complements of the hues of which the intermediate is composed. (eg) complement of red orange will be blue-green.

Complement of primary = binary

Complement of secondary = primary

Complement of intermediate = an intermediate

Some pairs of complementary colours are yellow and violet, green and red, blue and orange, yellow green and red violet, blue green and red orange, blue violet and yellow orange.

How to emphasize colours

- By placing a colour next to its complement. When warm and cool colours are placed side by side they intensify or emphasize each other. The complements have the greatest power to force or intensify their opposites when they are both bright. As one or both colours become dull, the tendency to force the complement is lessened.
- By combining the colour with a neutral black or white will emphasize colour more than grey.
- By repeating near it a large amount of the same hue in a lower intensity. For example a little bright green surrounded by dull green would be more emphatic.
- By repeating in some other part of a composition a small note of the same hue in a brighter intensity.

Neutral grey

It is the result of mixing any pair of complementary colours. It has a neutralizing effect and may be used instead of a complement to dull a colour.

Munsell colour system

A. H. Munsell worked out a colour system that eliminates much of the guesswork in colour study. In the Munsell plan the dimensions of colour are shown upon a sphere. (Figure 3.). The hues appear around the circumference of the sphere. Values in neutral grey are shown upon a vertical pole – the axis of the sphere. The "North Pole" is white, and the "South Pole" black. As the hues become lighter in value, they are placed higher on the spehre; as they grow darker they appear lower, toward the "South Pole". Chroma or intensity is represented by paths or arms running from no-colour, or neutral grey, out to the circumference and beyond it.

Munsell found that if the hues were in proper balance around the sphere and this were rotated upon its neutral aixs at the high rate of speed, the hues would blend together to form a neutral grey. Because of this discovery he definitely discarded the previously accepted division of the hues into three primaries - Red, Yellow, and Blue - and the three secondaries - Orange, Green, and Violet – as this gave an excess orange and yellow. He decided to use five principal hues in order to make use of the decimal system. The chosen hues were named Red, Yellow, Green, Blue and Purple. The hues intermediate between these were named Yellow-red, Green-yellow, Blue-green, Purple-blue, and Red purple. He discarded the names of Orange and Violet because they were not distinctive as colour names but were also related to name of flowers and fruits.

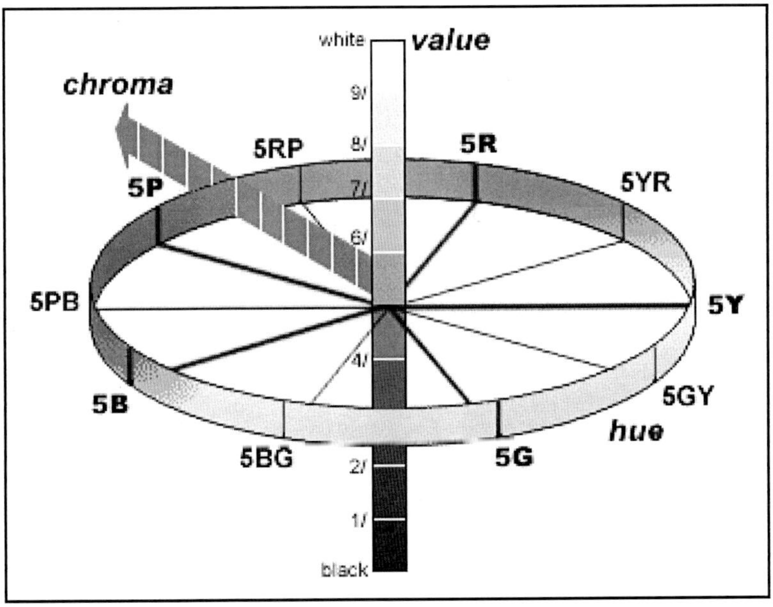

Instead of the twelve-hue circle we now see ten major hues divided into five principal hues and five intermediate hues.

Numerals are used to designate the hues lying between the principal and intermediate hues. Principal blue would be 5B; intermediate hue blue-green would be 5BG. The hues lying between 5BG and 5B are designated as follows; 6BG, 7BG, 8BG, 9BG, 10BG (the mid point between 5BG and 5B), 1B, 2B, 3B, 4B, 5B. The 6BG has a little more blue in it than 5BG; 9BG is four steps from 5BG and six steps from 5B; 10BG is just half way between B6 and B. The other steps 1B, 2B, 3B, 4B- all show more blue and less blue-green until they read 5B.

Values, in the Munsell plan, have numbers. Ten steps are charted between black and white. Absolute black (which the eye cannot see) is o, and is written $N_0/$. Absolute white is $N_{10}/$. Halfway between black and white is Middle value, or $N_5/$.

The full strength of the weakest hue-blue-green determines the circumference of the circle, and all other hues extend beyond the circumference in the degree of their relative strength. The scale of red chroma is written $R_{/1}$, $R_{/2}$, $R_{/3}$ etc. Chroma is an almost neutral grey but is recognizable as a warm grey and each succeeding step is nearer to the strongest visible red.

In the Munsell notation, colour symbols are expressed as follows $\text{Hue}\frac{\text{Value}}{\ }\text{Chroma}$. Thus, the five principle was hues as they appear in the fullest intensity now obtainable, with permanent pigment would read as follow: $R_{4/14}$, $R_{8/12}$, $G_{5/8}$, $B_{4/8}$, $P_{3/12}$. The five intermediate hues would read: YR 5/ 12, GY 7/10, $BG_{5/6}$, $PB_{3/12}$ and $RP_{4/12}$.

A study of colour theories and qualities is essential for planning colour scheme for a room. It requires great deal of knowledge and thought for achieving success in their use, because we find infinite variety of colours both in natural and artificial objects.

Psychologist's theory of colour (Visual perception of colour)

The experiments of psychologists have shown us three aspects of colour in vision; First, that colours can affect the mood of an individual; second, that colour have the property of seeming to advance or to recede; and third, that colours have very definite effects upon each others.

Colours can have such strong effects upon the emotions that colour therapy is now used with remarkable success in the treatment of nervous disorders. It will be seen that the group of cool colours, that is, those related to the blues and greens, have a quieting influence, and as the colour grows colder and darker it may become really depressing. On the other hand, the warm colours-those grouped around in red and orange hues - have a cheerful, comforting effect, which may increase to stimulation and excitement when the colours become very bright and near to red.

In pigment and in light there are three primary colours, but in vision there are four colours that are primaries, or elcments. That is to say, there are no colours which, when mixed in the eye, will produce red, yellow, green, or blue. Since the psychologist has four primaries, his colour chart is built upon the plan of a square instead of the familiar triangle of the two other systems. The secondaries are orange, yellow-green, blue-green, and purple (Violet). The colours which are complementary to each other in vision are not the same as those found to be complementary in the mixing of colour pigments or in mixing of coloured lights.

Visual perception of colour

Yellow	light and gay
Yellow green	cheerful

Green	restful and refreshing
Blue green	cool and passion
Blue	cold, subduing, dignified and meditative
Purple	subduing, depressing
Red	warm, stimulating or imitating
Orange	warm and stimulating

Symbolism of colours

White	light – purity, joy and glory
Red	fire and blood-signified charity
Blue	heaven – signifies truth
Green	nature-signifies hope of eternal life
Purple	signifies sorrow and suffering
Black	signifies death, mourning

Historical meaning of colours

Yellow or gold	**honour and royalty**
Silver or white	faith and purity
Red	bravery and courage
Blue	piety and security
Black	grief and sorrow
Green	youth and hope

After image

The visual effect of one colour upon another placed near it may be so strong that in the eye of an observer other non existent hues will appear. A new colour, called the "after-image," appears in one's eyes about half a minute after he has gazed fixedly at colour. The after-image is complement of the original hue, and it will change the appearance of that original colour, even while one is looking at it.

Physicist's theory of colour

The science of physics deals with colour as a property of light. Within the visible spectrum of light, colour is determined by wavelength; starting at the longest wavelength with red, we proceed through the spectrum of orange, yellow, green, blue and violet to arrive at the shortest visible wavelengths. When these coloured lights are present in a light source in approximately equal quantities, they combine to produce white light – light that is apparently colourless.

The physicist regards the seeing of colour as a psychological sensation which provides a more or less crude and inaccurate indication of the relative intensities of the wave-lengths to which the eye responds. Because the colour sensations which these wavelengths arouse in the eye are only approximately correct, colours in physics are denoted by their intensities and by their wavelengths rather than by colour names of all the colours. Red has therefore the longest wave length and violet the shortest. The physicist determines the quality of light radiation by spreading the wavelengths present in light into a spectrum, and measures the intensities of the different wavelengths. By this method a clear and physically complete analysis of the quality of light radiation is obtained.

It is found that, in the mixing of coloured light, all the hues, as well as white, can be secured from three primary colours, but they are not the same three colours the painter must use as primaries in pigments to secure all the hues. In coloured lights, red, green and blue-purple are the three primaries instead of the red, blue, and yellow of the painter.

The three secondary colours, as they are seen in light, are yellow, red-purple, and blue. These secondaries are produced as follows; yellow light is secured by mixing red and green lights; red-purple results from a mixture of red and blue-purple; and blue light is made by mixing green and blue-purple. The terms "magenta" and "violet" are often used in this field to indicate red-purple and blue-purple.

3.4. How to use colours (Principles of design in colour)

The successful use of colour is extremely complex and interesting. In different combinations one often finds that:

- *Colours are beautiful for the purpose for which they have been chosen.*
- *Colours are so combined as to enhance one another's beauty.*

There is no such ugly colour or beautiful colour. Colour is beautiful if it is used in the right place and in right amount. It may be a floor covering upholstery material, wall painting, decorative art pieces etc.

3.4.1. Balance in colour

Balance or the feeling of rest underlines the well known "Law of Areas". The law of areas is also known as "*The Law of Backgrounds*". This Law states 'large areas of colour should be quiet in effect, while small amounts may show strong contrast; the larger the areas quieter the colour and smaller the area the more striking the contrast may become. This contrast may be done due to a decided difference in hue, in value or in intensity'.

There should be a balance of bright and dull colours as too much as any one may appear monotonous. Too much of brightness may irritate, while too much of dullness may be depressing. For example, in a child's room, warm colour may appear cheerful but a combinations of it make it more appealing. (eg) pink curtains with red and white checkered may go together.

A small quantity of light value will balance a large amount of a dark value or small amounts of dark can balance large areas of light.

The hues which are directly opposite to each other in the chart form a natural balance because they complement each other in the eye. For example, imagine a room furnished in tan and brown with accents of bright red-orange. Unless there is a cleverly balanced distribution of light and dark areas, the room might become monotonous. Add some of opposite hue, such as blue, green or blue green, the effect will be more satisfying through the introduction of balancing colour.

Balance of colours can also be achieved by selecting the varied amounts of bright and dull colours and by arrangement of these colours.

By repeating some of the same colours, colours or values can be balanced, in various parts of an arrangement - this is also called a *'crossing'* which has the tendency to give a feeling of rest. For example, imagine a dining room in which walls and wood work are ivory white and the furniture mahogany. Let blue–green draperies hang at the windows on one side of the room. This is not complete. If some echoes of blue-green appear in the accessories against the wall or chair seats or rug, it would give a pleasant effect.

3.4.2. Proportion in colour

This principle applies to colour as much as to sizes. Colour combinations are more beautiful when the amounts are varied, than when they are equal. Usually the greek proportion holds good here but if the colours are very different in their forcefullness, they should be arranged according to the "Law of Areas", and the brighter colours used in smaller amounts.

3.4.3. Rhythm in colour

In colour, rhythm and balance through crossing or repetition implies an arrangement of colours along which the eye can move easily from one colour to another. Rhythmic colour results from the use of gradations in hue, value or intensity.

3.4.4. Emphasis in colour

It can be achieved by contrast of hue, light and dark and brightness. In any colour arrangement there should be one outstanding colour effect. Even if it is a quiet, simple or complicated scheme the main colour should cry out, perhaps in different degrees of distinctness or in various values and intensities.

The background should be quiet to make the objects effective against them. The effect of every other colour used in the arrangement should be subordinated to the main colour to prevent confusion.

3.4.5. Harmony in colour

Colour combinations with harmony or unity give more pleasure to the eyes. They give the impression that all the colours really belong together. The most beautiful colour schemes are those which give a single impression and impression of warmth with a note of coolness or of coolness with an accent of warmth. For example, in a bedroom showing an impression of warmth with a note of coolness may be given in the walls and wood work in a soft ivory tone, the drapery material with a conventional floral design with a warm coloured, background with sunny golden yellow, masses of flowers a bit of purplish blue and green give contrast and add distinction to the room, rug being greyed coppery tone, bed cover light copper, and furniture mahogany. The cool colour of the draperies may be repeated in pottery, pictures and in a painted box.

The standard colour harmonies are of two types namely, related colours and contrasting colour.

3.4.5.1. Related colour harmonies

In this colour scheme, related colours are used. Colour schemes sharing common characteristics with one dominating colour are used in these schemes. Colours are closely situated to each other on the colour wheel and have one common colour. The related colour harmony schemes can be divided into:

1. One - hue harmony or monochromatic
2. Analogous harmony
3. Accented neutral colour harmony

Monochromatic colour harmony

Monochromatic : "Mono" means one and "chroma" means colour. Here only one colour is used in different hue and intensities. The primary colour can be integrated with neutral colours such as black, white, or grey. However, it can be difficult, when using this scheme, to highlight the most important elements. For instance, red can be used with its various intensities giving vermillion, carmine, crimson etc. and various values in high key giving Alps red, peach and values in low key giving Indian red, brown, burnt sienna etc. With monochromatic schemes, the key to success is to provide enough contrast through either hue or intensity to make it interesting. This scheme helps to give a spacious feeling to an interior and provides unity for a composition and a quiet background for objects and people within. It is always a safe one to use but is more effective for dress or for a comparatively small area but in large area it may

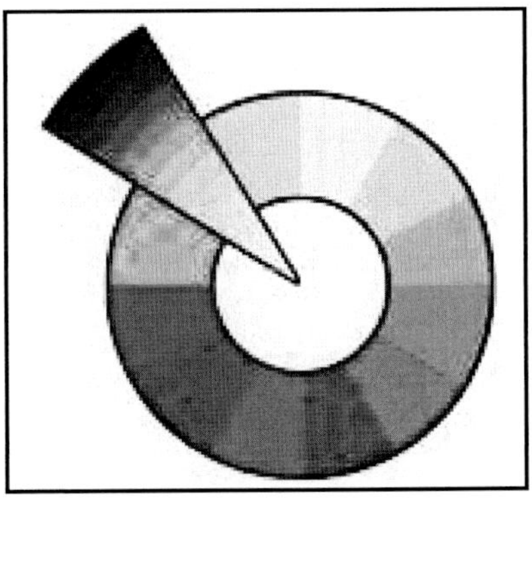

become tiresome. Additional interest may be gained if there is a contrast in the textures to the combined. The neutrals black, white and grey may be used in any harmony.

The factor to be consider in the use of this colour scheme is the way the different tints and shades are used. Normally the lightest of the colour (highest value) should cover the largest area and at the highest level, the mid value of the colour at the middle and the darkest at the lower level and so on. For example, when the tints and shades of blue are used in a bed room, it should have the following pattern;

Ceiling	White
Walls	Sky blue (light blue)
Draperies	Royal blue
Bed cover, table cover etc	Stripes / Checks / prints in royal blue, turquoise blue and greyed blue against a white background
Floor covering	Navy blue
Accent	A wall picture / flower arrangement / lamp shade in rust / orange / mustard orange colour.

Advantage	The monochromatic scheme is easy to manage, and always looks balanced and visually appealing
Disadvantage	This scheme lacks colour contrast. It is not as vibrant as the complementary scheme.
Tips	1. Use tints, shades, and tones of the key colour to enhance the scheme. 2. Try the analogous scheme; it offers more nuances while retaining the simplicity and elegance of the monochromatic scheme.

Analogous Colour harmony

In this colour scheme, colours situated next to or near each other on the chart are used. They are usually most agreeable when they are limited to those colours in between the primary. For example, green, blue green; yellow, yellow green; green, yellow green; blue green, blue etc. The colours should always be in a different value or different intensities.

Analogous colour scheme is much more interesting than a monocromatic colour scheme. It is also a simple and easy colour scheme to choose and adopt even for an inexperienced interior decorator or an untrained housewife. Unlike the previous colour scheme, adjacent colour scheme can be used in any room irrespectively of its size. It is suitable for both small and large rooms. All that is required is to choose the colours lying adjacent to each other in a colour wheel. While choosing the adjoining colours, one can choose either all warm or all cool colours, if it is desired so. For example, a combination of yellow, yellow orange, orange and red orange makes up a warm adjacent colour scheme. A combination of blue purple, blue, blue green and green provides a cool adjacent colour scheme. At the same time, combination of both warm and cool colour scheme is also possible in an adjacent colour scheme. When the adjacent colours of blue green, green, yellow green and yellow or blue purple, purple, red purple and red are combined, they provide a colour scheme which has both warm and cool

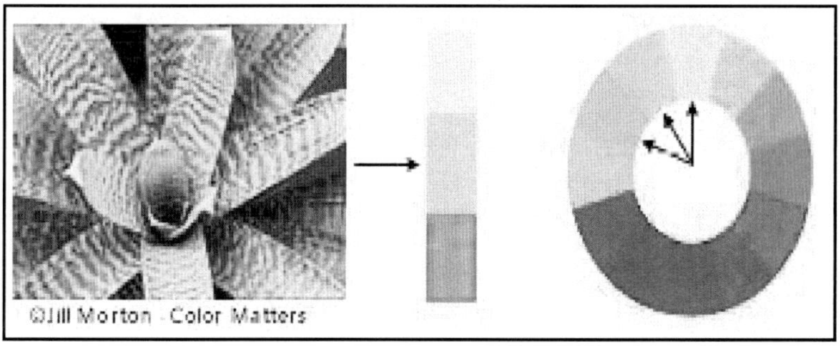

colours. Thus this colour scheme provides a wide variety of choices to an interior decorator. Whatever may be the choice of colour, the point to be kept in mind is that the lighter colours and their tints to be used at the higher level, mid values at mid level and then the darker value / shade at the lower level and so on, as was mentioned earlier.

Advantage	The analogous colour scheme is as easy to create as the monochromatic, but looks richer.
Disadvantage	The analogous colour scheme lacks colour contrast. It is not as vibrant as the complementary scheme.
Tips	1. Avoid using too many hues in the analogous scheme, because this may ruin the harmony.. 2. Avoid combining warm and cool colours in this scheme.

Accented neutral colour scheme

Neutral colours such as beige or white with an accent colour for breaking the monotony is used in this colour harmony. It has its plus points in the fact that it presents the interior with neutral background which enhances the objects and people in the interior, and for that reason is very useful for the people wishing to display their collection of objects of arts. The white neutral scheme became popular recently because of its adaptability to both traditional and contemporary style. A neutral scheme allows for easy colour accent changes by the simple process of altering pillow covers and small objects. It is clear that a colour may be neutralized or destroyed by mixing it with its complementary colour or grey, (eg) use of yellow and purple together with tints and shades.

3.5.5.2. Contrasting colour harmonies

Differences in colours are the bases of the contrasting colour schemes. Two colours which are extremely opposite, one might be cool and the other warm, are chosen for the colour schemes. The colours give great variations from highly saturated values to very dull combinations. If two contrasting colours are placed side-by-side, one appears to advance while the other seems to recede, producing a vibrant effect. Contrasting colour harmonies are of four types:

1. Complementary harmony
2. Double complementary harmony
3. Split complementary harmony
4. Triad harmony

Complementary colour harmony

When colours directly opposite to each other in the colour wheel are used they form complementary harmony. Few complementary colours are

- Yellow and Purple
- Red and Green
- Orange and Blue
- Yellow orange and Blue purple
- Red orange and Blue green
- Red purple and Yellow Green.

These colours need not be used in their pure form, they can be used in many values or intensities. A complementary colour scheme can be developed from a monochromatic colour scheme accentuated with a complementary colour or an even balance of two colours. They are most pleasing or least satisfactory depending on how they are used. For example, the reddish hues, need careful handling, as they are so much stronger than their complements. Either they or the complement should be dull, or very light or dark. Of all the contrasting colours, red and green are perhaps, most difficult to combine beautifully.

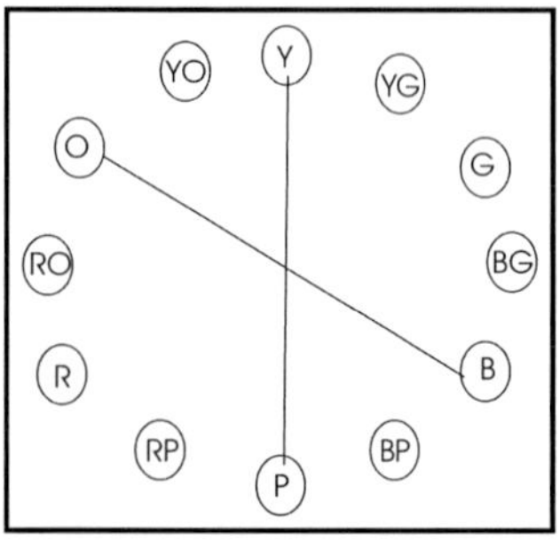

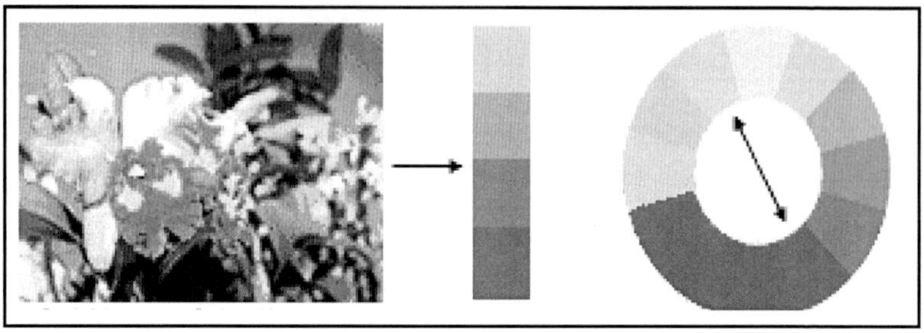

Advantage	The complementary colour scheme offers stronger contrast than any other colour scheme, and draws maximum attention.
Disadvantage	This scheme is harder to balance than monochromatic and analogous schemes, especially when desaturated warm colours are used.
Tips	1. For best results, place cool colours against warm ones, for example, blue versus orange. 2. If you use a warm colour (red or yellow) as an accent, you can desaturate the opposite cool colours to put more emphasis on the warm colours. 3. Avoid using desaturated warm colours (e.g. browns or dull yellows). 4. Try the split complementary scheme; it is similar to the complementary scheme but offers more variety

Double complementary colour harmony

This results when two directly adjacent colours and their complements are used together. Examples are

Purple and red purple with yellow and yellow green

Red and red orange with green and blue green

In this there should be one outstanding hue for larger areas and it is dullest of all. The next may be little brighter but still dull, the third colour used in only a small amount must be half neutralized and the fourth one for the smallest accents may be in or near its brightest intensity.

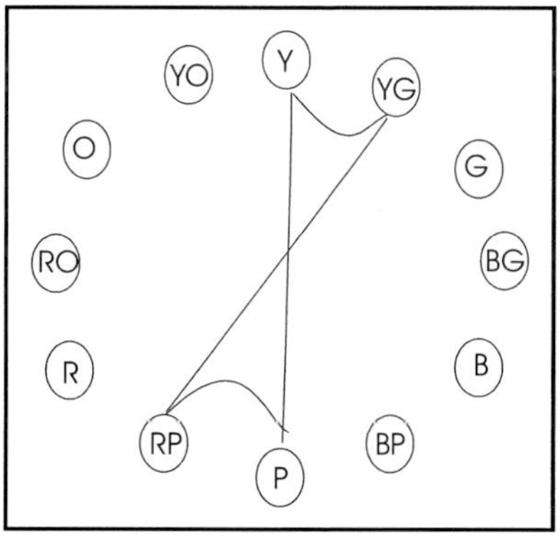

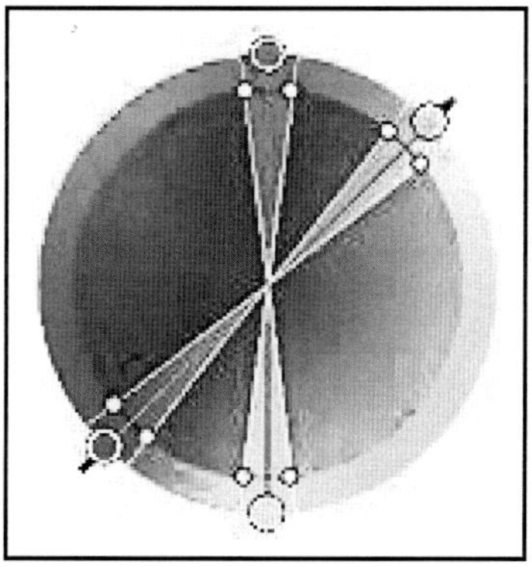

Advantage	This scheme offers more colour variety than any other scheme
Disadvantage	This scheme is the hardest scheme to balance
Tips	1. If the scheme looks unbalanced, try to subdue one or more colours. 2. Avoid using pure colours in equal amounts

Split complementary colour harmony

This harmony involves the use of three colours. Combinations of a primary or an intermediate colour with the colours on either side of its complement form split complementary harmonies. Examples are

Yellow with red purple and blue purple
Yellow orange with blue and purple

As the term implies, one splits or divides the complement of a hue into its component parts and omits the complement itself. Thus the yellow, red purple and blue purple combination is secured by splitting the complement of yellow, which is purple into red purple and blue purple. These are the colours on either side of purple which, when mixed form purple. Since a primary is an element, it does not have component parts. Either side of it do not enter into its composition.

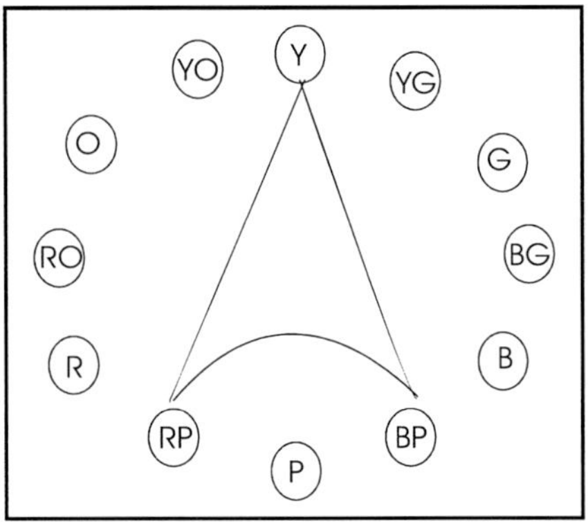

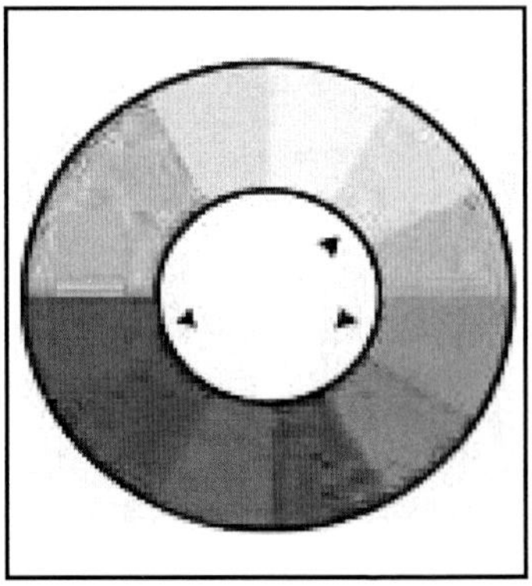

Therefore, one cannot start to plan a split complementary harmony with a binary colour, because its complement is a primary, and it is impossible to split a primary because there is only one colour in its composition. The colours sometimes mistakenly combined as split complementary harmonies are green, red orange, and red purple; purple, yellow orange and yellow green; orange, blue purple and blue green; in all of these combinations the effect is likely to give an impression of discord rather than harmony. A true split complementary scheme is a harmony of similar colour with a note of a contrasting colour. The amounts of the different values and intensities should be adjusted as in any other contrasting harmony.

Advantage	The split complementary scheme offers more nuances than the complementary scheme while retaining strong visual contrast.
Disadvantage	The split complementary scheme is harder to balance than monochromatic and analogous colour schemes.
Tips	1. Use a single warm colour against a range of cool colours to put an emphasis on the warm colour (red versus blues and blue-greens, or orange versus blues and blue-violets). 2. Avoid using desaturated warm colours (e.g. browns or dull yellows), because this may ruin the scheme.

Triad colour harmony

On the prang colour chart, equilateral triangles create four triads. These are: Primary triad, made of the three primary colours, red, blue and yellow; the secondary or binary triad- green, orange and purple and the two intermediate triads – yellow orange, blue green and red purple ; yellow green, blue purple and red orange. While triads are the richest of all the harmonies if they are well used, they are the ones, which need the most careful treatment.

Advantage	The triadic colour scheme offers high contrast while retaining harmony.
Disadvantage	The triadic colour scheme is not as contrasting as the complementary scheme
Tips	1. Choose one colour to be used in larger amounts than others. 2. If the colours look gaudy, try to subdue them.

Factors affecting the use of colour scheme for rooms

Since colour is a source of universal pleasure, every one of us should have beautiful colours in our homes and learn to enjoy them. It is necessary for all of us to have some knowledge of colour so that they are used to one's delight and to fortify them against dullness elsewhere.

While planning colour schemes for the rooms, it is necessary to consider them for the entire home as one unit to obtain an unifying effect. A colour plan for the entire home in which each room is independent of the others, has less unity than a related plan. It is wise to start planning from the living / drawing room first, then dining room and finally the bedrooms. Once these areas are planned, then the plan for the passages, corridors can be carried out. The colour schemes for these areas can be different from the rooms to produce variety.

Style and purpose of the room

The foremost factor in the selection of a colour scheme for any room is the room itself its size, shape and exposure. Analysis of a room is therefore, the first factor in making a colour scheme for it. While considereing the size, small rooms gain spaciousness and appear larger with light, cool and receding coours in the background and on the furniture too. On the other hand, the warm advancing colours reduce the size of the room and make a room to seem smaller and cramped. In large rooms, warm/advancing colours are more appropriate than a cool / receding colour scheme. A receding colour will not make the large room to appear larger, but may also give a feeling of being empty and under-furnished. A well-planned colour scheme can help to alter visually the size of the room, if it is desired so. Similarly, a long narrow room can be made to appear wider and of better proportion if the end walls are decorated with warm advancing colours and side walls with cool receding colours.

The room's shape can also be changed in similar ways – a rectangular room can be made to appear like a square one and a square to be a rectangular one. This can be obtained by alternating receding and advancing colours on the four walls of the room, thereby changing the shape of the room. Thus the room can be made to appear in better proportion.

Another aspect of the room that affect the choice of colour is the amount of sunlight that it receives. Rooms with too much light need dark subdued colours. The rooms facing west, south and south-west receive the maximum sulight and therefore, become very warm, especially in summers. In contrast to these rooms, rooms in the eastern and northern direction receive comparatively lesser sunlight. These rooms are cool, specially in winters. To counter this effect, cool colours in former rooms and warmer colour in the latter rooms should be opted.

The style adopted in a room determines the use of colour. Certain styles, such as traditional or conventional are best expressed by the authentic colours of the natural dyes that were used with the original furniture.

Fashion

Fashion is an important aspect of civilized living. It influences or in a way, limits all the things we use or enjoy. It is, therefore, not surprising that colour schemes are also affected by fashions. One has to keep up with colour fashion by visiting shops or reading magazines. In fact, it can be said that a person will find in the market, only those colours which are in fashion, though she might prefer other colours for her house. Thus, fashion in a way limits the choice of colour only to the available ones in the market. Thus, availability of colour according to fashions is another factor deterring the colour scheme of interiors.

Individual preferences

Personality of people also influences their colour choice. Women who are too feminine may choose soft cool colours like pinks, peaches, while a masculine room may be in wine red, brown or navy blue. A living room which is an activity - centered room, would require a colour scheme with electric blue, lemon and white with a small quantity of bright red. An elegant room, similarly, can be done with the neutral shades like grey, brown, beige, etc. along with the toned or greyed blues or pinks. Thus the colour scheme also exhibits the individual preferences of a person.

3.6. *Colour schemes for different rooms*

One of the most fascinating tools to work with, in decorating your home is the element of colour. We may have to choose from thousands of colours and the possible combinations are infinite. Several factors will guide our selection of colours and some of them are discussed below.

Living room

A living room should express cheer and hospitality along with restfulness and relaxation. Therefore, its colour

A living room with a good combination of warm colours

scheme needs to be cheerful but not over stimulating. Colour choice should be determined by facing of the room. Colour of the walls should go with furniture and fabric in the room. A beautiful living room creates a lasting impact as it is the first impression of the owner's personality, taste and style. Fairly light, warm colours are usually the most desirable for living rooms except in a summer home or in a tropical home, where a simple cool scheme such as white walls and a blue ceiling and floors is refreshing. For a temperate climate, white, brown, and coral with walls of pale greyed lime make a cheerful colour arrangement.

Dining room

The dining room in a formal home is naturally in the same character as the house so its colour scheme is conservative and dignified. Colours such as lettuce green, shrimp pink, butter yellow, lemon yellow, watermelon rose, or tomato red have refreshing and deicious implications. The addition of white is desirable, particularly if white is used on the table.

A beautiful combination of analogous colours

Bedroom

Bedroom is one of the important rooms of the house and it is considered as a necessity of the house. Most of the time is spent, on relaxing, watching T.V or listening to the music, reading etc. in the bedroom. Therefore, it is necessary that the bedroom should have light colours like blue, pastle green, etc. The size of the room has a tremendous impact on a decorative scheme. Ceiling of the room should have white colour. A bedroom colour scheme is usually more personal than any other, its dominating colour might well be the favourite colour of the occupant. In deciding upon this colour the exposure and the amount of light in the room should not be overlooked.

A master bedroom used by both husband and wife should contain colours, expressive of both. A man's room or a boy's room should be bright and masculine, with rich characterful colours, possibly combined with natural wood. A woman's room or girl's room should be bright and feminine and harmonious with her own colouring.

Direct complementary colour harmony

Monochromatic colour harmony

Children's bedroom may require bright colours since it has many special features; open floor space for games, work tops for home work and crafts, adjustable shelves, good

Triad colour combination in child's bedroom

lighting, washable durable surfaces, sturdy beds that can survive the transistion from crib to open bed, etc. Walls of the children's bedroom should be finished with washable paint rather than wall paper, since few small children can resist to the peel off the paper. Dull colours should be avoided.

Bathroom

Bathroom walls and fixtures should usually be white, for hygienic as well as aesthetic reasons. In general, coloured fixtures have proved to be tiresome. However, one bright clear positive colour is needed in a bathroom; it should be used on the floor or on the upper walls and ceiling and in towels, mats, curtains, and shower curtains. Bathrooms are often decorated in colours that suggest water—blue, green, violet and grey.

Kitchen

Kitchen is often termed as the nerve center of the home. Natural light is an important issue when it comes to choosing kitchen colours. Day light has always been the cook's ally and even with the sophistication of modern artificial lighting, there is no substitute for its clarity. Restful white and other light enhancing tones also tend to increase the sense of space. White and cream have powerful connotations of cleanliness, freshness and efficiency which reinforce their prevailing use in kitchen décor. In modern kitchen design, grey is one of the most popular neutrals.

A modern kitchen with the neutral colour scheme

Exercise

Student Projects / Assignment

1. Use the material in this book to prepare a training programme on "Use of colours in interiors" to Home maker. Assume that our trainees do not have any basic knowledge about use of colours and their effects on human emontions. (Hint: have several sections beginning with basic concepts, followed by self help skills and some practical demonstrations).

2. You are the senior colour consultant of an interior designing firm. What colour / furnishings would you suggest for an elegant commercial complex, that consists of an office room, guest room, recreational area and a front office.

Suggested colour schemes for a home Scheme I

Room	Walls	Upholstery	Draperies	Accessories	Floor coverings	Furniture	Remarks
Living room	Dove grey	Blue grey (checked) small red cushion on the upholstery	Blue grey (self)	Table lamps, vases and sculptures	Red carpet	Light wood	Blue and grey are cool, restful colurs; their attraction is heightened by the red carpet. This colour scheme is a primary triad, the yellow being accented in the light wood furniture and red accents in the form of small cushions
Bedroom	Pale pink	White top with pink and white gingham frill	Pink and white checked	Table lamps and pictures	White bed rug	White wood	An ideal colour scheme for a girl's room, the cool soft colurs give a restful effect
Dining room	Pale turquoise	-	Hand woven cotton striped in blue, green and yellow and a small amount of black	Brighter yellow accessories	Dark green linoleum	Mahogany or rosewood orange upholstered seats	Pale colour gives a feeling of serenity, warmth and cheer is introduced through the vivid orange.
Guest room	Pale blue	Turquoise bedspread, tan upholstered chair with yellow cushions	Yellow	Pictures, table lamps, etc	Tan	Mahogany	This colour scheme gives the room a sunny appearance, serenity is introduced through the pale blue walls
Kitchen	Pale blue	---	Cream and orange patterned	---	Orange	Cream	A colour scheme which is ideal for a kitchen with dreary outlook

Scheme II

Room	Wal s	Upholstery	Draperies	Accessories	Floor coverings	Furniture	Remarks
Living room	White	Turquoise	White background with turquoise and green print	Potted plants, porcelain or ivory figurines, table lamps	Forest green	White cane	The colour scheme has been selected from the draperies; turquoise, the basic colur has been used for the upholstery, green has been repeated in the carpet, white serves to unify these two colours
Bedroom	Pale green	Green and yellow bed spread	Yellow draperies	Accents of orange, picture, table lamp	Yellow bed rug	Mahogany	A cool, serene colur scheme accents of orange and warmth
Dining room	Cream	---	Deep yellow and green striped	Pictures, vase etc	Yellow linoleum	Light with green seats	This colur scheme creates a cool effect and there is illusion of space
Guest room	Cream	Apricot and green bedspread upholstered chair in red	Apricot	Pictures etc	Red bed rug	Light wood	A cool scheme, warmth is introduced through the addition of red.
Kitchen	Pale green	---	Pale yellow	---	Deep green linoleum	Cream	A cool colour scheme, pleasing and not harsh on the house wife's eyes.

3. Carry out a survey of the colour schems used in the residential complexes and prepare a report about the choice of colours and the reasons for the same.

4. Analyse the colour schemes used in the kindergarten classrooms and prepare a report suggesting colour schemes for children's classrooms.

Choose the correct answer

1. Colours that are obtained as a result of mixing two primary colour are known as

   a. quaternary colour b. intermediate colour c. secondary colour

2. Warm colours tend to

   a. reduce the size of the object.

   b. increase the size of the object

   c. complement the size of the object

3. Addition of white to any colour is known as

   a. tint b. shade c. neutral

4. Addition of black to any colour is known as

   a. shade b. tint c. neutral

5. A value scale has __________ gradations

   a. 9 b. 8 c. 7

6. The brightness or dullness of a colour is referred to as

   a. intensity b. value c. hue

7. The number of triad combinations that can be evolved from a prang colour wheel is

   a. three b. five c. four

8. Identify the triad in a given combination

   a. yellow, red and blue   b. yellow, red and green   c. yellow, red and purple

9. Use of a single colour in varying tints and shades is

   a. monochromatic colour harmony   b. contrasting colour harmony   c. split complimentary colour harmony

10. Colour scheme formed by using colours that lie adjacent to each other

    a. monochromatic   b. contrasting   c. analogous

Fill in the blanks

1. Yellow, Red and ________ are the primary colours as per prang colour chart (green, blue).
2. Binary colours can also be termed as __________ (conventional/secondary colours).
3. Combination of one primary and one secondary colour results in ________________ (quaternary colours/ intermediate colour).
4. Purple, Green and Blue are ____________ Colours (warm, cool).
5. Use of lighter colours for larger areas and darker colours for smaller areas is given in (law of areas/law of equimarginal/utility).
6. Children's room should have ________ colours (bright/dull).
7. Intensity of a colour can be changed by addition of ________ colour (contrasting/adjacent).

8. Warm colours have ____________ effect (receding/advancing).
9. ____________ is the highest in value (white/black).
10. Repetition of colours to achieve balance is termed as __________ (crossing/rhythm).

State True or False

1. Colours can indicate the personality of an individual.
2. Munsell colour system and prang colour system describe the same dimensions of colours.
3. A psychologist analyses colour as that of an artist .
4. All colours have same reflective properties.
5. Colour dissonance deals with usage of new colours.
6. Intensity and chroma of the colour indicates the level of saturation of a colour.
7. Complimentary colours always have different dimensions.
8. The quantum of natural light influences the choice of colour scheme of a room.
9. Monochromatic colour scheme is the best choice for a child's bedroom.
10. Colour of the floors should necessarily be always darker than the walls.

Match the following

1. Pigment theory	Receding colour
2. Psychologist theory	Emotions
3. Munsell theory	Prang colour chart
4. Purple	Wavelength of colour
5. After image	Yellow, Red and Blue
6. Triad	Balance of colour
7. Crossing	Light colours for larger areas

8.	Law of areas	9 gradations
9.	Value scale	Non-existent hues observed by the eyes
10.	Physicts theory	Repetition of colours.

Short answers

1. What are the qualities of colour?
2. Write a short note about the types of colour.
3. Explain "crossing" of colours.
4. Give an account of warm and cool colours.
5. What is a value chart?.
6. How will you change the intensity of a colour?
7. What is a monochromatic scheme?
8. Explain the visual perceptions of colour.
9. What is a contrasting colour harmony?
10. Explain split complimentary colour harmony?

Long Answers

1. Suggest a colour scheme for an adolescent girl's bedroom and justify your choice of colours.
2. Explain with an illustration the Prang colour chart.
3. Explain with an illustration the Munsell colour chart.
4. What colours would you suggest for a children's bedroom?
5. Discuss in detail the types of colour harmonies.
6. What are the factors to be considered while selecting a colour scheme for a house?

❑❑❑

CHAPTER

4

Furniture Arrangement

4.1. Introduction

Furniture provides transition between architecture and people. In the most basic sense it is a tool for relieving the stresses of gravity. It exists to provide comfort in the things we do- working, eating, sleeping and relaxing. We expect each piece of furniture to fulfill certain aspects. Furniture is the nucleus around which the entire decorating scheme resolves. It is generally seen that features such as accessories, soft furnishings, wall hangings, foot mats and floor coverings are planned and selected only after the furniture items for a room are finalized. A scantily furnished room will appear empty and barren. When a person enters a room, it is the furniture arrangement that makes an impression and extends a warm and friendly greeting. It can be said that it is the furniture which gives character to a room and other features add to its ornamental value. Furniture also acts as an architectural element by organizing the space within a room- defining conversation area and traffic paths, suggesting separation of areas and so forth. Furniture enables us to improve our personal tastes in our life. We manipulate the character of the furniture and their arrangements to define the type of living we expect a room to foster.

4.2. Terminologies

Antiques : A term loosely applied to all old furniture. It should be confined to periods ending with Sheraton's style in Europe and with Duncan Phyfe's in America.

Ball-and-claw : A carved foot found mostly on Chippendale designs. It is a form of ornament originating in China, and is supposed to represent a bird's claw grasping an egg.

Baroque : A fantastic furniture style of the 16th Century to the mid-18th Century marked by exaggerated scale, curves, and movement, and was always symmetrical.

Batten : Strips of wood used as a brace or cleat across one or more boards.

Bergere : A French armchair with closed upholstered sides and back.

Bookcase headboard : A headboard with built-in storage for books, radios, reading lights, etc. A modern form which has been given period interpretations.

Buffet : French term referring to sideboard used to store china, silver, and linens. Top surface used as a counter in self-service informal dining.

Bunk bed : Twin beds mounted one above the other; sometimes detachable for use separately.

Bureau : Low chest of drawers, generally used in bedroom with mirror. Originally a writing desk or table with drawers.

Butt Joint : The term refers to a joint on which the squared end of the one member is butted against the side or the end of another member.

Canopy : The frame or tester over a high four-poster bedstead, with or without its covering material.

Casters : Small, swiveling rollers attached to the base or legs to facilitate moving a piece of furniture, first used in the early 19th Century.

Chest : A piece of furniture with stationary top and drawers and/or doors in front. Originally a trunk-like box with a hinged lid.

Chest-on-chest : A chest of drawers in two sections, the smaller on top the larger one.

Chesterfield : Overstuffed couch or sofa with upholstered ends.

China Cabinet/Closet : Cupboard, with glass sides and front. Used to store and display fine china. Term often abbreviated to China.

Chinese Chippendale : 18th Century furniture style of the Chippendale School using Chinese motifs and decoration

Coffee Table : A low table used in front of the sofa to hold a coffee service.

Coffer : Hinged-top chest used as seat, table, or trunk for valuables.

Couch : An arm less back less lounge or sofa for daytime resting; generally with head rest at one end.

Cupboard: Cabinet or box with doors; for storage. The special types and names are numerous, springing from the special uses and locations. Sometimes a cupboard is considered an architectural feature only, the free-standing equivalent being a cabinet.

Curio Cabinet: A case with glass door, panels, shelves; used to display art objects.

Davenport: Small writing desk. In current American use, an upholstered sofa.

Divan: Upholstered couch without arms or back, originating in Turkish form of piling rugs for reclining.

Dovetail: Method of joining boards at right angles by interlocking wedge-shaped tenons and mortises. Generally used in drawer construction. Also, a butterfly-shaped inset used to join boards lengthwise in table tops and floors.

Dresser: Derivative of the French term, dressoir. Originally a table used to dress meats. Evolved into cupboard for utensils and dishes. In United States term applies to chest of drawers with mirror.

Easychair: Less frequently-used term for lounge chair.

End Table: A small table used at the end of a sofa.

Footboard: Panel in the lower end of a bed, or the entire end.

French Polish: Process of finishing with a high gloss by applying successive films of shellac in spirits.

Game Table: One of the earliest specialized types of tables developed for games, such as dice, cards, chess, or draughts, backgammon, etc.

Headboard : Simple panel at the head of the bed.

Lacquer : Oriental lacquer is a high dense finish acquired by tedious padding up and rubbing down of many coats of sprits, shellac. This has nothing to common with modern lacquer, which is a compound of cellulose derivatives. These dry so rapidly that they must be sprayed by compressed air. Such lacquers now posses many qualities not found in varnish or shellac finishes, such as the resistance to heat, moisture, and acids. It can be rubbed to a clear satiny finish

Lounge : Type of couch in late 19th Century work, often with one high end as a pillow.

Love Seat : Double chair or small sofa. Also, "courting chair".

Mortise: Hole in wood, into which the tenon or tongue fits.

Motif: Distinctive feature or element of design or ornament; theme.

Nest of Drawers: Quantity of small drawers or boxes contained in a case; a diminutive chest of drawers, chiefly English, 18th and 19th Centuries.

Nest of Tables: Set of several tables, designed in fit over one another.

Peg: A wooden nail used to hold furniture parts together; sometimes exposed to create decorative interest in Early American pieces.

Recliner : Lounge chair with adjusts to various positions, including reclining; usually incorporated a hidden footrest.

Rocking Chair : A uniquely American piece of furniture developed in the Colonial period, it consists of a chair mounted on curved runners which create a rocking motion when the unit is occupied.

Room Dividers : Any piece of furniture or any other article which performs the architectural function of partitioning a room.

Secretaire : Closed desk, usually with drawers below and bookcase above. In Europe, sometimes called "bureau."

Sectional Furniture : Furniture which comes in complementary parts which can be grouped in a variety of arrangements or used separately. Term generally refers to upholstered furniture.

Settee : A long seat with side arms and back, sometimes upholstered; light-scaled forerunner of today's sofa.

Sideboard : Originally an open-shelf dining room piece (literally a side board or boards) the sideboard later consisted of doors and/or drawers below, sometimes open shelving above for the display of plates, etc.

Sofa : Long upholstered seat for two or more persons. The name "sopha" is of Eastern origin and was first used about 1680 to designate a divan-like seat in France.

Swivel Chair : Revolving seat on a fixed frame, used for desk chairs, dressing chairs, music stools, etc.

Tufting : Means of anchoring the cover on upholstered furniture or mattress by sewing through the filler, often with buttons; arranged to form a pattern (rows of squares, "biscuit tufting," or staggered to create a diamond form, "diamond tufting").

Veneer : A thinly-cut slice of decoratively-marked wood glued to a stronger, thicker, solid wood or plywood backing.

Wardrobe : A large utilitarian cabinet used to hang clothes.

4.3. History of furniture

The development of civilization presents a fascinating approach to the history of furniture. A brief history of the furniture design briefly discussed in the following paragraphs, will give an idea about its gradual evolution from the scratch to the present form.

Initially the flat surface of the bark of a cut tree was used by people either as a seat or a table. A typical household inventory included a few simple chests (with no drawers), stools and settle benches. Tables consisted of huge boards temporarily laid across trestle bases and dismantled after meals. Chairs were stiff-backed, not upholstered, and consequently uncomfortable, reserved expressly for the Lord of the Manor.

Furniture forms evolved only gradually. The furniture started standing on legs, accommodated hinged doors and finally arrived the drawer. However, the furniture was still massive, heavy and immobile. Then came the *Renaissance* which marked the beginning of an architectural and decorative style called *Baroque.* It added little to furniture comfort and changed the face of furniture design. Court style gradually filtered down to the provinces, first to the homes of the country nobility and finally to the public at large.

The eighteenth century is considered the great age of furniture making both in England and in France. Design reached a degree of excellence. This century dawned with the graceful *Queen* Anne style (1702-1714) and reached its maturity and waned with the elegant Georgian styles that had become better known by the names of its cabinet makers - Chippendale (1718-79), Thomas Sheraton (1751-1806) and George Hepplewhite (1770-1786). Fig. 4.1. illustrates the furniture styles of various periods.

During this time trade was flourishing and hence a greater number of people got exposed to better furniture with bigger homes. The furniture then was evolving from heavy, rigid, block like forms into objects of great refinement and beauty.

Use of materials and furniture styles at various periods

Period	Materials	Style
1100-1660	Oak	Romanesque Gothic
1660-1714	Walnut	Renaissance Late Renaissance Baroque (Louis IV Williams & Mary, Queen Anne)
1714-1760	Mahogany, Walnut, Laquered Gilded & Painted wood.	Baroque Rococo (Chippendale, Louis XV)
1760-1830	Satinwood, Mahagony, Painted & Laquered	Classical Revival Louis XVI
1830-1900	Rosewood, Oak, Mahagony, Satinwood, Plywood.	Victorian, Art Nouveau
1900-1970	Rose Wood, Teak, Oak, Mahogany, Plywood and Plastics	Victorian, Classic and Contemporary
1971-2000	Pure wood, Plywood, moulded plastics, recycled wood of agricultural waste.	Conventional / Traditional, Period, contemporary, Eclectic

Source: Seetharaman, P and Pannu, P. 2005. Interior Design and Decoration pg. 214

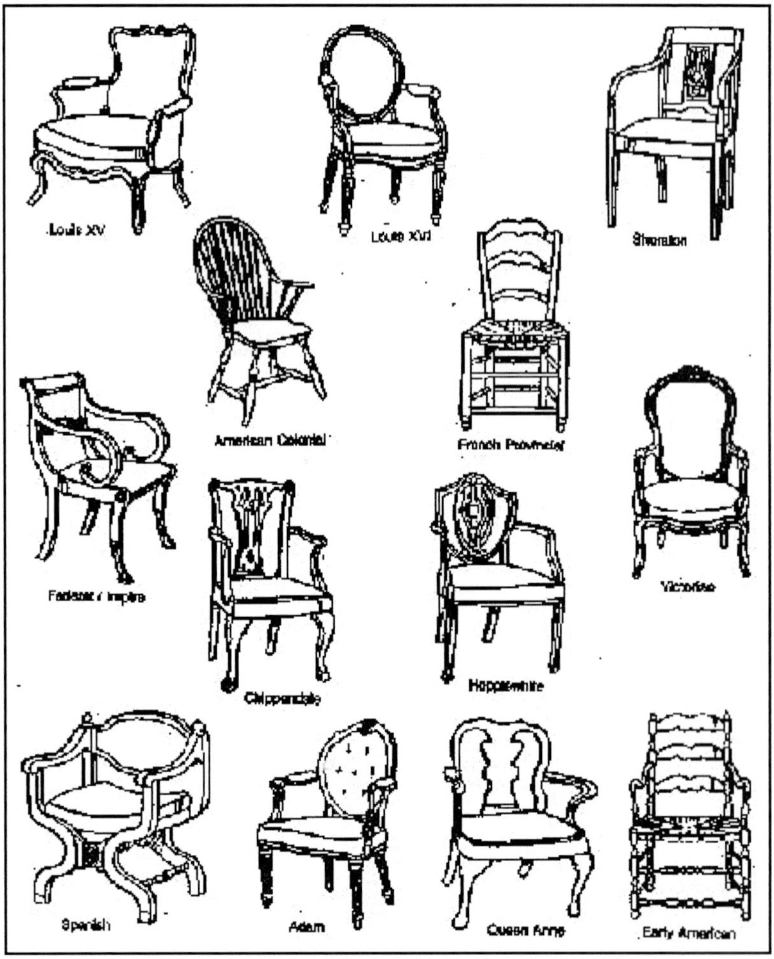

Fig. 4.1 Furniture styles

4.4. Selection of furniture

The vast array of furniture currently available testifies to a wide divergence in the ways people live. There are mass produced furniture that reflects and enhance every pattern and style of living. Furthermore, increasing number of people are finding satisfaction in constructing their own furniture - either freely or from components or renovating furniture others have discarded. In order to sort through many types of furniture and to find what pleases you the most, you should build a personal scale of values that will allow you to evaluate furniture as it relates to your particular necessities and aesthetics. Deciding on physical requirements is the first step although it seems like a rather prosaic one. Considerable thought should be given to how and what situations you are going to use your furniture and who will use it. A single person household will obviously have finite different needs than the family with more members.

Before selecting furniture, one should also consider how much space is available, what scale of furniture will relate well to the room and the possible arrangement that can be done to suit the aesthetics of the room. In stores, catalogues, magazines, books and from your friends' home, you can identify many kinds of chairs, tables, cabinets and furniture systems both old and new, compare and contrast them noting the excellence and weakness of each. When you have opportunity, sit on, look on it and feel the furniture you are going to use it, so find out what looks good and is comfortable to you. Whether furniture is for sleeping, sitting, eating, working or playing, practical considerations should not be minimized. Certain important factors to be considered while selecting furniture are given below:

Factors to be considered

- Convenience
- Mobility
- Comfort
- Flexibility
- Space requirement
- Materials and construction
- Length of service

4.4.1. Convenience

Convenience applies to efficient storage and to the ease with which we can move. For example, the furniture such as dining chair or beds that must be pulled out from the wall for making up the bed. Almost all the furniture are moved from time to time, so it should not be heavier than necessary for use, strength and appearance. Larger pieces, especially if they are heavy, should have castors and gliders.

4.4.2. Mobility

Mobility is a facet of life in our society and many households must cope with packing, shipping and resetting at frequent intervals. Furniture that is light weight, collapsible or capable of dismantling may provide the answer. Some people who move often find it easier to buy cheap or second hand furniture that can be sold and left behind. This experiment makes it more difficult to personalize a space but it offers an exciting challenge of designing a new environment every few years.

4.4.3. Comfort

Comfort relates to pieces on which we sit or sleep as well. The height of tables and desks are determined based on the anthropometrical measurements. Most of the furniture is made on standard measurements for an average person. A person who is above or below average should select furniture to suit his comfort. Children's furniture should be according to their height and measurement. Sometimes comfort overrides every other factor in choosing a particular item of furniture. The classic example of this is, ugly broken down Easychair whose owner would never part with it. The age of household members becomes important here, for example, elderly and young people have definite but quite different requirements for comfort.

4.4.4. Flexibility

Flexibility pertains to furniture that can be used in more than one room or for more than one purpose. Until recently most furniture was designed very specially, such as typical dining sets a few decades ago. Only the chairs would be moved about freely, but no matter where they were placed they carried a 'dining room' character. Now many pieces are multipurpose. For example, a table desk may tilt to make a drawing table and without its drawer components, would serve as a small dining table. Money and space should not be wasted in using unfunctional furniture in the house as both these resources are limited.

4.4.5. Space requirement

Space requirement become an increasingly important factor as homes grow smaller. Accordingly many contemporary designers have eliminated protruding mouldings and curved legs, so that pieces can be fitted together snugly; as in-built storage units to the floor or hung in walls; designed cupboards and drawers to fit the contents flexibly ; employed materials such as metal, plywood, foam etc. that reduce size; developed foldings, stackings, resting tables and chairs and in some cases reduced both size and scale to a minimum. Using the multipurpose pieces such as sofa cum bed, we can have more comfort in less floor area. The floor area is also freed when furniture is attached to walls.

4.4.6. Materials and construction

Furniture items are made from wide range of base materials and accessories or fittings.

Materials

Wood: Wood is the traditional and oldest material. It has natural beauty. It comes in variety of types: hard wood, softwood, plywood, veneer, solid wood, inlays and carvings.

As wood is extremely absorbent it requires some protective finish to prevent it from absorbing moisture, dirt or grease. Furniture is thus finished with painting, polishing or varnishing.

Metals: Metals in the form of iron and steel have been widely used for bed steads and for the springs of furniture. Due to its characteristics like fireproof, strength and ease of shaping, it is now increasingly used for the legs and frames of modern furniture and for tables which have tops of heavy materials, marble or ceramic tiles now-a-days. Aluminum, chromium and brass are also used. To prevent corrosion of metals protective coating need to be given by anodizing, electroplating, transparent lacquers or enamel coating to maintain it easily.

Plastic : Furniture made from plastic is unbreakable, dent proof and scratch proof. It is light in weight and comes in attractive colours. Other plastic materials used in modern furniture are laminated plastics and reinforced plastics. They are durable and very easily cleaned.

Cane: This material is light in weight and cheaper than wooden furniture and is used in bedrooms as head boards of beds and in sun lounges. It is not as durable as wooden furniture.

Glass: Unbreakable fibre glass is an elegant material and is fire proof and is used as table tops in modern interiors.

Upholstered furniture: Generally wooden furniture and other furniture is not very comfortable to sit because of the hardness of these materials and hence it is finished with cushioned surface called 'upholstering'. Stuffing materials like tow, sisal, coconut fibre or animal hair are used to produce softness and may be finished by beautiful fabrics. Tension springs are often used while upholstering.

Construction

Proper construction and materials will affect the appearance, durability and price. The furniture thus made should

- be free from rough, unfinished edges or surfaces.
- be free from surplus adhesive.
- have the correct joints that fit well. (e.g. mortice and tenon, dovetail and dowel).

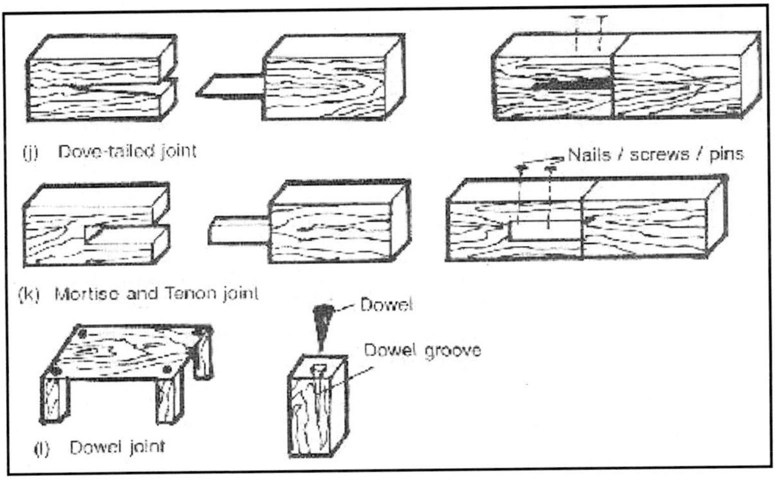

Fig. 4.2 Types of joints

- stand firm on the floor and be rigid in use.
- have drawers that slide smoothly.
- have doors which fit properly.
- have efficient locks, latches, hinges, washers, wheels etc.
- have handles conveniently placed.
- have castors with no sharp edges.

4.4.7. Length of service

Length of service depends on both physical and psychological durability. The physical life of furnishings of course is determined by materials, construction and finish. Psychological longevity, relates to the like or dislike of a quality in a furniture. It makes no sense to buy a piece of furniture solid enough to last for generations if you are going to hate it within a year or two. It may be better to choose well-made, well proportionate items in which the materials have been honestly and suitable used.

When furnishing temporary quarters or anticipating a period of mobility such as business, training programmes or military service, you may find solid expensive furnishings to be actually a handicap. Built-in furniture also has drawbacks in these situations because it may be too large to move.

4.4.8. Cost of maintenance

Cost of maintenance includes cleaning, repairing, refinishing and reupholstering. The choice of appropriate materials can lighten cleaning burden, while strong materials for construction lessen the need for repairs. Durability of finish and care of refinish are important. Painted furniture whether wood or metal needs new paint every few years; transparent finishes on wood; supplemented by wax or polish last a long time and some of the new synthetic finishes such as aluminium, chromium also last long. Upholstery fabrics may serve from two to twenty years or more depending upon the materials and use. The use of zippered covers wherever possible facilitates both cleaning and repairing easier.

4.5. Types of furniture

4.5.1. Built in and unit furniture

More often than not, built-in furniture promotes flexible living although this may seem like a contradiction. Because the furnishing takes less room than movable pieces, they leave maximum amount of free space around and between them. Built-in furniture can also minimize dust-catching crevices, give a feeling of permanence and security and break up the look of typical rooms. At the same time, it reduces the visual clutter brought by many isolated pieces of furniture, which takes time to set to their best positions. Like built-in furniture, unit or component furniture answer our designs for coherence and spaciousness. Some of the built-in furniture are discussed below.

4.5.2. Beds

Reducing physical strain to a maximum is the major purpose of the beds. Individual vary in their specific ideas about sleeping comfort. The typical foundation consists of either inexpensive, light weight, flat springs or more bulky, expensive coil springs, but a flat plywood foundation can also be comfortable if the mattress is thick enough, particularly for people who enjoy a very firm surface.

Today the least expensive are thin pads of polyurethane foam. The better grades have 4 to 6 inch cores of polyurethane or latex foam or innerspring covering with padding. Inner spring mattresses are more popular because people are familiar with them. They vary in number of coils, in their design or in the type of the thickness of padding.

Most commonly used varieties of beds include water bed and built-in beds. A water bed consists of a heavy duty plastic water bag, a solid frame that supports the bag, a watertight liner between the bed and frame to guard against floods and a special heating pad that warms the water to a comfortable temperature. Water beds are firm and strongly supporting because they can shape themselves exactly to body contours, but some people find disconcerting their quick reactions to change in position. They also weigh a tremendous amount when filled and must be emptied for moving and there are problems in adjusting sheets, blankets and bed covers.

Built-in beds offer a certain reassuring protectiveness and bring many conveniences close to hand- lighting, possibly a slanted end for reading in bed; book cases and stereo components onto which things can be placed. The main difficulty is in moving the bed and in making it. Sometimes storage facilities are combined with bed. Children, especially smaller ones require different kinds of sleeping furniture. Bunk beds are popular. Infants must have well protected sleeping spaces to prevent them tumbling out.

4.5.3. Sofas

We have chosen the inclusive term sofa to a seat for two or more people but many other names are also applied to such piece of furniture. The varied types of seats are given below.

Chesterfield: It refers to an over stuffed sofa with upholstered back.

Couch : Couch originally meant a sofa with a low back and one raised end; now-a-days the name is synonymous with sofa.

Davenport: It is used in United States to describe an upholstered sofa often convertible into a bed.

Divan: Divan is a Turkish term for large low couches with no back or arms with one high end for reclining .

Love seat : Love seat means a small sofa or double chair for two people.

Settee : Settee refers to a double seat with a back, sometimes with arms, often upholstered.

Settees: These are wood settees, used in colonial days before a fire to trap heat.

Sofa: Sofa comes from an Arabic word. Any long upholstered seat for more than one person is named as sofa in United States.

Fig. 4.3 Types of sofa

Lounge: Lounge once referred to a type of couch with no back and with one high end for rest.

4.5.4. Chairs

For most of the people, the greater part of our working hours are spent sitting down. We work, study, relax and travel in a seated position only. Maximum comfort results when weight and pressure are distributed and tension eased. The characteristic features of a good chair are given below.

- The height of the seat is somewhat less than the length of the sitter's lower legs, so that the feet rest on the floor and the legs be relaxed.

- The depth of the seat, is a bit less than the length of the upper leg to avoid putting a pressure point under the knee.
- The width of the seat is ample enough to permit some movement.
- The seat is shaped so that pressure is not concentrated on the small weight bearing edge of the pelvis.
- Both seat and back are tilted backwards slightly.
- The angle between seat and back is 95 degrees or more.
- The chair back must be in a position to support the sitter's back.
- The position of the seat and back adjustable for different persons and for different ways of relaxing.
- A place to rest the head and relax neck and also should have support for arms.

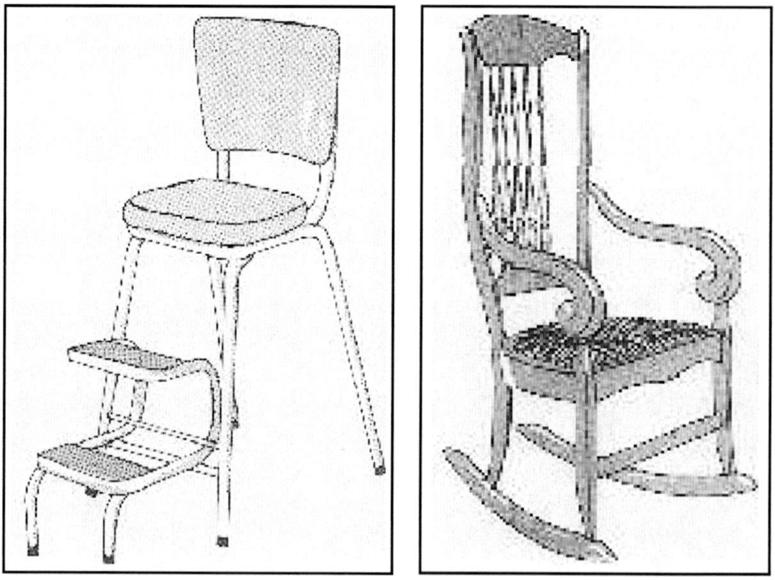

Fig. 4.4. Types of chairs A – Step chair B – Rocking chair

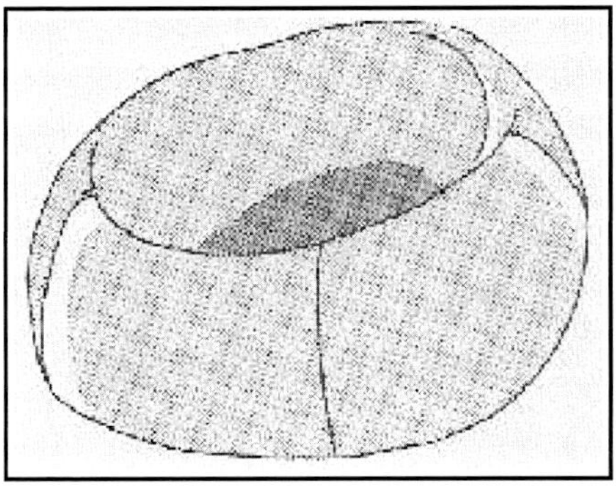

Fig. 4.4. C – Bean bag chair

4.5.5. Tables

As with chairs, each home needs a variety of tables that differ in function and therefore in size, shape, height and materials. The different types of tables are discussed below.

Dining tables

Sit down meals require a table that is sturdy enough not to be jarred by the unpredictable movement of children, that has a top large enough to give each person at least two feet of elbow room and high enough to allow leg room between the chairs and lower surface.

The surface of dining table will be an important feature in its selection because this covered or uncovered will form background for China, Crystal, Silver and Linen.

Shape is the major consideration in choosing a dining table. Most are rectangular and can be pushed snugly against a wall or into a corner and is slightly less costly to make. In the right place however a round or oval table will give an inimitable friendly feeling. It is important to check dining chairs and tables together, because often their legs interfere with each other, the heights of the two are not co-ordinated or the space between the chair and table is unsufficient for sitter's comfort.

Coffee tables

Usually we have a feeling that no sofa is complete unless faced with a long, low table on which ashtrays, books, magazines, newspapers, accessories, plants, flowers and snacks abound.

Occasional tables

It might be said that the old fashioned living room table that once sat in the middle of the room disintegrated into many little tables; convenience now seem to demand a horizontal surface, however small within reach of every seat. Thus we often find a table at each end of the sofa and one for each group of chairs. Unlike coffee tables, occasional tables seldom interfere with the legs of sitters and may provide shelves or drawers for supplementary storage.

Card and game tables

Although rarely handsome, the folding or break down card table is a wonderful invention. Most people find it more comfortable to play cards and other games at table several inches lower than those meant for eating.

Kitchen tables

These differ from dining tables in having greater strength and durability often used for eating and meal preparation. These are compact efficiency tables in a kitchen.

Desks

An efficient desk has two essential properties, a suitable writing surface and an accessible storage for storage of papers and supplies. It should be obvious that every household needs atleast one writing place but the size, complexity and location of the table differ in households. A desk can be a table with one or two drawers, a compartment in modular unit a piece of furniture designed for serious work.

4.5.6. Storage units

Storage is a major problem today. Living quarters have steadily became smaller while attics, spare rooms, basements and sheds have disappeared now. Many favour the uncluttered, cleanlined look and having the proverbial, "place for everything". Convenience, visibility, accessibility, flexibility and maintenance are just as important in kitchen, group spaces, bedrooms etc.

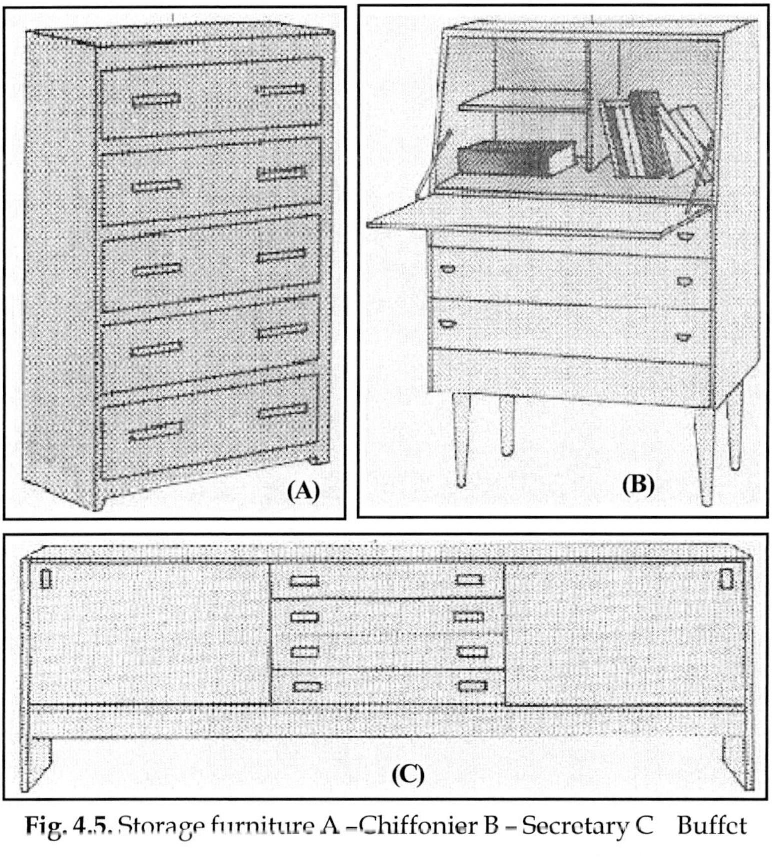

Fig. 4.5. Storage furniture A –Chiffonier B – Secretary C Buffet

4.5.7. Book shelves

The simplest piece of storage furniture are bookshelves. Despite of the fact that books come in many different sizes and shapes, easily adjustable shelves can store them efficiently. Books on open shelves do get dusty but they make a handsome display and also absorb noise. Now-a-days bookcases have display space for all sorts of objects that have aesthetic value or interest.

Nearly every room can profit by some book / magazine storage. In the kitchen, a single shelf may store all the family's cook books, while a book case or a few shelves in the living area and in bedrooms suffices to hold current reading materials.

4.5.8. Drawers

Chest of drawers work best when they are strongly joined, dust proof drawers that slide easily and handles that can be grasped without difficulty. Shallow drawers at the top are a great convenience, flexible dividers for them well justify their cost. Relative small units that fit together increase flexibility of placement. Drawers combined with shelves and cabinets of different sizes can store a multitude of variously shaped items.

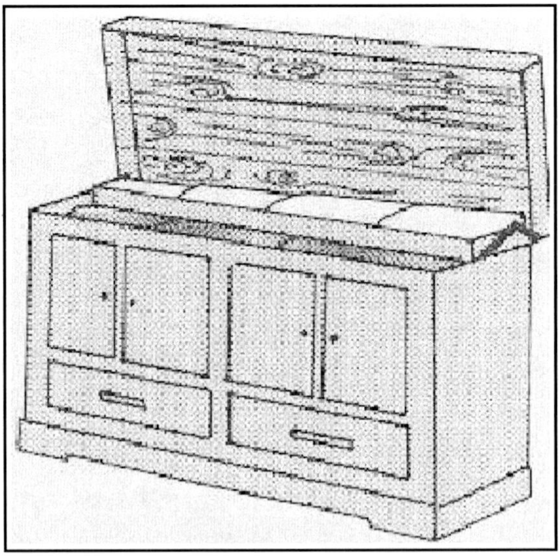

4.5.9. Cabinets

Although they appear infrequently outside kitchen, dining space and bathrooms, cabinets with doors and adjustable shelves or vertical dividers are welcome in every room.

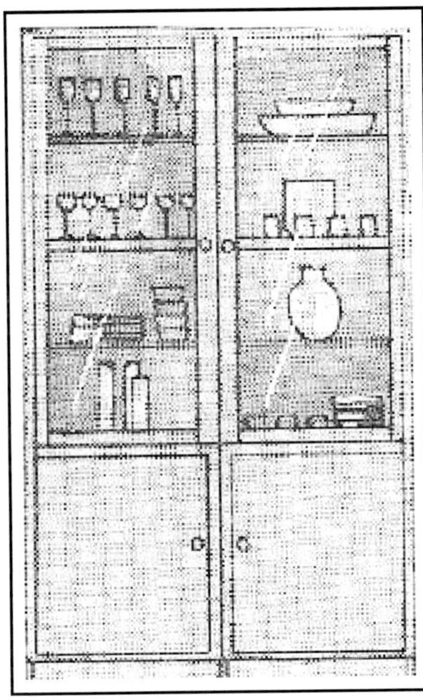

Cabinets are also provided for radios, stereo components and television sets. Now-a-days, audio visual equipment is often integrated with cabinets and bookshelves or in-built into the wall. It may become a striking design element.

4.5.10. Outdoor furniture

Interest in outdoor living has led to many kinds of weather resistant furniture in a surprisingly wide range of materials. Red wood, cedar, cyprus are long-lasting and attractive. Some of the newer plastics stand weathering quite well and are suitable for use in outdoors.

4.6. Characteristics of modern furniture

Modern furniture is now a style in its own right. The features of modern furniture are;

- Simple and restful
- Light in weight
- Colourful
- Durable
- Portable and space saving
- Compact
- Can be separated and joint together are referred as modular furniture. They all look like one piece e.g. Sectional sofas
- Beauty in size, shape and texture
- Easy to maintain
- Functionalism- the present trend towards built in furniture – sofas, book cases, radios, beds and tables is an interesting development.
- Specially designed furniture for physically challenged when necessary.

4.7. Furniture sizes and shapes

The working knowledge of the sizes and shapes of specific pieces of furniture helps immeasurably in arranging a room, as does familiarity with recommended clearances between pieces, between furniture and walls and so on. The given table clearly reveals the sizes and shapes of the furniture.

4.8. General rules that apply to furniture arrangement

- Select furniture that is scaled or in proportion to the room and to the family using the furniture.
- Avoid using too many furniture in a room.

Table 4.1. Furniture sizes and shapes

Type of furniture	Size recommended	
	Small (Depth x Width)	Large (Depth x Width)
Living room		
Sofa	2'6" x 6'	3' x 9'
Love seat	2'6" x 4'	3' x 5'
Easychair	2'6" x 2'4"	3'4" x 3'4"
Pull up chair	1'6" x 1'6"	2' x 2'
Coffee tables (oblong)	1'6" x 3'	3' x 5'
Coffee tables (round)	2' dia	4' dia
Coffee tables (square)	2' x 2'	4' x 4'
Occasional table	6" x 10"	3' x 1'8"
Card table	2'6" x 2'6'	3' x 3'
Flat top desk	1'6" x 2'8"	2' x 3'6"
Secretary (chest of drawers)	1'6" x 2'8"	2' x 3' 6"
Upright piano	2'x 4'9"	2'2" x 5'10"
Grand piano	5'10" x 4'10"	9' x 5'2"
Book case	9" x 2'6"	1' x 4'
Dining area		
Table (square) 4-8 people	2'6" x 2'6"	5' x 5'
Table (rectangle) 6-12 people	2'6" x 2'6"	5' x 5'
Table (round) 4-10 people	3' x 5'	4' x 8'
Arm chairs	1'10" x 1'10"	2'x 2'
Buffet	1'8" x 4'	2' x 6'
Serving table	1'6" x 3'	2' x 4'
China cabinet	1'6" x 3'	1'8" x 4'
Bedroom		
Twin bed, head and foot board	6'6" x 3'3"	7'6" x 3'8"
Full bed, head and foot board	6'6" x 4'6"	7'6" x 6'
Cot	5'9" x 3'	-
Nightstand	2' x 4'	2'6" x 4'6"
Chest of drawers	1' x 1'3"	2' x 2'
Wardrobe and closet	1'7" x 3'1"	2' x 6'
Easychair	2'4" x 2'4" x 2'4"	2'8" x 2'8"
Pull up chair	1'3" x 1'6"	1'6" x 1'9"

- Place large pieces of furniture such as sofas, beds and so on before trying to place smaller pieces.
- Arrange all furniture with purpose and function in mind, grouping those pieces which are needed for an activity.
- Balance is the basis of good furniture arrangement. Each side of the room should be equally heavy to produce a feeling of equilibrium. Opposite walls in particular, should balance well. Each wall too should be balanced with equal weight on each half. The highest part should usually be at the center, either formal or informal balance may predominate in a room.
- Unity in line, texture, scale and colour is necessary within the groups. At the same time, variety is needed to stimulate interest.
- Do not place furniture on traffic lanes.
- Place larger pieces of furniture against the wall.
- Place furniture around a center of interest (ex. Fire place, T.V. etc.).
- Scatter upholstered pieces of furniture among wood pieces.

4.9. Steps in arranging furniture

Good furniture arrangement begins with analyzing your space and the contents of your room. When planning the arrangement of a room, think about how many people use the room, how traffic flows, and how the room is used.

The first step in planning your space is to *determine the focal point of the room*. Find the dramatic element that draws your immediate attention. If your room has an attractive feature, such as a fireplace or picture window, center your furniture arrangement around it. If your room doesn't have one, create a focal point with furnishings. Dramatic window treatments, an interesting display of artwork, or a beautifully decorated bed can help define the space.

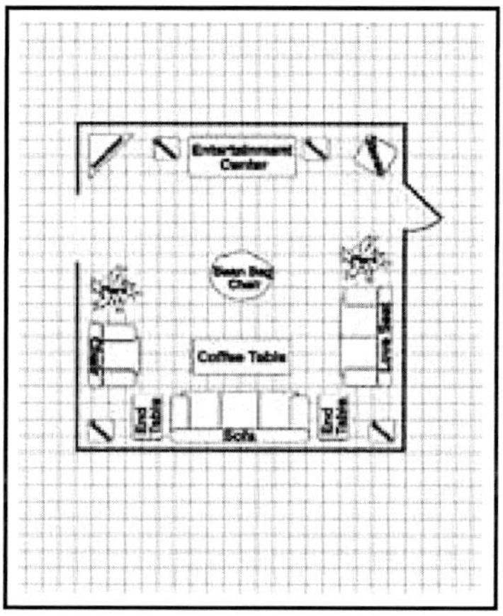

After determining the focal point, *draw a floor plan of your room using graph paper and the provided furniture templates.* Use one graph square for every foot of actual space. Be sure to include windows, staircases, doors, fireplaces, and the focal point of your room.

Measure major furniture pieces and make a template of each piece. After you have cut out the templates, colour each in the hue of the piece it represents; then you can get a good idea how colour is mixed throughout the room. Move the templates around to find the best arrangement before moving the first piece of furniture.

Achieving Balance and Visual Interest

Balanced rooms are more pleasing to the eye and make more effective use of the available space. To keep your rooms from looking one-sided or dull, remember:

- Make sure all the tall or heavy pieces don't end up in the same area of the room. Mix bigger and smaller pieces throughout the room, but keep in mind the scale of the items you put beside each other. You wouldn't want to place a dainty round table by your oversized, comfy armchair. A large chair will require a larger end table. So how do you achieve a mix of bigger and smaller items? Remember that a grouping of smaller items can balance out a weightier item. Two small armchairs and a table, balance a larger sofa.

- Balance does not simply apply to the size and scale of the furniture. Be sure to mix colour and pattern throughout the room as well.
- Avoid leaving pieces of furniture sitting alone in the room. Connect pieces by placing tables or lamps nearby. For example, if the sofa is positioned in the middle of the room facing the fireplace, anchor it by placing a table behind it.
- Use different heights of furniture and accessories. As someone looks around your room, you want their eyes to move up and down.
- For added interest, attempt to pull furniture away from the walls. If you have a sofa placed against a wall, consider placing a table behind it and pull it into the room.
- Angle furniture when possible to take the rough edges off, of a room. A desk or dresser usually looks better angled across a corner than straight against a wall. Angles make the room warmer and present a casual, lived-in style.
- If your room has a curved mantel or a large bay window, a round or semicircular furniture arrangement may complement it.
- If your room lacks architectural detail, you may want to add moulding or a French door to create visual interest.

- Remember rooms are more inviting if they are not overfilled with furniture. If you have a piece that throws off the room's balance or is seldom used, consider moving it to another room, storing it, or giving it away.

Many of us need to use an area in our homes for more than one purpose. For example, the living room often acts as an everyday gathering spot for family, a place to entertain guests, a space to watch television, an area for the kids to play and even a room for guests to sleep in a crunch. Here are some ideas to help you define separate areas within a room:

- Use furniture, such as tables or upholstered pieces, to outline separate, functional areas of a room. A sofa can separate a reading space from a television viewing space.
- Open bookcases divide areas, and they also lend an illusion of spaciousness.
- In the bedroom, instead of anchoring a bed against the wall, try using the headboard as a divider for sleeping and dressing areas.
- Use area rugs to help define areas within a room. You can mix rugs of different patterns within the same room as long as the colour coordinates. Using two rugs of the same size may tend to divide the room in equal halves. Unless the areas you want to create have equal proportions, select rugs of differing sizes to create more interest and contrast.

4.10. Arrangement of furniture in different rooms

Furniture arrangement is a matter of co-ordinating furniture with both people and architecture. To do this well, we need to consider the alternative ways in which furniture can be positioned and the amount of space needed for these placements.

Living room

Living room expresses the spirit of home and a warm welcome to the guests. It should be cheerful, gay and conducive for various activities such as entertaining guests, family room for recreation with music corner and television, study or reading and so on. In living room, furniture must be around the center of interest. For example, a beautiful flower arrangement, around which furniture can be arranged. A comfortable sofa and several chairs are the most essential pieces of furniture in a living room.

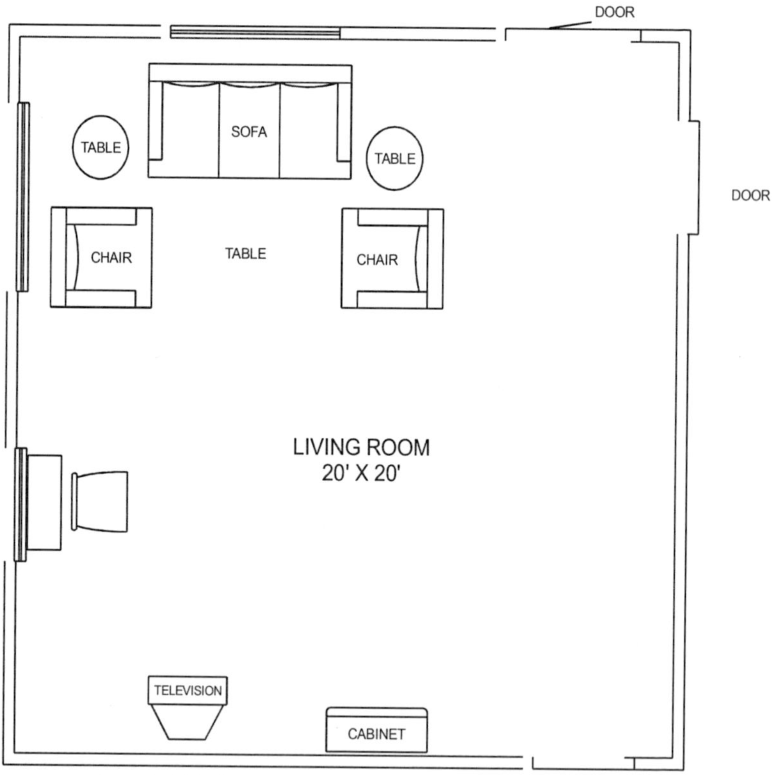

Fig. 4.6(1). Furniture arrangement in a living room

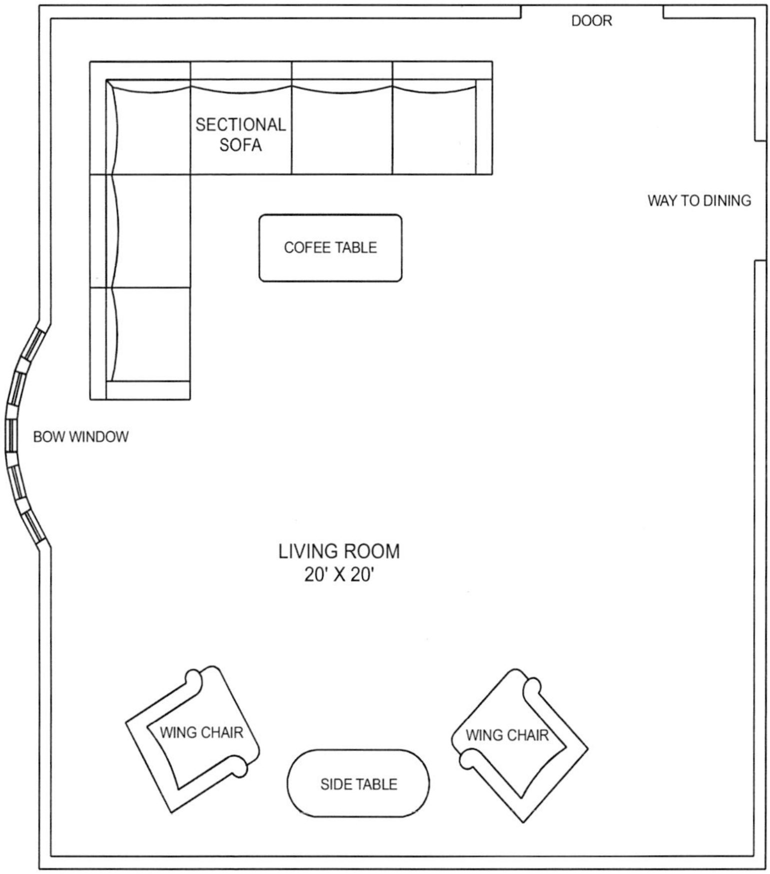

Fig. 4.6(2). Furniture arrangement in a living room

Provisions should be made for reading or study. A desk and straight backed chair of adequate height and a lamp need to be provided in this area as well as book cases, adjustable rack are also the basic requisite.

Recreation is also a part of living room activity. Space must be allocated for placing the television set, the radio, the CD player or tape recorder etc., Thus the traffic lanes should be proper, since many activities are carried out in a single room.

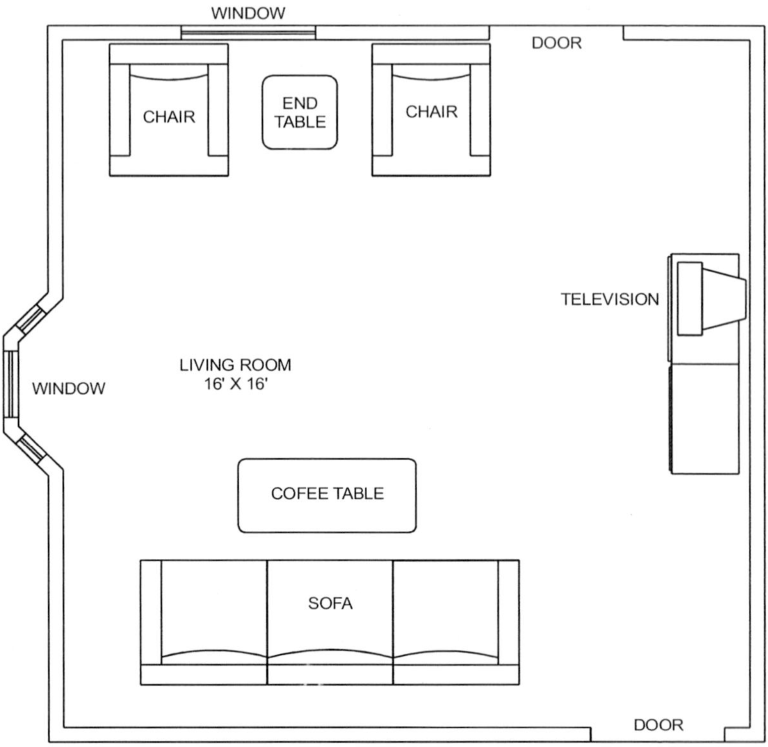

Fig. 4.6(3). Furniture arrangement in a living room

Dining space

Dining tables and seats no matter what room they occupy can be arranged in many ways:

- A rectangular or round table in the centre of a dining room or large kitchen or at one end of the general group space, increasing the importance of meals and simplifies serving.
- A table with one end against the wall takes less floor space and fits into the room architecturally.
- A table and seating in a corner, especially built-in requires minimum space and have the advantage of staying in position but they complicate moving in and out as well as serving the meal.

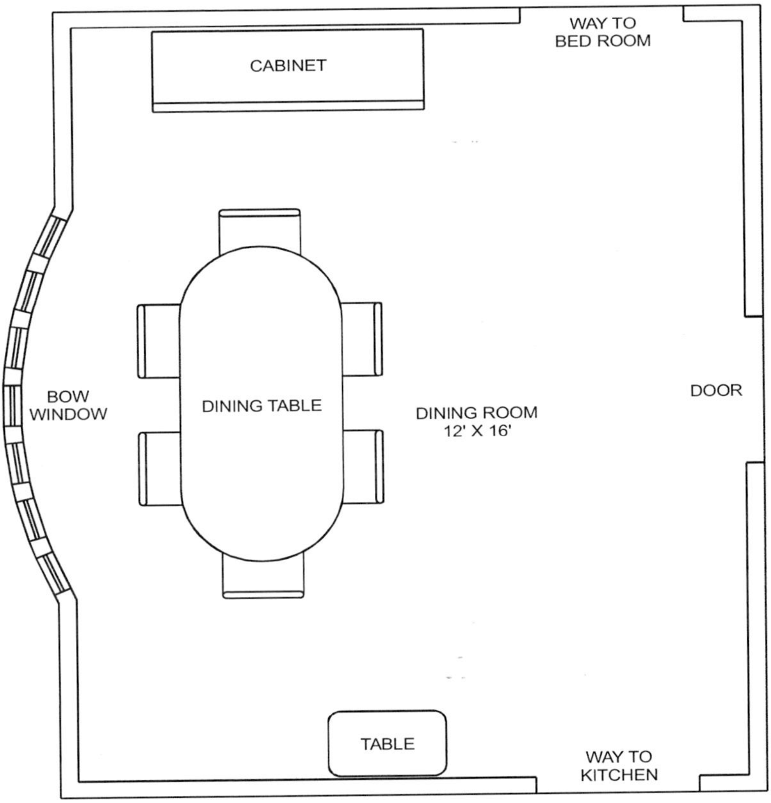

Fig. 4.7(1). Furniture arrangement in a dining room

Bedroom

The two major facts in arranging bedroom furniture are circulation paths and the placement of bed or beds. The most used traffic paths links the entrance door with the closets and drawer units, so these should be as short and direct as possible. Beds are large and inflexible. Moreover, convenience usually enforces certain tips of placement.

- Beds are typically (but not necessarily) placed with heads against a solid wall. Adequate space should be left on sides for ease in making up the bed.

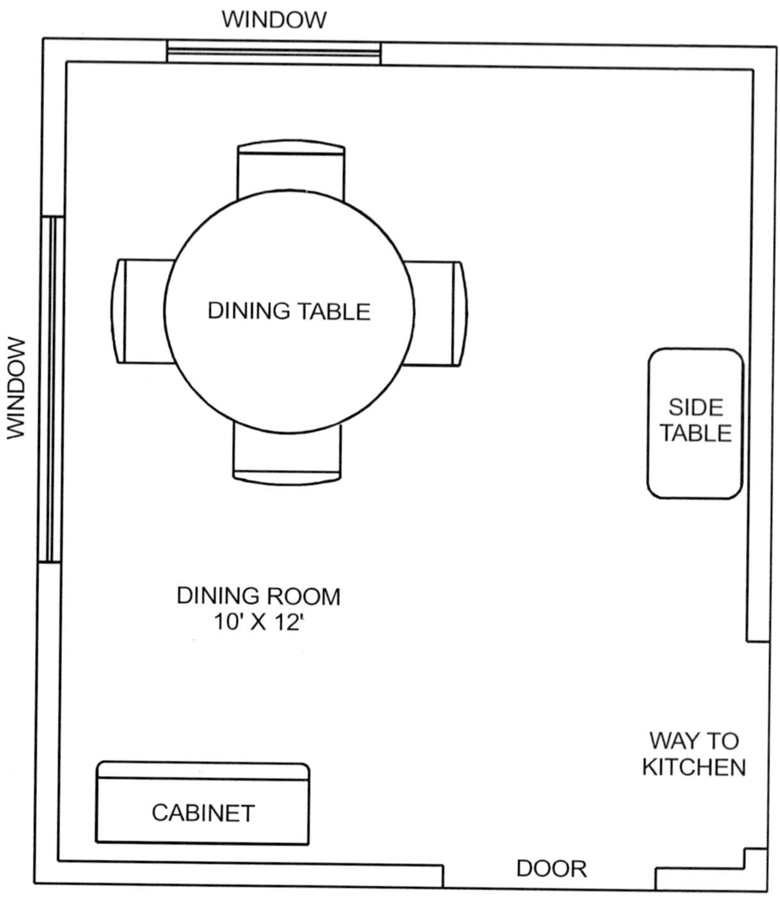

Fig. 4.7(2). Furniture arrangement in a dining room

- Single bed placed broadside against a wall or in a corner gives more space and can double as seating units but they should be on easily rolling castors to facilitate making up.
- Double decker beds will save space very efficiently but upper bunk will be difficult to make up.
- Drawer units are best next to or in closets, near window if they have mirrors above.

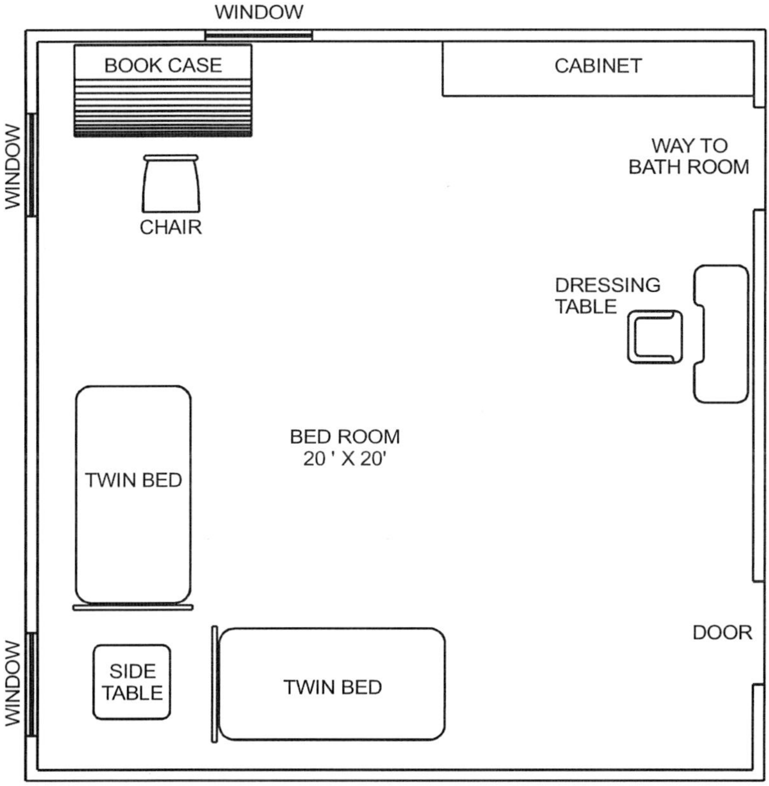

Fig. 4.8(1). Furniture arrangement in bedroom

- Drawers combined with cabinets and possibly a desk constitute a compact unit.
- A chair adjacent to closets and drawers unit completes the dressing center.
- An Easychair, a lamp and a small table set near the window form a pleasant reading spot in a bedroom.

Guest room

A guest room is used occasionally. It can be given an extra benefit of serving as a study room, TV room or a hobby room. The beds in such multipurpose rooms should have

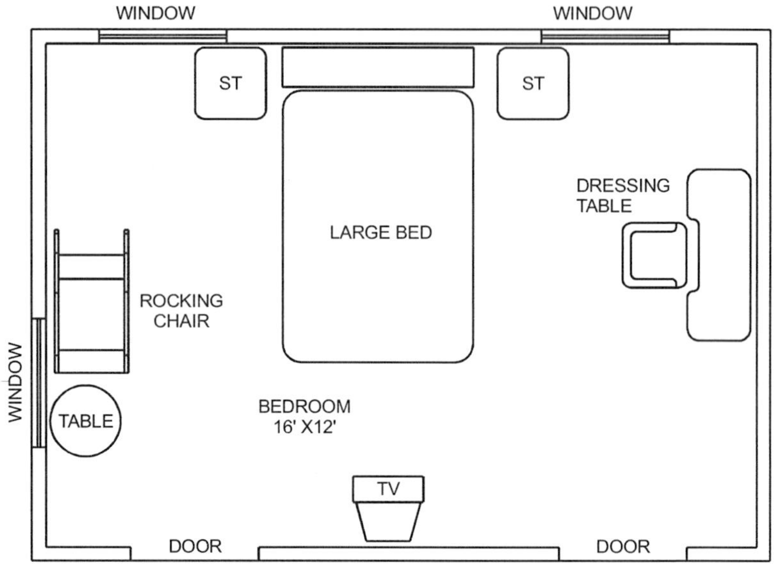

Fig. 4.8(2). Furniture arrangement in bedroom

no head board and should be placed at right angles with a lamptable between them. In small rooms, furniture should be kept along the walls and centre of the floor kept clear.

If sofabeds are kept in the guest room they should be placed in relation to other furniture, so there is enough room to open those at night. Small movable furniture may be placed nearby.

Children's room

The children's bedrooms are planned according to their activities and age. All the furniture should be kept close to the wall for a lot of free space in the centre of the room. The boy's room should provide storage for toys, books and shelves for modern ships and planes. If two boys share a room it will be a good idea to put bunk beds or two tier beds for saving space. A toys chest can be placed at the foot of the bed. Then a bedside table, a chest of drawers in a corner with a desk near the window will be a good arrangement. A nice idea will be to paint pictures of the contents on drawers to train children to put their things at proper places. A black board in boy's room will be a practical idea for a young artist. Adjustable types of furniture is a good investment. The unit or cabinet holding toys can hold books later on. Shelves, book cases, wallhung cabinet and desks are necessary for creating an uncluttered look in children's room.

4.11. Summary

Furniture lends a certain character to a room which determines whether we call it a modern or traditional. This chapter gives an ideal about the various terminologies related to furniture. A brief history about the furniture styles will enable us to have an understanding of the evolution of furniture. Some of the factors such as mobility, comfort, flexibility, space requirement, materials and methods of construction, length of service and cost of maintenance are considered for the selection of furniture. Different types of furniture are used for the creation of beautiful and comfortable room according to the family size and income level. Preliminary plans of orderly arrangements of furniture for various rooms such as living room, bedroom, guestroom, dining room and children's room can be done with effective space management.

Questions

Choose the correct answer

1. Choice of furniture for a family depends on

   a. Flexibility

   b. Comfort and convenience

   c. Mobility

   d. All the above

2. Chesterfield is a type of

   a) Chair b) Sofa

   c) Stool d) Storage furniture

3. Chest of drawer is an

   a) Outdoor furniture b) Storage furniture

   c) Modular furniture d) Built-in-furniture

4. The important criteria for the choice of outdoor furniture is

   a) Mobility b) Weather resistant

   c) Colour fastness d) All the above

5. Any furniture used in interior should be

   a) Comfortable to the user b) Foldable

   c) Harmonious d) None of the above

Fill in the blanks

1. Upholstering refers to ___________ (cushioned surface/highly polished surface).
2. Secretary is a type of _________ (storage furniture/ sofa).
3. Outdoor furniture should be _________ (weather resistant/ water repellant).
4. Where space is a limitation ___________ furniture is used (foldable/ plastic).
5. Heavy pieces of furniture should have _________ for easy mobility (castors, adjustable back).
6. Any furniture is said to be comfortable when designed based on user's __________________ dimensions. (anthropometric, maximum).

7. The height of the chair / Seat is determined by the ______________ (length of lower legs/length of upper legs).

Write short answers

1. List the factors to be considered while selecting furniture for a family.
2. Explain the term modular furniture.
3. Define the term 'upholstering'.
4. List different types of bed.
5. State the characteristics of modern furniture.
6. Name any four kinds of furniture used for seating.
7. What are the materials used for making furniture?

Long Answers

1. Explain with an illustration the furniture arrangement in a living room.
2. Explain the characteristics of modern furniture.

❑❑❑

CHAPTER 5

Furnishings

5.1. *Introduction*

A house that is furnished well would give an attractive and comfortable look, thus it requires a careful thought on usage of variety of fabrics, soft furnishings that include upholstery, slip covers, draperies or curtains, carpets, bed linen, table linen etc. The success of the scheme depends upon the skillful handling of colour, space, texture, pattern and light in the interiors. The harmony of color, design and texture of fabric must be maintained. In addition, the style of furniture, the size of the room, the use of the room, and the size and shape of the windows are important considerations while designing soft furnishings in home environment. Furnishings must be used in a distinctive style, it must give warmth and comfort. Furnishings will be subjected to different types of wear and tear and the fabric from which it is made should be suitable for the purpose. Thus soft furnishings are used in windows, doors, furniture, floor, etc.

5.2. *Terminologies*

Down : Feather from the breast of the duck used as filling for quilts.

Bed pad : Under blankets are called bed pad.

Puff : Soft, light weight, very resilient comforters are called a puff.

Blanketing : A heavily napped fabric of wool, cotton or manmade fibres in blends, woven 60 or 80 inches or more in size in plain or twill weave.

Bed linen : Any cotton, linen, or nylon sheeting for use on bed.

Comforter : A quilted bed covering made with a layer of stuffing between two fabrics of taffeta, brocaded satin, sateen or printed muslin.

Taffeta : Plain weave, smooth, stiffened fabric in silk, rayon, cotton or man-made fibres, solid colored or printed.

Quilt : A bed covering usually thinner and less resilient.

Upholstery fabrics : The fabrics that are used for covering upholstery furniture, cushions and slip covers are named as upholstery fabrics.

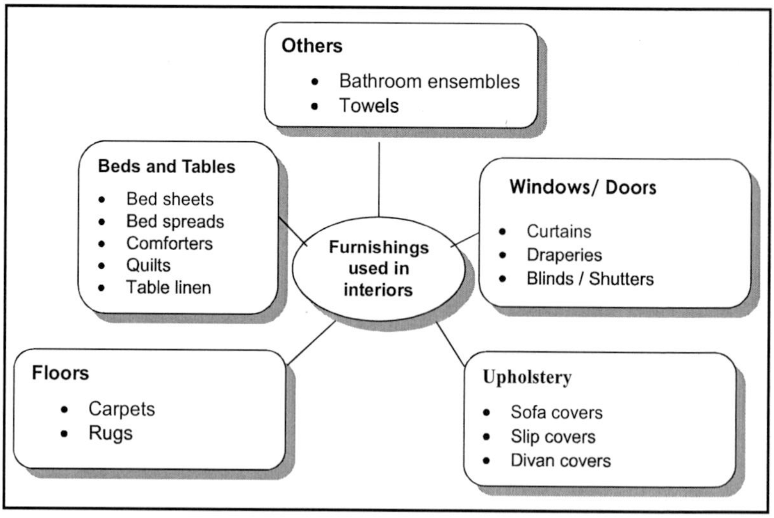

Fig. 5.1. Furnishings used in interiors

Slip covers : They are detachable covers fitted over upholstered chairs, stools etc.

5.3. Fabrics used as soft furnishings

A great variety of fabrics are used for furnishing interiors. These fabrics are spun from fibres, which may be natural or man made. Their physical and chemical properties decide its nature such as softness, durability, elasticity, lusture, resistance to fading, soiling etc.

Natural fibres such as cotton, linen, hemp, jute; animal fibres such as silk, wool, alpaca, camel hair, mohair; man-made fibres like rayon, viscose, acetate fabrics, nylon, orlon, dacron, acrylic fabrics, polyester materials and mixed fibres like cotton-rayon, cotton-polyester and so on are used for producing furnishing fabrics.

The weaves used determine the strength of fabric. There are numerous varieties in the method of interlacing of warp and weft yarns, some of the weaves commonly used are plain weave, rib weave, basket weave, satin weave, pile weave etc. The woven fabrics need to be finished to acquire an attractive appearance. The finishes used are bleaching, dyeing, printing, tentering, calendering, sanforising, mercerizing, singeing, embossing, napping, crease and shrinkage resistance, water repellency and spot resistance treatments.

5.4. Characteristics of different types of fabrics

The fabrics used for furnishing the house are discussed below.

Silk has natural luster and strength of its own. Heavy silk is crease and wrinkle resistant, drapes very well but is very expensive.

Wool is warm and expensive as silk. It needs good maintenance and must be dry cleaned.

Cotton known as 'king of fabrics', is absorbent, hygienic and easy to wash. It wrinkles easily and absorbs crease and dirt.

Brocades are finely woven fabrics of silk in which sometimes gold or silver threads are used. They are used for producing elegance and luxury.

Damask is a mixed fibre woven fabric of cotton and rayon. It can be used for curtains, upholstery and table linen.

Corduroy is made from a combination of cotton and man-made fabric.

Tapestry denotes all closely woven upholstery material. It is generally expensive.

Synthetic fabrics like viscose, nylons, acetates etc. are highly inflammable and are wrinkle, crease and moth resistant. They are easy to maintain.

Whatever the types of material available in the market, careful selection in terms of suitability and durability lies in the hands of homemaker.

5.5. Selection of fabrics

While selecting fabrics for a room, the following are the points to be remembered:

- The colour scheme of the house should be noted before selecting fabric for upholstery or drapery.
- Textures, weights and weaves of the materials must be chosen based on purpose. Chairs need thick, tough and hard wearing fabrics while curtains must be light and permit some light to pass through.
- Fabric must be tested for fading and shrinkage.
- It must be chosen for its decorative value.
- The warmth or coolness that the fabric has to provide must be considered.

- Consider the protective qualities such as fire resistance, crease resistance etc.
- Consider the durability and comfort which the furnishing is going to provide to the residents.

The size of the table, bed or window must be measured before going for purchase and sufficient allowances must be made for hems, gathers etc.

5.6. *Soft furnishings used in interiors*

Soft furnishing such as curtains, draperies, upholstery materials, carpets, bedspread, blankets, table linens etc. are used commonly in almost all houses.

Upholstery materials

The fabrics that are used for covering upholstery furniture, cushions and slip covers are named as upholstery fabrics.

The common upholstery fabrics are the

- *Printed textiles* : Ex. Chintz, cretonne, linens, jouy prints, warm prints, etc.
- *Decoratively woven materials:* Ex. Damasks, brocades, armures, reps, denims etc.
- *Pile fabrics :* Ex. Velvets, velveteens, corduroy etc.
- *Smooth* silks and satins.
- *Crewel* and needle point embroidery.
- *Mohair* and other wools.
- *Durable* quilted cottons.
- *Plastic* and leather.

Any textile fabric used for upholstering must retain freshness, resist hard usage. Inconspicuous patterns and colours that will not show soil should be chosen.

Slip covers

Slip covers are detachable covers fitted over the upholstered chairs, stools etc. They give a clean and fresh appearance to a room. The cover may reach almost to the floor level with a pleated or gathered skirt or a tailored, fixed under the chairs with the help of fastenings such as hooks, eyes, zips or touch and close fasteners.

Loose covers may be used to cover shabbiness, to cover the original upholstery and to change the appearance of the room. Slip cover fabrics must harmonise with the decorating scheme of the room in pattern, texture and colour. The fabrics may be medium-weight materials such as poplin, denim, corduroy, taffeta, velveteen, silk, sateen, etc.

Cushions

Cushions may be used to increase the comfort of chairs and sofas and to bring colour, pattern and texture to the room. They are decorative as well as useful. They can be shaped to fit the seat or be used as scatter cushions. Other types of cushions include boxed cushions cover, bolster and cushion.

Boxed cushions

Box cushions are relock-shaped cushions with squared-off edges. They are normally made from foam rubber pads and are often used on the seats and backs of chairs in place of traditional upholstery.

Bolsters

Bolsters are elongated pillows which stretch to the width of the bed and are with two circular ends which can be piped. They are usually used in diwans and as pillows for the bed.

Cushions may therefore be in all shapes, sizes, filled with feather, foam, plastic or rubber and covered with a variety of materials, matching or contrasting with the materials.

Floor coverings

Floor coverings have been made from textile fibers for more than five thousand years. Throughout civilization, rugs and carpets have formed a part of the history and culture of races and nations. Priceless handmade carpets and rugs woven hundreds of years ago in the Far East are exhibited today in museums as representative of the patient labor and creative art of weavers whose skills have been passed on through many generations. The term 'rugs' and 'carpets' are sometimes used synonymously, but the form or the size in which these coverings are manufactured differs. The differences between carpets and rugs are given below:

Table 5.1. Carpets and rugs

Carpets	Rugs
Carpets are mostly sold by yard.	Rugs, are available in specified size.
Carpets are fastened to floor.	Rugs are not fastened to floor.
Carpets are mostly machine made.	Rugs are hand tied or machine made.
Carpets are finished only on two sides.	Rugs are finished on all the four sides with fringes on two sides or on all sides.
Carpets may or may not cover the entire floor area.	Rugs does not usually cover the entire floor.
Carpets consist of backing or foundation material to enable fastening to the floor.	Rugs generally do not have a backing material.
Carpets are not easy to move from one place to another.	Rugs are easily moved from one place to another
Carpets are difficult to clean.	Rugs are comparatively easier to clean

Classification of carpets

Carpets can be classified into many categories based on manufacturing methods.

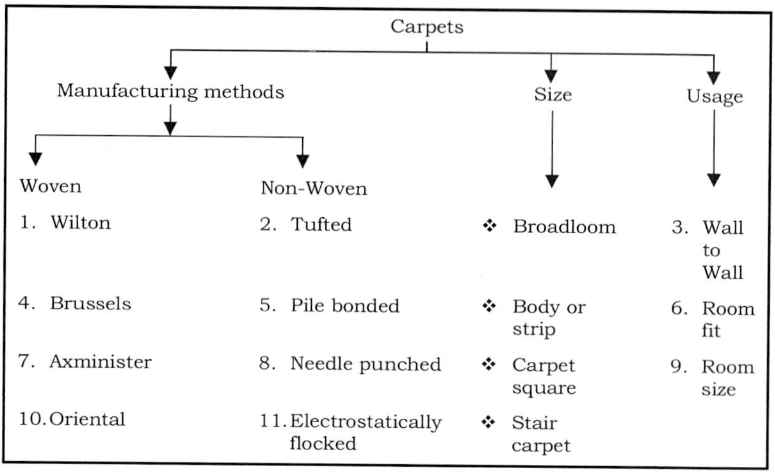

Fig. 5.2. Classification of carpets

Carpets

Wilton carpet

These are made in plain and patterned varieties. The pattern is made by Jacquard weave. The use of Jacquard enables one coloured thread at a time to be drawn as a pile, while the remaining threads, 'deads' are hidden in the backing of the carpet. Hence only two or three colours are generally used to avoid wastage of pile yarns which are carried along as backing. Then the pile is cut and closed, confining spillages to the surface and is often made up of 80/20 wool/nylon.

Brussels carpet

Brussels is an uncut patterned wilton carpet and 'cord' is an uncut plain wilton. Although Brussels carpets are less popular than the cut pile wilton carpet, they are very hard wearing for contract use. Looped or uncut pile carpets probably give 5-10% more wear than the same quality cut pile, but they do not have the same softness or resistance as the cut pile carpets.

Axminster carpet

Axminster carpets are woven in such a way that the pile is almost entirely on the surface and the backing has a distinctive rib; no dead threads are carried in the backing and the pile is longer and less close than in Wilton. The other varieties include Spool axminster, Gripper axminster, Chenille axminster.

Non-Woven carpet

The pile yarn is inserted into a pre-woven backing by a long row of needles and a loop is formed. This may be left uncut or cut. Mixtures of high and low piles, cut and looped areas, may be found in the same carpet. The pile is firmly held to the backing material by an application of natural or synthetic rubber adhesive, tufted carpets do not fray and may be cut to any shape.

Pile bonded carpet

These generally have a pile of nylon or polypropylene which is stuck into a PVC backing. There is a variety of techniques and either a corded or cut pile surface may be produced; pile bonded carpets are also available as tiles. Pile bonded carpets do not fray and may be stuck to the floor.

Needle punched carpet

These are resin impregnated or heat treated materials used in sheet or tile form. A thick web of nylon, polypropylene, acrylic or polyester fibres either as 100% or as blends, is fed into the needling sector of the machine. By the reciprocating movement of several rows of barded needles which penetrate the web, the fibres are entangled and consolidated.

Electrostatically flocked carpet

These are produced by projecting electrically charged fibre downwards into an adhesive coated backing material.

Broad loom carpet

It is woven on extra wide looms and are normally between 2 m and 5 m wide but it is possible to get one variety as much as 10 m wide.

Body or strip carpet

It is usually 68-90 cm wide, and has no border so that the pattern matches when the strips are joined for fitted carpets. The pile of a carpet lies slightly in one direction, so care must be taken when joining the carpet that all the pile lies in the same direction, if not, a slight variation in shade can be noticed.

A carpet square

It is a loose carpet with all edges finished. It does not fit the floor exactly and can be turned round to even the wear.

Stair carpet

It often has a border and may be 45 cm, 56 cm, 68 cm or 90 cm wide, while broadloom carpeting can be used on very wide staircases. These variations enable the same designs to be used along corridors of different widths from the stairs.

Wall to wall carpet

It covers the entire floor area and extend from one wall to another. As these carpets are fixed, it cannot be fixed or reversed and traffic lanes begin to wear over a period of time. These carpets are difficult to clean.

Room fit carpet

These are cut to fit the shape and size of the room. An unusual idea is to use room fit carpets, is to cut an oval shaped piece from under an oval shaped dining table, so that the area under the dining table is bare.

Room size Carpet

These carpets are available in standard sizes like 6′ x 9′, 9′x 12′ or 12′ x 15′. These can be readily used in most of the rooms and hence are generally used in majority of the interiors.

Rugs

Oriental rug

Although our present day rugs are used chiefly as floor coverings, room size, scatter size and mats or hangings, the old oriental rugs were created for other purposes as well. These include prayer rugs, hearth rugs, grave rugs, wedding rugs, mosque rugs, saddle bags etc. Of these very few of the oriental rugs produced before 1795 are on the commercial market today, but many are displayed in museums. These older oriental rugs are valuable because of their age, beauty and intricacy of design. Those made in the last hundred, years are accepted as "Old Orientals" and although scarce, are still obtainable.

Oriental rugs are classified according to the country and the section from which they originated. They are divided into six groups; Persian, Turkish, Cancasian, Turkoman, Indian and Chinese. These can further be sub classified according to their weave and also by their method of looping or knot tyeing that is characteristic of oriental rug construction.

Persian rug

Work rugs made from middle East are referred to as Persian rugs. These rugs demonstrate a high degree of creative ability, skill and artistic achievement.

Indian rug

Indian rugs include hand tied rugs, numdahs, and druggets. The hand tied rugs come from Lahore, Banaras and Rajasthan. The numdahs are made of felted goats hair and designs are embroidered by hand. Druggets also are made of wood mixed with cow's hair. Indian rugs should be dry-cleaned, not washed.

Chinese rug

The pile is deep and rich. Blue and tan are common colours. Dragons and flowers in circles are characteristic motifs, although the Chinese designers create patterns to meet the style.

Room size rug

It is the one that comes within 12 inches or less from walls on all sides.

Area rug

It is a smaller rug used to emphasize a certain area. In large rooms they are used to separate different activities like reading, dining etc.

Scatter rug

It is a very small rug used to complement a room feature- i.e., in front of bed, dressing table etc.

Accent rug

It is placed on wall-to-wall carpet for emphasis. Usually this rug has definite colour and pattern.

Factors to be considered

There are several decisions a consumer has to make when a floor covering is selected – decisions as to colour, design or pattern, suitability, quality and price.

- Choosing of carpets / rugs depends on personal choice, condition of floor and budget in hand.

- It should be at the right size of the room.
- It should be moth proof, fire resistant and wear resistant.
- It should fit into the decorative plan (colour and texture)
- It should be of durable material, resilient, abrasive resistant, colour fastness and easy to care for.
- It should not shed link, show tracking or crush.
- Buy from a reputed dealer.
- Check the fibre, weave, backing and thickness of pile.

Pillow cover / Pillow slips

These are made to match the sheet and are usually packed two to a set. Bolster pillows are also available.

Size of pillow (inches)	Size of pillow slips (in inches)
Standard 20 x 26	22 x 36
Queen 20 x 30	22 x 40
King 20 x 36	22 x 46

The hems should be 3 inches wide, straight and even. Seams should be evenly stitched and finished to prevent raveling.

Comforters

Comforters are stuffed or quilted bed coverings. It's a soft, light weight, very resilient comforter and this is called a puff in New England. Fillings for comforters can be made of cotton, acetate, wool, down, feather, acrylic and polyester fibres. The covering for comforter should be soft and pliable, with good draping qualities, wrinkle resistant and a durable press fabric.

Quilts

Quilts are thinner and expensive than comforters. They provide a warm, light bed covering but are expensive. The upkeep cost is also high. Quilts are usually filled with down. The sizes are approximately 84 cm x 127 cm and 144 cm x 127 cm. They are made from a less slippery material. Ex. cotton, sateen or brushed nylon.

Blankets

Blankets are made of various constructions and compositions, which provide different degrees of warmth, softness and durability. The yarns may be composed wholly or of blends of cotton, wool, nylon, acrylic or polyester. All types of blankets are made in four sizes and the dimensions are fairly standard.

Standard Blanket Dimensions

Type	Size (in inches)
Twin size	66 x 90 72 x 90
Double full size	80 x 90
Queen size	90 x 90 95 x 90
King size	108 x 90

It is usual to provide one under blanket (sometimes called bed pad) and two or three top blanket for each bed. These are little shorter than sheets since they do not require tucking at the top. The bed pad need to be laundered or dry-cleaned occasionally.

Bed spreads

Bed spreads are used to cover the bed during the day and the materials from which the spread was made should not crease or snag since it is folded and put away in evening. The commonly used bed spreads are made of patchwork quilts, candle wick bed spread, woven coverlet or Indian prints, chintz, calico, plaids or checked material.

Some materials used for bed spreads are cotton taffeta, chenille, upcloth, cotton crepe, unbleached muslin, quilted material etc. Bed spreads may be of the fitted or throw-over type. A loosely fitted box like slip cover reaches the floor and it is desirable. These bedspreads may be straight, pleated or frilled. The throw cover bed spread can be held in place under the pillow, and then carried over to the back of the bed.

Bathroom linens

Face and bath towels, washclothes, tank toppers, lid covers, window and shower curtains and bath mats are the commonly used items. Bath mats are usually made of terry cloth, chenille or rubber. Bath rugs are made of nylon in solid colour with patterns. A dense nylon pile is locked with rubber coating to a cotton duckback to hold the pile tufts in place and to make rug skid –resistant.

Table linens

Cloths for dining table include dinner cloths, banquet cloths, luncheon cloths, dinette, tea sets, place mats, napkins, table pads etc. The size suggested for dining linen are 54 x 54, 54 x 72 or 63 x 80 inches.

Linens are used extensively in dining table because

a. it looks clean
b. it is some what lustrous
c. stains can be removed from it easily
d. it wears and washes well

Table linen should be durable and washable cotton for everyday use. Damask, embroided linen and cutwork table mats are good for special occasions. Organdie looks crisp and attractive on a dining table. Table linens should not absorb stains readily. The points to be considered while selecting are appearance, suitability, serviceability, durability and minimum care.

Towels

Towels also form all essential part of furnishing. They include bath towels, hand towels, dish towels and glass towels. These towels usually come in terry cloth, made of cotton or a blend of cotton, rayon and polyester. Terry cloth is characterized by looped-pile surface.

Bath towels

It comes in solid colors, prints and sheared loops on one side of the towel. These are made in a range of sizes;

Type	Size (in inches)
Regular size	25 x 46
Queen size	28 x 58
King size	36 x 70

Hand towels

These are made wholly of cotton, or wholly of linen. Honey comb weave is used while constructing. They appear in sizes 16 x 26 and 18 x 36 inches and also in 11 x 18 inches.

Dish towels and Glass towels

Dish towels may be made of cottonade, crash, damask, glass cloth, terry cloth etc. Crash is excellent for dish towel and glass towels. Glass towels are intended for drying glasses and thus should be free of lint. The towel must be lighter in weight than regular dish towels.

Dish towels come in sizes of 15 x 30, 17 x 32 and 18 x 32 inches. Glass towels are 20 ½ x 31 ½ and 22 ½ x 33 inches.

Bed furnishings

Bed linen include sheets, pillow cases, mattresses, pillows, blankets, comforters, quilts bedspreads etc. Bed linen should be comfortable, have a good appearance, be durable and withstand abrasion while on the bed and during laundering.

The characteristics of fabrics used must be smooth but not slippery, absorbent, cool and be able to withstand creasing. Bed linen may be made from linen, cotton or synthetic fibres.

Sheets

Sheets for a single bed of 85 x 190 cm, a single sheet should be 177 x 274 cm; for a double bed of 135 x 190 cm, the sheet should be 238 x 274 cm; for a king-size bed of 182 x 200 cm, the sheet need to be still larger and are frequently 274 x 297 cm.

Sheets should be long enough to give a good tuck in and a good turn over. The term 'resheeting' normally refers making up bed with clean linen. Sheets have wider hem at the top than at the bottom.

Mattresses and pillows

Mattresses should be comfortable and durable. In earlier days stuffed hair, mattresses made of wool or flock are used and are absorbent and liable to be attacked by moth and other pests. Now these mattresses are replaced by spring, latex or plastic foam type.

Pillows consists of various fillings like feathers, rubber or plastic foam, synthetic fibres and kapok and are usually covered with closely woven material. The most usual size is 48 x 73 cm.

Tapestry

A jacquard woven fabric in cotton, wool, or man-made fibres. The design is woven in by means of colored filling yarns. On the back, shaded stripes identify this fabric. It is used for draperies and upholstery. Thus it is an ornamental textiles with a long service record.

5.7. Summary

Fabrics are an integral part of every room in the home. They contribute so much to the general atmosphere that they should be chosen carefully and used aesthetically. Every note of texture and colour from the functional dish towel to the formal elegant draperies in the living room express the taste and culture of the inmates. Terminologies used in furnishing, factors to be considered for selection of different fabrics for different uses, and the characteristics of these fabrics have been discussed in detail in this chapter. Fabrics have a wide range of applications in interiors such as – floor carpets, rugs, wall finishes, wall coverings etc.

Exercise

Student Project / Assignment

1. Conduct a market survey to assess the recent trends in furnishing materials and prepare a report on their availability and appropriateness to different income groups.

Choose the correct answer

1. Dish towel should

   a. absorb moisture b. be crease resistant c. be colour fastness

2. Rugs are
   a. smaller versions of carpets
   b. cut strips of unused carpets
   c. miniature size of carpets

3. Wall to wall carpets are used in
   a. staircases b. pathways c. conference rooms

4. Comforters are
   a. stuffed bed coverings b. blankets c. bedspreads

5. Towels should be made of __________ for better absorbency
   a. plain weave b. twill weave c. pile weave

Fill in the blanks

1. ______________ rugs are used in conversation area. (area/scatter).
2. Table linens should be made of __________ (satin/ blended materials).
3. Terry towels are made of __________ weaves (pile/ sateen).
4. ________________ rug is used to emphasis object placed on a wall to wall carpet (scatter/accent).
5. Needle punched carpets can be used to create __________ (elaborate designs/holes on carpet edges).

Short answers

1. State the differences between a carpet and rug.

2. What are the qualities required for the following items

   a. Bath towels
   b. Bed spreads
   c. Table linens
   d. Bathroom linens

3. Discuss about the factors to be considered while choosing furnishing materials for a home.

4. Write a note on the classification of carpets.

5. Give an account of the rugs used in interiors.

6. What are the factors to be considered while selecting floor coverings?

7. Define the following

   a. Tapestry
   b. Upholstery
   c. Bolsters
   d. Rugs
   e. Carpets
   f. Quilts
   g. Comforters

❑❑❑

CHAPTER

6

Lighting

6.1. Introduction

Lighting is one of the most routine features of our homes- so routine, in fact, that we usually take it for granted. Most of us live without second thoughts with the standard-issue, built-in-lighting that comes without abodes. Of course, we supplement the overhead lighting in each room with lamps and fixtures of every ilk, yet we often don't choose these sources of light for the right reasons. They may look good, or solve an immediate problem by providing the illumination that is needed for a specific task, but are they really the right light?

Light as an element of design should be used for visual comfort and to achieve desirable emotional responses. Factors related to visual comfort are those, which enable one to see easily, accurately and in comfort. Emotional responses are influenced by the manner in which light has been used to communicate ideas about colour, texture, shape, form and line. To understand the benefits of effective lighting in a home, there is a need for an understanding of how man responds to light. Human seeing responses improve as lighting levels are increased. Good lighting can make a house warm and friendly, lively or restful. Bad lighting results in a dreary or glaring interior and can be dangerous.

6.2. *Understanding lighting*

Objects are seen because of the light they reflect back to the eye, and the amount reflected varies according to the colour. The lighter the colour, the more light it reflects. White reflects 80% for example, reds and blues 10-20%

Table 6.1. Reflectivity in percentage of the incident light

Colour and materials	Reflectivity (%)
White	100
Aluminium; white paper	80-85
Ivory; deep lemon yellow	70-75
Deep yellow; light ochre; light green; pastel blue; pale pink; cream	60-65
Lime green; pale grey; pink; deep orange; blue grey	50-55
Powdered chalk; pale wood; sky blue	40-45
Pale oak wood; dry cement	30-35
Deep red; grass green; wood; pale leaf green; olive green; brown	20-25
Dark blue; purple red; reddish brown; slate grey; dark brown	10-15
Black	0

Source : Grandjean, E.(1985) Fitting the task to the Man – An ergonomic approach, Taylor and Francis, London, pp. 285

Reflection of light also depends on the quality of a surface – a glossy one reflects more than a matt one, a clean one more than a dirty one. Under electric light, reflection of colours is not the same as in daylight. The light from a normal household bulb causes red and yellow surfaces to appear brighter than in daylight and green and blue surfaces to appear darker. Fluorescent lamps have varying effects on colours.

Light and shade give depth to an object; the way the shadows fall depends on the way the light is distributed. Soft shadows, with the light directed from above, are best for general purposes. For decorative effect, lighting from behind an object throws it into relief in a dramatic way; side lighting models its profile; and front lighting emphasizes its detail. Lighting in below can be used for unusual effects.

6.3. Terminologies

Accent lighting is interchangeable with decorative lighting and refers to the illumination directed at a specific object or area of a space to draw attention to it. It is used to enhance certain features or furnish in a space, such as architectural elements, shelves, armoires, and collections of objects, decorative accessories or art.

Ambient lighting is interchangeable with background or general lighting, and refers to the indirect illumination that fills the volume of a room and creates a general foundation of adequate lighting for all the activities in a room or space.

Chandelier is often the focal point of the dining room. As such it should be hung about 30 inches above the tabletop and should be at least 6 inches narrower than the table on each side.

Compact Fluorescent Lamp (CFL) is a generic name used for a whole family of small, single-ended fluorescent lamps with a folded, bridged, or spiral glass tube design and with high color rendering (CRI>80) and a long life (>8,000 hours).

Cove Lighting is a lighting system comprises of light sources shielded by a ledge or recess, and distributing light over the ceiling and possibly the upper part of the wall. Cove lighting often provides a soft, warm feel to an architectural space. Light from the cove lighting fixtures is directed upward and is distributed over the ceiling and/or the upper wall of a room. The reflected light off the ceiling usually provides very even and pleasant light throughout the room. It creates comfortable ambient light that helps to balance the space. Most people have a very positive reaction to the indirect lighting provided by cove lighting. Sometimes cove lighting can offer opportunities to be a little creative and make an aesthetic statement. This can be especially true if the cove lighting fixtures provide colored light.

Cove lighting can be used very successfully in a great many locations: art galleries, bathrooms, bedrooms, churches, conference rooms, dining rooms, game rooms, hallways, hotel rooms, kitchens, libraries, living rooms, museums, offices, restaurants, studies, and taverns. The top of the cove should be located about 10-14 inches from the ceiling and designed in such a way as to allow the light coming from the cove to "wash" as much of the ceiling as possible with light

Colour Rendering is the effect which the spectral characteristics of a light source have on the appearance of coloured objects illuminated by it.

Contrast is the subjective assessment of the difference in appearance of two parts of a field of view seen simultaneously or successively (hence brightness contrast, colour contrast, simultaneous contrast). Objectively the relative difference of luminance between two parts of a field of view.

Dimmer is a device in an electrical circuit used for varying the brightness of lamps in a lighting installation. Dimming controls are ideal for almost any type of room because they can change the amount of lighting to suit each mood or activity and they can help you look good. The use of dimmers with incandescent, xenon, and halogen light sources also *increases* the life of the lamps and *decreases* the use of electrical energy.

Downlight is a small light fixture recessed into the ceiling that usually concentrates the light in a downward direction.

Emergency Lighting is lighting used when the normal lighting fails.

Filament is a tungsten wire that incandesces or lights up when an electric current runs through it.

Flexible Track Lighting System is a low voltage or a line voltage lighting system where the suspended track (sometimes called a monorail) holding the light fixtures in place and also conducting electricity to those fixtures can be bent into creative shapes.

Fluorescent Lamp is a low-pressure mercury electric-discharge lamp in which a phosphor coating on the inside of the glass tubing transforms some of the ultraviolet energy created inside the lamp into visible light.

Four-Way Switch is a wall switch that allows three switches like this to control one lighting system. Whenever you flip one of the four-way switches in a given circuit, the light changes its state; that is, if the light was on, it then turns off and if the light was off, it then turns on.

Foot-candle is a unit for measuring illumination that refers to the amount of light falling on a surface one foot from a standard candle.

Fluorescent lamps are a type of discharge lamp, which means that light is produced by the passage of an electric current through a vapor or gas instead of a tungsten wire, as in incandescent lamps. In this case, a fluorescent phosphor coating on the inside of a bulb transforms the electric energy into light. *General illumination* is also called background or ambient lighting and is the foundation of a lighting plan.

Glare is a condition of vision in which there is discomfort or a reduction in the ability to see significant objects, or both due to an unsuitable distribution or range of luminance or to extreme contrasts in space and time.

Glare Index is a number representing the amount of discomfort glare in a lighting installation to which upper limits are given for a variety of room sizes and surface reflection factors resulting from 10 selected light distribution (BZ classification).

Halogen lamps are incandescent lamps, filled with halogen gas, that employ a tungsten filament. These lamps burn brighter and get much hotter than standard incandescent lamps.

Incandescent lamps are electric lamps in which a tungsten filament is heated by an electric current until it glows. This type of bulb is most commonly found in homes.

Illumination is the density of luminous flux incident upon a surface. The unit of illumination is lumen per square metre ($1m/m^2$) which is known as lux (lx).

Louver is a type of "screen" made of translucent or opaque material and geometrically designed to prevent lamps from being viewed directly within a given angle. Louvers are intended to minimize direct or indirect glare.

Lumen (lm) is the luminous flux emitted within unit solid angle (one steradian) by a point source having a uniform intensity of one candela.

Luminous flux is the light given by a source, or received by a surface or transmitted by a medium irrespective of the way in which it is distributed spatially as regards direction. The unit of luminous flux is the lumen (lm).

Pendant can provide both task and general lighting. Equipped with shades or globes to avoid glare, they are suspended from the ceiling over dinette tables, game tables, kitchen counters, or other work areas. When used over end tables or night tables, they free up the space occupied by table lamps. In general, pendants should be hung about 30 inches above the tabletop and be about 12 inches narrower than the table on all sides.

Recessed Downlight is a small light fixture recessed into the ceiling that usually concentrates the light in a downward direction.

Task lighting is also called focal lighting. It is bright, directed light that provides illumination adequate to accomplishing specific activities, such as reading, writing, playing games, or working on crafts.

Torchiere is a floor lamp that directs light up to the ceiling rather than down, so it reflects off the ceiling to create a dramatic source of illumination.

6.4. Sources of natural and artificial lighting

The light in the house during day time is received from the sun being reflected from the sky, ground, water, building etc. At night we rely on artificial sources of light which is reflected by walls, ceilings, floor and furniture, part of the light is also absorbed by the objects. Therefore how much light is available will depend upon how much light is reflected.

6.4.1. Day lighting

Day lighting in interiors is possible by providing sufficient number of doors and windows through which light is admitted, use of proper reflecting surfaces and by control of glare. The size, location and number of windows determine the quality and quantity of light made available in a room. Large windows and sky lights may be used for better distribution than small conventional windows. By use of appropriate surface, the reflectance of light can be increased or reduced to suit the activity in the room.

Glass fixed on a window, however, may absorb or reflect as much as 35% of the light that falls on it. Although the thickness of the glass does not seem to have much effect, it is the smoothness that does. A rough surface absorbs radiant energy more readily than a smooth one. Much light is absorbed by dirt on the glass and thus it must be kept clean. Glass helps in diffusing the light as it distributes the light and provides more illumination at the farther side of the room.

The use of shades and draperies also influence the amount of daylight that is available in a room. It has been found that drawing the roller shade so that the upper half of the window is covered, cuts off sixty percent of the daylight, but only fourteen percent is lost when the shade is restricted to the upper fifth. By contrast, the light transmitted through the lower panes is reflected from the ground, and surrounding areas which may absorb more light than what they reflect.

Opaque shades may cut out 98 percent of the light while translucent shades transmit 18 percent. Curtains and draperies may cut off as much as 75 percent of the light. Removing the valence may double the available day light at the farthest side of the room. Many heavy draperies and curtains increase the shadows and tend to produce a spotty condition that may result in glare, whereas a clear window and very thin curtain materials diffuse the light and soften the shadows. If draperies are desired for purposes of decoration, the windows must be more in number and larger to make up for the loss in light (window area equivalent to one-fourth of the floor area is desirable). However, glare due to natural lighting may be reduced by growing enough shrubs, trees; roof overhangs etc. to suit the requirements.

6.4.2. Artificial light

Two most common sources of light used in our homes are incandescent bulbs and fluorescent tubes. Light from the incandescent bulbs or tubes is produced by the glow from a tungsten filament heated by electric current, so they are known as filament lamps. With fluorescent lamps, the light is produced by the glow from a phosphor coating on the glass inside the tube, activated by an electric discharge through gases. Both types are rated according to the electric power (wattage), they use. This depends on the electrical (voltage). Most household lamps are designed to use the given wattage at 240 volts.

Table 6.2. Characteristics of filament and fluorescent lamps

Filament lamps	Fluorescent lamps
Vacuum or filled with inert gas	Vacuum – coated with fluorescent powder of various colours
Fine filament inside heated to incandescence	Ultraviolet radiations fall on the powders to give light Wide choice of colours available Some tubes have reflectors inside
Coiled coils have higher operating temperature and more glare than same wattage single coil	Hot cathode lamps require low starting voltage, so more convenient for general use. Cold cathode lamps start instantaneously, lasts longer but are more difficult to install as they require high voltage
Average life 1000 hrs, long life 2000 hrs, life reduced if not suspended from cap, by vibration, wrong voltage etc.	Average life of hot cathode lamp 5000 hrs, life of cold cathode lamp 15,000 hrs.
Low in cost, different sizes suitable for many types of fittings Give direct (clear), or diffused (pearl) light of varying intensities Can produce sparkle and highlights give warm light with little distortion of colour	Initial installation cost higher than filament, but running costs lower Give diffused lighting with flat appearance, textural interest and highlights can be provided by supplementing with filament lamps Gives three times as much light as filament lamps of equal wattage
Particularly suitable for pendant lights, wall brackets, table and floor standards, spot lights	Suitable for cornice lighting and obscure corners
Poor efficiency compared with fluorescent lamps	Higher efficiency
Tubular shaped or architectural lamps 30-56 cms long	Variation in length of tube 15 to 244 cm long, large areas can be lit from a single point.

6.4.2.1. Bulbs and tubes

Bulb filaments have either single coil or more concentrated type of coil, which will give upto 20% more light for the same wattage. Most bulbs are fitted into the light socket by means of two pin bayonet caps (BC), but Edison Screw Caps (ES) are becoming popular now-a-days and are used only for special bulbs, such as reflectors.

Pear shaped bulbs is also called as GLS (General Lighting Service) bulbs. Those with a clear finish give a hard, sharp light and should be used only in opaque fittings or in fittings that are designed to give a sparkling effect.

A pearl finish gives softer shadows without any loss of light output. Pearl bulbs are suitable for most fittings. Mushroom shaped bulbs have a white finish from an internal silica coating. This gives a very even light with white shadow, and the glow from the filament cannot be seen. Reflector bulbs with internal silvering are expensive.

Filament tubes can provide strip lighting that is not too powerful. This is an advantage where a fluorescent lamp would be too bright in contrast with other lamps in the room. Architectural type linear filaments are often used for strip lighting under glass shelves in display cabinets or for lighting mirrors. Very powerful tungsten halogen filament lamps are available and are mostly used for flood lighting.

There are different colours of white fluorescent tube varying from cool blue white to warm pink white. These different colours produce different effects on the colours in a room. Compact fluorescent lamps (CFL) are now available in the market. Though they have been available for about decade, recent improvements in the design and colour resolution of these bulbs have increased their desirability for home use. Now their colour rendering properties are similar to the warm, mellow tones of incandescent light and they come in shapes and sizes that are effective for home use. A 9-watt CFL produces light roughly equivalent to 40 watts of incandescent illumination, while a 13-watt CFL is approximately equal to 75 watts work of incandescent light.

6.5. Methods of lighting

6.5.1. Direct lighting

If light shines directly on an object, it is said to be lighted by direct light. These direct 90% or more of their light towards the object in the form of a cone of light. Light sources of this kind throw hard shadows, with a contrast between light and shadow of 1:10 or much more. This kind of lighting results in discomfort, eye fatigue or interference with clear vision because of glare.

Advantages

- Good balance between ambient illumination of the room and accent lighting.
- Relatively good energy efficiency even in large spaces.
- The smaller direct component required makes it easier to control reflective *glare* in computer screens.
- Renders three dimensional objects well without harsh shadows.

Disadvantages

- Relatively high installation and maintenance costs.
- Users often need instruction on how to use the system effectively.

Glare

Physiologically speaking glare is a gross overloading of the adaptation mechanism of the eye, brought about by over exposure of the retina to light. Lighting can produce two kinds of glare - discomfort glare and disability glare.

Discomfort glare may be caused by an over bright source – such as bright sunlight or an unshielded light bulb or too much contrast between an object and its background and can result in eye strain and headache. Disability glare can make seeing difficult or even impossible. It often occurs when an object is placed too close to a bright light.

To avoid glare

- Do not use unshielded lamps, and shade the lamp to screen it from eye.
- Do not place lamps and objects to be viewed too close together, and keep the contrasts and brightness in the room within a level comfortable to the eye.
- Use of curtains with sheer fabrics or blinds that either pull up or down to half shield the glare of the natural light.
- Bring light from two or more directions.
- Provide a low level of general illumination to diminish contrast in a room with strong task lighting. For close work the working area should be no more than five times as bright as the darkest part of the room. A ratio of one to ten is never desirable.

6.5.2. Indirect lighting

These throw 90 per cent or more of their light on to the ceiling and walls, which reflect it back into the room. This system requires the ceiling and walls to be light coloured. Architects sometimes prefer this type of lighting because it can be used to emphasize architectural features, as well as produce a pleasant aesthetic effect.

Advantages

- Distributes light more evenly than do direct lighting systems.

- Eliminates glare and shadows.
- Reduces electricity use.

Disadvantages/Limitations

- Higher fixture cost in some installations.
- Requires greater floor to ceiling heights.

Application

Indirect lighting systems are best suited to office, classroom, and retail applications. Floor-to-ceiling heights of 2.4 m are acceptable, but a minimum of 2.7 m is recommended for optimum light distribution. Lower light levels are acceptable with indirect lighting systems.

6.5.3. General diffuse lighting

General diffuse lighting emits light in fairly equal proportions in all directions and up and down. The fixture providing diffuse lighting is usually a glass globe variety. To prevent glare the globe should be large and dense enough to completely conceal the lighting source.

6.5.4. Semi-indirect lighting

Semi-indirect lighting directs 60 – 90% of the light towards the ceiling and upper walls, using the ceiling as the main reflective source, the other 40% to 10% is directed toward the work place. A lamp providing semi-indirect lighting with a diffuser is preferred for reading and study.

This type also emits light in highest percentage upwards to the ceiling for redirection downwards. It provides less foot candles per watt in the center of the room than others, but illumination is spread over a large area than others and has a less of soft shadow.

6.5.5. Semi-direct lighting

In semi-direct fixtures sixty per cent of the light is directed down to the work surface and the remaining amount is directed upward.

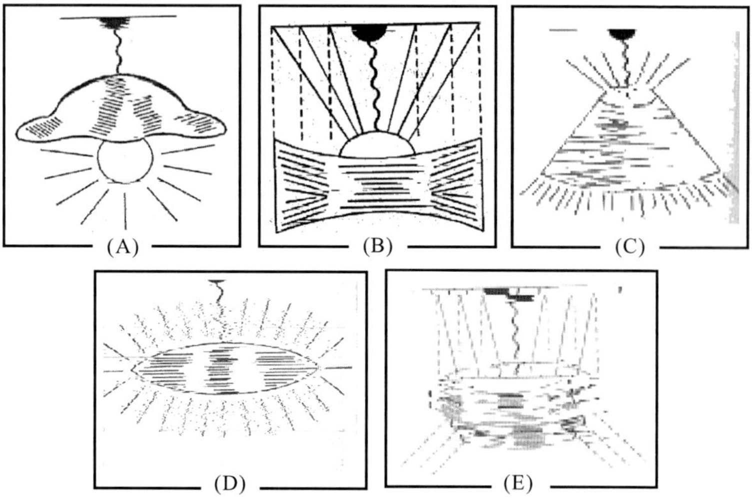

Fig. 6.1. Types of lighting

A - Direct lighting B - Indirect lighting
C - Semi direct lighting D - Diffuse lighting
E - Semi indirect lighting

6.6. Architectural and non architectural lighting

Lighting fixtures can also be classified into architectural and non-architectural fittings based on their nature of fittings. Architectural lights are structural fittings that are a component of the building and do not lend itself for transportation. They are built-in-fixtures.

Non-architectural fittings are those which can be transported / moved from one place to another.

Architectural lamps

i. *Valance lighting* are those lighting fixtures on the walls and are concealed behind a valance.

Table 6.3. Types of architectural and non-architectural lamps

Architectural lamps	Non-Architectural lamps
Valance lighting	Table lamps
Bracket lighting	Floor lamps
Cornice lighting	Pharmacy lamps
Soffit lighting	Specialty lamps
Luminous lighting	
Track lighting / spot lighting	
Plant lighting	
Ceiling and wall fixtures	
Floor lights	
Pendant	

ii. *Bracket lighting* are located on the wall especially above a sofa.

iii. *Cornice lighting* refers to the lighting fixtures located at the junction of the wall and ceiling and generally throws light in downward direction.

iv. *Soffit lighting* refers to the lights fixed in a horizontal built-in-panel to aid a better view. These lights are also fixed in the kitchen above the sink or counter along the bathroom and direct light downwards.

v. *Luminous lighting* are fixed in the ceiling and provide light in downward direction. These lights have plastic textural panels to provide diffuse lighting to the area.

vi. *Track lighting / spot lighting* are fixtures that are fitted to a track and can be moved along the track to provide lighting over a particular area. They can also be positioned at any angle to become a down light, spot light or accent light for art and collectibles.

vii. *Plant lighting* are fixtures used for indoor gardens, near foliages and are generally used to highlight the plant.

viii. *Ceiling and wall fixtures* refers to the fittings on the wall and ceilings that generally direct lighting downwards.

ix. *Floor lights* are used to provide special effects to interiors and are generally used in dance clubs.

x. *Pendant* is a suspended ceiling fixture normally used in a dining area and its length can be adjusted according to the usage.

Non-architectural fittings are not integral part of the structural design and are usually of transportable type.

Lamps that can be moved from place to place and can be used to harmonise with the style of the room. They can be table lamps, floor lamps, study lamps, candle and kerosene lamps etc. With the modern techniques, new varieties of portable lamps are available to suit the occasions and are generally used in the interiors for carrying out various tasks and also for decoration.

Table lamps show individuality and style, at the same time they serve as sources of light. Variety, mobility, and ease of installation add to the appeal of such lamps. The choice of lampshade is very crucial. Diameter of the lower edge dictates the spread of light below. The height of the bulb within the shade also affects the circle of illumination.

Floor lamps offer great flexibility. The traditional floor lamp provides a continuation of levels, serving either as a reading light or as a source of soft ambient light.

Pharmacy lamps offer options for tasks such as reading and sewing. Lamps with adjustable arms provide greater range and flexibility. Bright torches available in halogen and incandescent versions bounce light onto the ceiling for a dramatic form or indirect light specially for high ceiling rooms.

Speciality lamps in new varieties are constantly appearing in the market. These lamps can fill a definite need while remaining movable and requires standard wiring. A lamp designed for an artist's table can be called a speciality table.

6.7. General principles of good lighting

- It must provide plentiful but glare free light for all kinds of tasks.
- It must create sufficient contrast between dark and light areas to prevent dullness and monotonous.
- Prevent accidents especially at such hazards as in staircases.
- Protect our health by minimising eye strain.
- Contribute beauty and individuality to our home.
- Ensure absence of harsh shadows.
- Maintain aesthetic appearance.
- Provision of spot lights for tasks like sewing, reading etc.
- No source of light should appear in the visual field of any worker during working operations.
- As far as possible all lights should be provided with shades.

6.8. Lighting requirements for various areas

One can determine how many lumens of light is needed in the house by arriving at general conclusions using a simple method

Area of a room	x	Lumens required per sq. ft.	=	Lumens required for good lighting

On an average 70 lumens per square foot on floor space is sufficient for the entire home. A plain household candle gives about 12 lumens and 100 watts bulb emits 1630 lumens.

Incandescent Lamp Wattage	Approx. Lumens
4	20
7	45
10	56
15	95
25	232
40	360
60	615
75	960
100	1100
150	2850
200	3800
300	6280

Recommended lumens for different areas in a home

Area	Lumens/sq.ft.
Living room	80
Dining room	45
Kitchen	80
Bathroom	65
Bedroom	70
Hall way	45

Entrance and passage lighting

With good front door and porch lighting, the door itself, the keyhole, the ground immediately in front of door and the steps or step leading upto it will clearly be visible. It is a safety measure too, to identify the unexpected callers or intruders by illuminating the front entrance brightly. One can create a welcoming atmosphere by brightly lighting the entrance hall. One can use ceiling lights to highlight a painting or sculpture with spotlights. The entrance hallway should be well lighted by a ceiling fixture and other supplementary light as needed. A hall may have a direct or indirect ceiling light that can give brilliant, medium or subdued light as required. A pair of table lamps or a floor lamp may constitute a part of a group of furniture in a hall.

Planning points to be considered for lighting requirements

Activities: What will be happening in the room, and where will each specific action take place	Balance: Should the entire room be brightly lit, or would pockets of brightness and shadow be desirable? If the latter, make sure these pockets balance each other and do not detract from the room's functionality
Highlight: What features in the room need emphasis? Stunning architectural elements, such as magnificent mantels or intricate ceilings, should be bathed in light to show them off	Flexibility: To accommodate different activities in the room, make sure the level of general illumination is adequate and employ free-standing fixtures that can be moved at will
Deficits: What needs to be concealed? Faults, such as ugly architectural ornamentation or badly plastered walls, should not be emphasized with light.	Variety: A lighting plan that uses all the same fixtures or lamps can be both boring and inadequate, as it is unlikely that one type of item can satisfy all requirements. Use a diversity of light sources in a room, and choose attractive and creative options.
Ambience: What is the desired mood for the room? Dramatic or soothing? Businesslike or cheery and bright? The choice dictates the intensity and positioning of the light sources in the room	Decorative style: Make sure the light sources complement or match the decorative style of a room. If a light source is particularly stunning in itself, such an intricate chandelier or an artist made lamp, it can even be the focal point of the space.
Ambience: What is the desired mood for the room? Dramatic or soothing? Businesslike or cheery and bright? The choice dictates the intensity and positioning of the light sources in the room	Decorative style: Make sure the light sources complement or match the decorative style of a room. If a light source is particularly stunning in itself, such an intricate chandelier or an artist made lamp, it can even be the focal point of the space.

Living room

In every room in a home, there is a constant give and take between natural and artificial light. This ever changing dynamic unfolds over the course of an entire day and night. Thus the features of a room - such as its dimension and architectural details, the size, type, and number of its windows, its orientation to the world outside, and the way it is used throughout the day are all key elements, that must be considered from sunup to sundown when lighting that room. Ultimate, it is important to pay as much attention to the effect sunlight has in that room as it is to consider the impact that artificial lights have in the same space.

Today, we often spend the bulk of our time in open, airy rooms used for a variety of activities such as relaxing, watching television, reading, listening to music, and entertaining friends, or even working on hobbies, homework or special projects. We refer to these spaces with an assortment of terms, such as great room, family room, den or even the plain, old fashioned term living room, but in essence, they are hardworking, multipurpose spaces that have to accommodate a range of disparate endeavors.

Just as lighting draws attention to actors on a stage, it must highlight and accommodate the various parts of the set in these sorts of rooms. At the same time, the lighting must play up the room's best assets. It is necessary to focus adequate amounts of the right kind of light on various furniture groupings and at the same time complement and enhance the décor of the room. Reconciling these needs requires a combination of the three types of lighting (namely, general task and accent lighting).

Traditionally, a standard-issue lighting plan has been evolved for each of the public spaces in our homes. The living room contains several seating or activity areas, as it is a multipurpose space for most of us, and these are generally lit with floor lamps. An additional form of general illumination is usually present overhead, either in the form of tracks, a central ceiling fixture or recessed cans.

Dining room

In dining areas, or those portions of multipurpose spaces that are used for dining, the chandelier is still the fixture of choice. Not only it is a suitable, and often even superior source of light, it is an exceptional decorative asset that can go a long way toward expressing the specific style of a room. Today, pendant fixtures are available in a broad range of styles and are used with the same frequency as the chandelier. Recessed cans or tracks equipped with down lights can also be used to adequately light a dining table, which can be accented with flickering candles to change the ambience or mood.

Bedroom

Gone are the days when bedrooms were meant solely for sleep. Today they have become multipurpose rooms and or private sanctuaries for many members of the family. Consider all the activities that take place in this room, from reading, writing and watching television to rummaging around for what to wear and dressing. All these activities require a specific source of light, and if two people are sharing the space, it calls for sources of light that are flexible enough to be adjusted to two activities at once. As the activities of the room are tied to the perimeter of the room, this necessitates lighting sources that are tied to the layout of the room and the needs of its users. To read in a bed, besides typical bedside lamps, swing arm fixtures can be mounted to the wall, or for the most maneuverability, affixed directly to the bedpost with screw tightened vises so they can ride up and down for the best positioning. Finally don't forget to have two main light switches in the room, one by the door and one by the bed.

Study room

The home computer has become a ubiquitous feature of the households. Whether setting up a home office or simply turning a corner of the living room into the work area, the computer needs a permanent space. Task lighting – a concentrated pool of light – is essential, but tricky. The task light should be angled to fall on the work area. It is also as important to correctly position directional task lighting so you avoid working in your own shadow. To do so, place lamps at the opposite side of the work surface from your dominant hand and far enough away so that the light falls across the work surface diagonally from the top left or right. In addition to it, it is best to surround you with ambient light, particularly lighting that does not cause glare.

Kitchen

Bright, concentrated light is an essential ingredient in the hardworking areas of a home. It keeps us alert, focused and even safe at what can sometimes be hazardous tasks, such as cutting vegetables with sharp knives. Task lighting is therefore the choice for areas where concentrated activities repeatedly occur in the home.

The kitchen – the hardest working area in most homes, the kitchen, is where we store, prepare and cook food daily. In addition, its often where the family congregates for meals. Lighting needs, therefore, include both task and ambient applications. In the food preparation area, the lighting plan is largely fixed due to the permanence of cabinets and appliances. Safety is a major consideration and effective task lighting is essential where sharp implements are used, water is boiled, gas is fired, and electric rings glow. An unnecessary shadow or moment of glare can cause injury. Further, the color the light casts significantly affects our perception of the food we are preparing. Down lights, recessed lights, and lights mounted on the lower surfaces of cabinets are often ideal for task lighting. These lights should be positioned towards the front edges of cabinetry rather than the back, since bulbs placed towards the rear of a cabinet will reflect off the wall and may not reach the part of the counter where tasks are executed. However, lights too far forward on the work at hand, which can compromise safety. So it is important to get the positioning of these lights right, and it often calls for old-fashioned trial and error. Over cook tops or stoves, lights can be installed under exhaust hoods or on the ceiling, either recessed or mounted on a track and pointed at the work area. Sinks and drain boards also need to be well lit, even if this seems unnecessary because they are often situated in front of large windows.

Bathroom

In the bathroom, you need plenty of even, shadow-free lighting for shaving, grooming, and applying makeup. In small bathrooms, mirror lights will illuminate the entire room, but in larger bathrooms, an additional ceiling fixture is needed for general lighting. A recessed infrared heat lamp will give you added warmth on chilly mornings.

Bath/Vanity Lighting Strips supply task lighting, while supplementing the general lighting provided by ceiling fixtures. Similar to the lighting in theater dressing rooms, these softly glowing strips of globe-shaped incandescent bulbs provide excellent lighting for applying makeup, shaving, and grooming.

Wall-Mounted Fixtures can furnish general, task, and accent lighting. Many are designed to match and supplement dining room chandeliers, or to provide hallway, bedroom, or living room lighting. Wall brackets are often used for task lighting at the bathroom mirror. They are available with a choice of incandescent, tungsten-halogen, and energy-efficient compact fluorescent bulbs.

Living room

					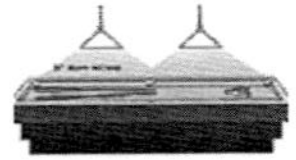
Fireplaces made of brick or stone can be emphasized with recessed downlights installed in the ceiling over the mantle to create an intriguing grazing effect across the surface. Wall sconces on each side of the fireplace are an attractive addition that draws attention to the fireplace area, while providing general lighting for the living room.	**Reading** requires task lighting that comes from behind the reader's shoulder. This can be accomplished by placing a floor lamp either at the right or the left of the reading chair. The bottom of the shade should be located at eye level to avoid glare.	**Paintings** can be highlighted with low-voltage, tungsten-halogen picture lights. These frame-mounted lights spread a beam of bright, white light across the face of the painting. **House plants** can be accented by aiming an uplight can at the wall behind the plant, creating a dramatic silhouette of the plant against the wall.	**TV, video games, and computers** require low-level general lighting that does not wash out the screen's image nor reflect into the viewer's eyes. Miniature track lighting can be installed under shelves to provide both general and accent lighting. Choose from accent spots, mini-lights, and compact or linear fluorescent light sources.	**Bars** can be lighted from above with recessed or track fixtures, or with miniature, low-voltage pendants that hover intimately over the bar. **Glass shelves and glassware** can be accented by two recessed adjustable fixtures. The use of low-voltage fixtures with tungsten-halogen bulbs will emit a bright white light that will make glassware sparkle, while providing added illumination for serving and cleanup.	**Game tables** require bright, even overhead lighting. Shaded pendants equipped with either incandescent bulbs or energy-efficient compact fluorescent tubes are one solution (see illustration). Or, install two recessed downlights over each half of the table.

Dining room

			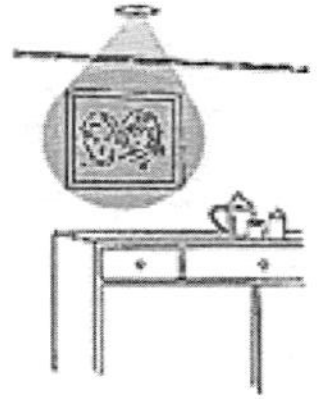	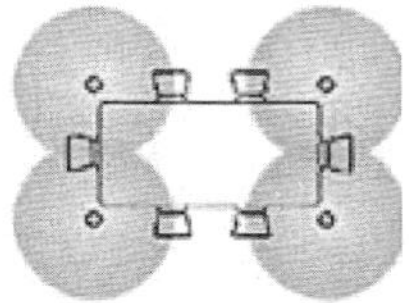
A buffet or sideboard can be flanked with wall sconces on either side. Choose fixtures that complement the style of your chandelier. Displayed objects can be accented with recessed downlights installed in the ceiling above.	**A chandelier** is the focal point of the dining room. Suspended over the dining table, it serves as a decorative style element that enhances the beauty of your fine furnishings. When the light is dimmed, a soft, glowing atmosphere similar to candlelight is created. If equipped with a downlight, the chandelier provides task lighting for the table and accent lighting for a centerpiece.	**A China cabinet, breakfront, hutch, or wall niche** can become a showplace for your prized collectibles by installing strips of low-voltage mini-lights under the shelves.	**A family portrait** can be dramatically lighted with recessed	**Recessed or track lighting** provides general lighting, while enabling you to highlight prized possessions throughout the room. A ring of four recessed downlights around the dining table supplements the light from the chandelier, while providing accent lighting for your tableware. The pure white light of low-voltage fixtures with tungsten-halogen bulbs will make your crystal and silverware sparkle.

Bedroom

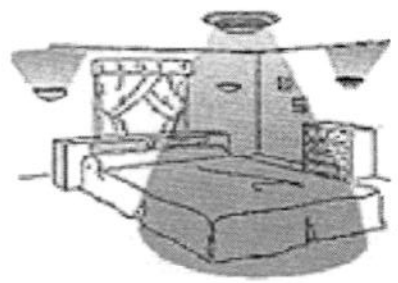	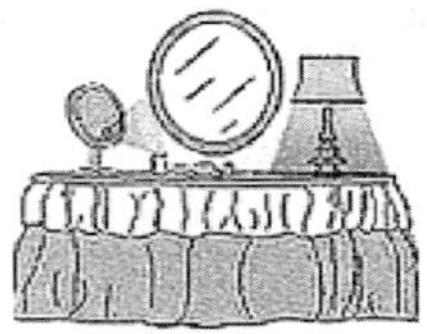	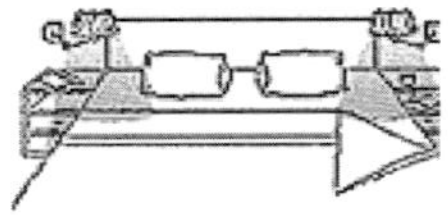	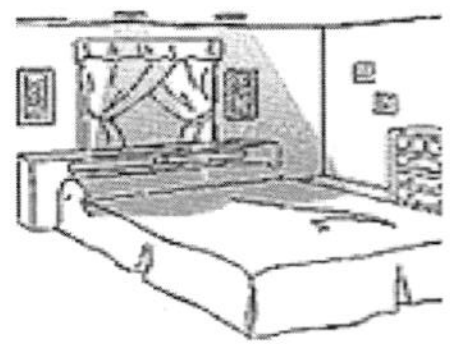	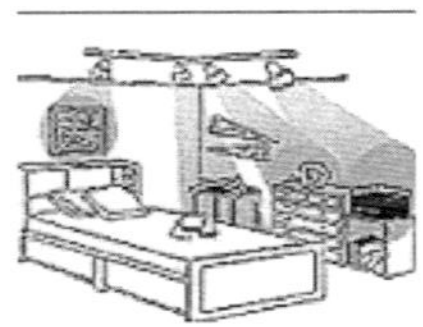
General lighting can be provided by ceiling fixtures, chandeliers, fan lights, recessed downlights, or wall sconces, giving you the illumination you need to dress and see into drawers and closets. 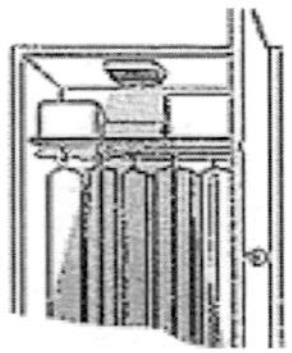 **For closets,** a recessed or surface-mounted closet light is suggested.	**At the dressing table,** an adjustable, lighted magnifying mirror will provide ideal lighting for grooming and applying makeup.	**Swing-arm wall lamps** on either side of the bed will provide adequate light for reading, while leaving night tables free for a clock-radio, books, or beverages.	**Another idea is to hang pendants** next to the bed, or install recessed downlights in the ceiling over the bed.	**Children's rooms will benefit from the use of track lights,** which can be swiveled, rotated, and aimed in any direction to shed light on play areas, hobbies, or homework. As the child grows older, the fixtures can be moved and redirected toward a stereo cabinet or sitting area.

Kitchen

	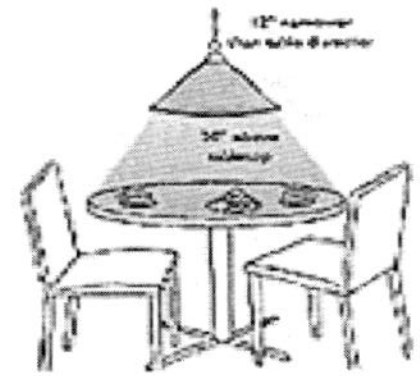	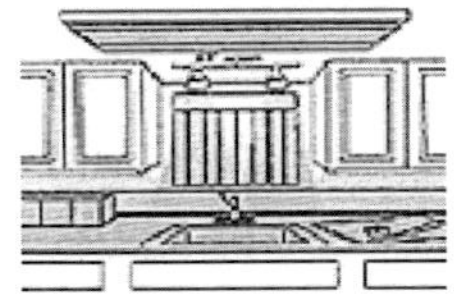	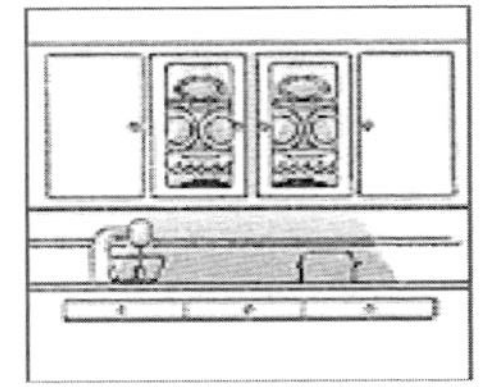	
At the sink and range, an individual recessed downlight, equipped with an energy-efficient compact fluorescent tube, will provide you with adequate task lighting when installed in the ceiling or in soffits over these two busy work areas	**Dinettes, nooks, and island counters** can be lighted with decorative pendants. When used with a dimmer control, these ceiling-hung fixtures will provide adequate task lighting for homework, hobbies, or family business and also allow to lower the light for dining or entertaining.	**A large ceiling fixture,** equipped with energy-efficient fluorescent tubes will supply plenty of well-diffused general lighting, but it may leave you working in your own shadow at the sink, range, and countertops. These areas need supplemental task lighting. For example, two track lights over the sink will give you the illumination you need for washing dishes and scouring pots and pans.	**Kitchen cabinets** can be accentuated by placing low-voltage mini-lights over, under, or inside cabinets. **Soffits and other concealed locations** can also be treated effectively with this type of lighting. These inconspicuous strips of miniature incandescent bulbs will highlight your cabinetry, while adding a warm, comfortable atmosphere to your kitchen.	**Undercabinet lighting** is ideal for countertops. Mount as close to the front of the cabinets as possible to avoid glare reflecting off work surfaces. Choose energy-efficient fluorescent fixtures (they generally range from 12 to 48 inches long) that cover at least two-thirds the length of the counter.

Bathroom

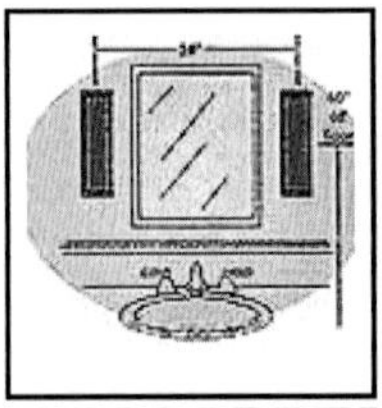			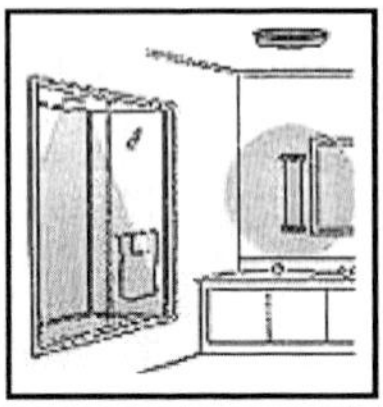
For small mirrors, decorative wall brackets on each side will illuminate both sides of your face evenly. You can also mount a wall bracket across the top of the mirror.	**Fixtures equipped with incandescent bulbs** behind glass or plastic diffusers provide the most flattering light. If you opt for more energy-efficient fluorescents, choose warm white tones They come closest to the color of incandescents.	**Theatrical lighting strips** around your bathroom mirror will give you the same excellent lighting the stars enjoy in their Broadway dressing rooms	**Tub and shower enclosures** can be adequately lighted by placing an enclosed damp-location recessed downlight in the ceiling. These downlights are also recommended over whirlpool baths or in saunas.

6.9. Summary

Light is a primary requisite of life. It is an art element as well as a utilitarian element. Light in interiors can create wonderful and different effects in the interiors. This chapter gives the reader an idea about the terminologies used in lighting, the source of lighting, methods of lighting and lighting requirements for various areas. To understand in a better manner appropriate illustrations have been provided in this chapter. Architectural and non-architectural system of lighting is also discussed in detail.

Exercise

Student Project / Assignment

1. Measure luminance's on a horizontal plane in the following places

a. outdoors, under a shady tree

b. on work benches in a class room

c. in a modern office at noon with the blinds open and the lights on and off.

How do the measured values compare with your subjective impressions of light /dark.

2. Carry out a lighting survey in an office. Draw a map of the office showing location of desks, luminaries and windows. Measure desktop luminance's and write them on the map.

Choose the correct answer

1. The colour that has the highest reflectivity of the incident light is

   a. ivory b. deep red c. white

2. The unit of measurement of lighting is

   a. lux b. decibels c. foot candle

3. CFL refers to

   a. compact fluorescent lamp b. convenience fluorescent lamp c. compact filament lamp

4. When the lighting fixtures are movable, they are known as

   a. architectural lighting b. non-architectural lighting c. cornice lighting

5. GLS refers to

   a. general lighting service b. general lighting segment c. ground lighting segment

6. The lighting that can result in higher amount of glare is

   a. direct lighting b. indirect lighting c. diffuse lighting

7. Tasks requiring higher amount of lighting should be supplemented by
   a. ambient lighting b. focal lighting c. accent lighting

8. Pendant is more suitable for
   a. living area b. dining area c. kitchen

9. Light is emitted from a fluorescent lamp from
   a. phosphor coating b. tungsten wire c. halogen gas

Filling the blanks

1. _______ bulbs provide higher light (fluorescent tubes/ incandascent bulb).
2. ________ switches are more commonly used in interiors (dolly/dimmer).
3. Glare can be eliminated by use of __________ (curtains/reflecting surface).
4. ___________ lighting is more suitable for a dinning room (track/chandelier).
5. ____________ lighting gives no shadow (indirect/ semi-direct).
6. Staircases should be lighted by providing lights from _______ (top/side ways).
7. ___________ prevents lights falling directly on the objects (lamp shade/mirror).

State True or False

1. Light requirement should be based on the type of activity.
2. Cove lighting can be used only in commercial interiors.
3. Walls sconce can be called as wall fixtures.

4. All rooms should have sufficient quantity of natural lighting.
5. Unshielded lamps helps in minimizing glare in interiors.
6. Colour rendering can be done by use of appropriate combination of lights.
7. CFL can be recommended in all areas of the house.

Short and long answers

1. Define the following terms
   Lux
   Lumen
   Foot candle
   Ambient lighting
   Accent lighting
   Glare
   Architectural lighting
   Non-architectural lighting
   Incandescent bulb
   Compact Fluorescent Lamps (CFL)
2. Explain the principles of good lighting
3. Differentiate direct and diffuse lighting.
4. How will you calculate the amount of lighting required for a room.

Long Answers

1. Give an account of the types of lighting in interiors.
2. State the characteristics of a filament and fluorescent lamp.
3. What are the factors to be considered while planning lighting in interiors?

4. Suggest a lighting plan for the following area
   a. Living room
   b. Bedroom
   c. Kitchen
   d. Dining room
5. Give an account of the types of Architectural lighting in interiors.
6. Light should be right but not bright - Discuss.

❑❑❑

CHAPTER

7

Window Treatments

7.1. Introduction

A window is an opening in the wall of a building that allows light and air to enter a room and people to see out. In early days windows were merely small oval or square holes in the walls. Very early windows were shielded with hide or cloth stretched over the opening or with wooden shutters. Later various types of windows were invented that allowed light but not weather to pass into a building. Mullioned glass windows, which joined multiple small pieces of glass with leading, paper windows, flattened pieces of translucent animal horn and plates of thinly sliced marble. Mullioned glass windows were the windows of choice among European well to-do, whereas paper windows were economical and widely used in ancient China and Japan. In England glass became common in the windows of ordinary homes only in the early 17th century whereas windows made up of panes of flattened animal horn were used as early as the 14th century in Northern Britain. Modern style floor-to-ceiling windows become possible only after the industrial glass making process was perfected. Evidence of glass windows panes in Italy dates back nearly 3000 years.

Modern windows were customarily large rectangles or squares with glass surfaces. Churches traditionally have stained glass windows. Today a window can be made in practically any shape and size desired.

Modern domestic windows come in many styles. The choice of design varies throughout the world, and is largely dictated by the prevailing weather conditions. Coastal climates tend to have smaller outward-opening windows due to the stronger winds experienced. Continental climates tend to have larger windows, many of which open inwards.

Windows are provided in the wall for sunshine, light and air circulation. Maximum number of windows should be provided on the external walls. The size and shape of the windows depend upon the activity performed in the room. The sill level is usually about one meter above the floor level and the tops of the doors and windows on the same level. Windows are classified into different types based on operation and materials used.

7.2. Types of windows

Sash window

The sash or double window is the most familiar type. Both upper and lower sections are movable.

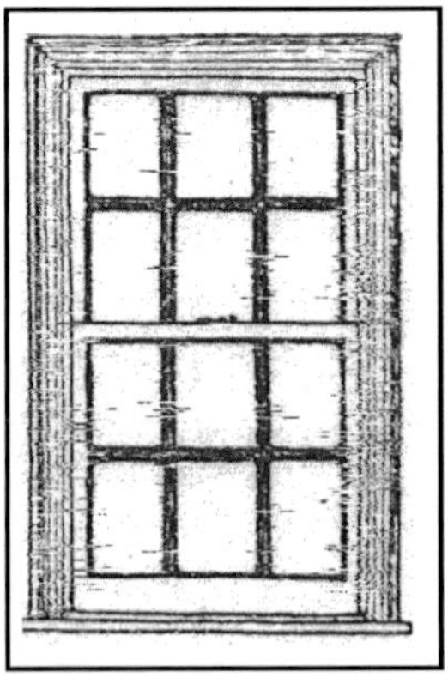

Fig. 7.1. Sash window

Bay or Bow windows

These are large curved windows designed to fit a given space or a group of three or more windows placed at an angle to each other. The window projects outside the external walls to form a projection called as a 'bay or bow'.

Fig. 7.2. Bay window

Dormer window

The dormer is a window in a gable rising from the sloping roof. These windows improve the appearance of a building.

Fig. 7.3. Dormer window

French window

Glass panelled doors are used between rooms or leading from a room to a patio or terrace. If a door or window opens in, it is best to use glass curtains with heading at both top and bottom. If they open out, draw curtains are most effective.

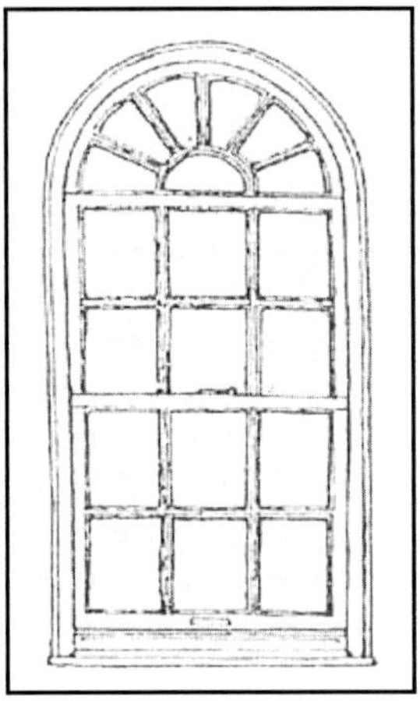

Fig. 7.4. French Window

Casement window

These are double or single window that swing like doors and can be opened in or out.

Fig. 7.5. Casement window

Sliding window

They are made of shutters which move horizontally or vertically on small roller bearings. The necessary cavities are provided in the frame or walls to receive the shutter when windows are opened.

Fig. 7.6. Sliding window

Corner windows

These are windows, single or in pairs, placed nearer to the corner than to the center of the wall.

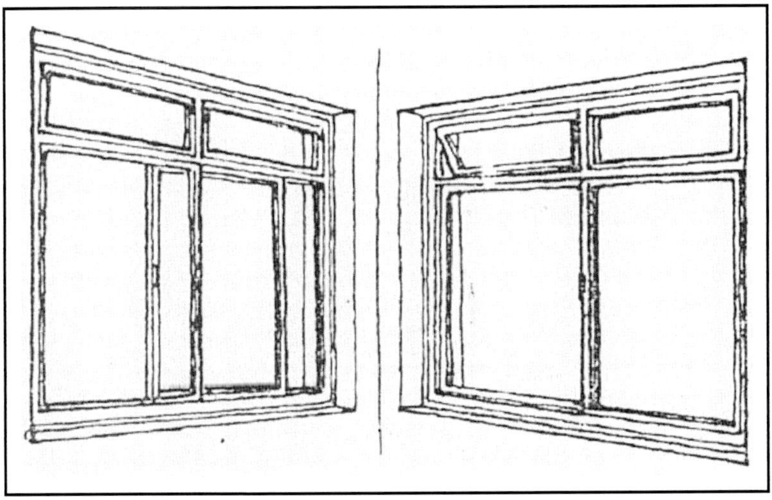

Fig. 7.7. Corner window

Pivoted windows

The shutters in these type of windows are made to swing round the pivots. The windows may be pivoted horizontally or vertically. No bars or grills are used in these type of windows.

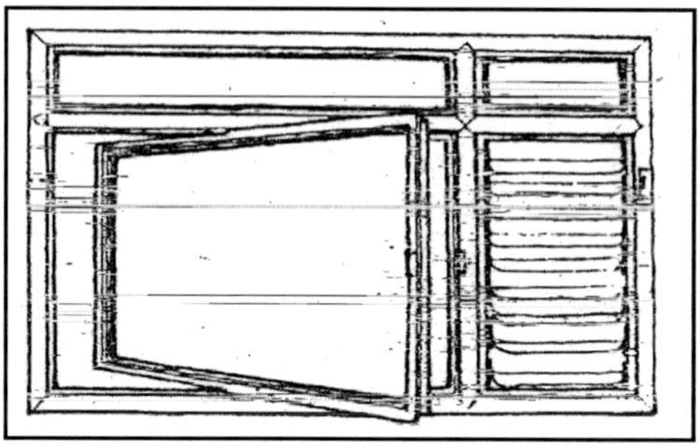

Fig. 7.8. Pivoted windows

Louvered windows

These windows consists of series of louvers made of wood, glass or metal. For economical construction, it is usually inclined at 45°. They gather dust easily and needs periodic cleaning. These are used mainly in bathrooms and workshops.

Sky light

These types of windows are usually fixed on the sloping surface of the roof parallel to its inclination. They bring

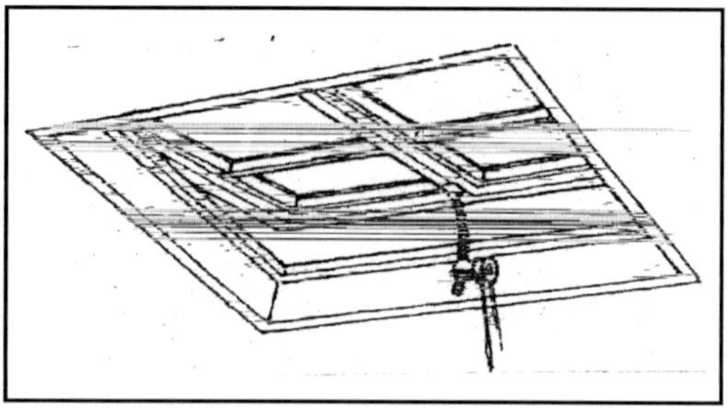

Fig. 7.9. Sky light

natural light into the room and are provided with glass panels.

Window treatments

Window dressing has undergone a sea of changes during the recent years. From the times immemorial people have been treating their windows and walls to keep out of the cold, first with skins and later with such coverings as window shutters and lengths of tapestry fabrics. In India and China, there are records of windows being draped in temples and palaces as far back as the 6th century. But it was not until the late Gothic era of Europe that the west began curtaining anything that was bare.

Window treatments offer large units of colour, texture and styling in a room. Whether to provide a inconspicuous background or to make a decorating asset, it should be remembered that the basic purpose of a window is to provide light and air. At times it may be desirable for sunshine to flood the room; at other times, it may be appropriate to block out strong sunlight. It may also frame a lovely view or exclude an unsightly one and it may be the means of ensuring privacy where privacy is needed.

Window treatments can be broadly classified as soft window treatment and hard window treatment. Soft window treatments include curtains and draperies and hard window treatments include shutters, screens, and blinds. Curtains and draperies have a broad coverage and provide large variety of window treatments. The treatment can be short or long; the material sheer or opaque, lined or unlined, plain or patterned; the decorative effect enhanced by ornamental rods, valences and swags. Appearance of course has a place, but what a person wants a window to do is the primary deciding factor. Windows can be dressed to disguise when not desired or to open up views when desired.

7.3. *Soft window treatments*

Curtains and draperies

Curtains and draperies have the following main functions:

- To screen windows at night, giving privacy to lighted rooms.
- Darken the room when necessary.
- Reduce heat loss and noise levels.
- Control light, air and view.
- Give a theme to a room.
- Bring character and atmosphere to the room by their line, colour, pattern and texture. Depending on the type of finishing, these may be used independently or to compliment with each other. Curtains and draperies are of different types and the common ones are discussed below:

Difference between curtains and draperies

Curtains		Draperies	
1.	Curtains are usually made of sheer and transparent materials, soften and diffuse light.	1.	Draperies are made of medium or heavy weight fabrics that prevent entrance of light and heat.
2.	Curtains cover a part or the full length of the window.	2.	Draperies extend from top of the window to the sill or more often 9"-12" below the sill.
3.	Curtains are hung by inserting the curtain rod or spring through the casing stitched on its top hem.	3.	Draperies are made with pleated headings and are attached to rods by hooks and rings.

Glass or Sash Curtains : These are generally made from softly gathered sheer fabrics that hang from a rod against a glass. The purpose is to ensure privacy, soften the interior and diffuse light. Glass curtains may be used with panels or draw draperies. The curtains and the draperies should be of the same length. These are usually made in simple designs and neutral colours. To get the required fullness, these should be 2 to 3 times the width of the window.

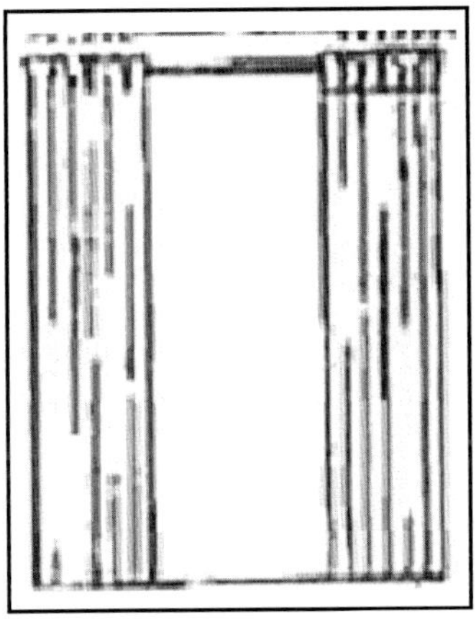

Fig. 7.10. Sash curtains

Tieback Curtains : In these straight panels are draped behind the valance and are held back to the frame of the wall with ruffles, ties or other decorative rings. Most often these are made in sheer materials but the tie back designs may be used in draperies as well.

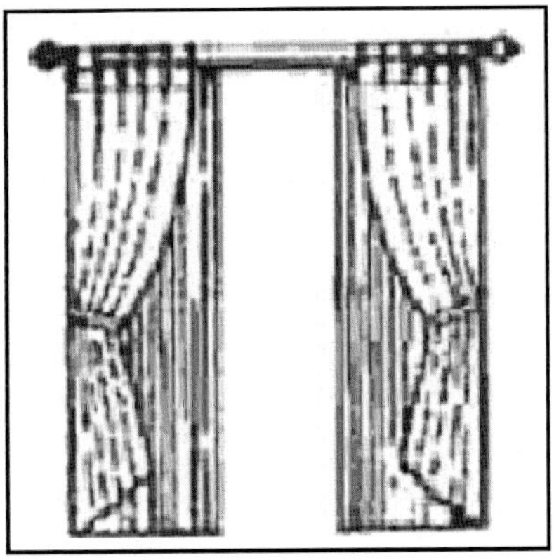

Fig. 7.11. Tieback curtains

Criss Cross Curta ins : These are a more decorative style of net curtains which is ideal for places where it is more important to distract attention from the outlook than to provide privacy. Two wide panels of the same width of the frame are fixed behind the valance. Such curtains overlap each other partially or fully and may be tied back. Sheer, fabrics having ruffles or fringes give a more interesting look.

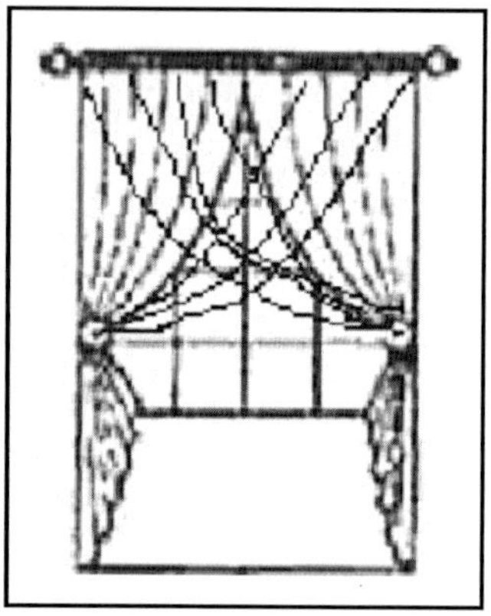

Fig. 7.12. Criss-cross curtains

Cafe curtains : The straight curtains hung from rings that slide along brass or a wooden curtain rod are called cafe curtains. These are short curtains that cover only the

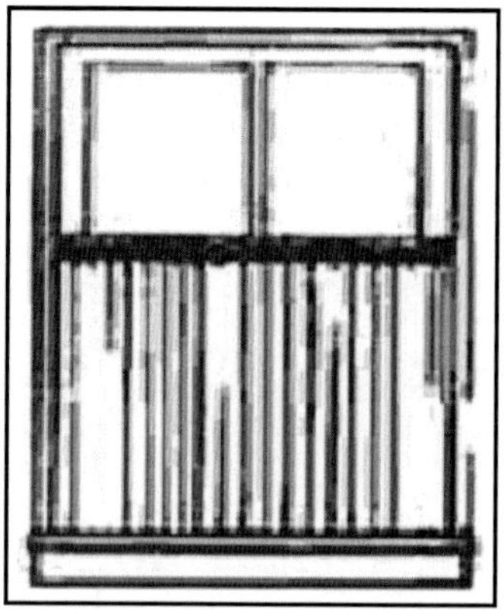

Fig. 7.13. Café curtains

lower half of a window for the sake of privacy, yet allow the light to come in from the top of the window. These are mostly kept permanently drawn and are not lined. However, when an expensive fabric is chosen or when no venetian blind or shade is used, these need to be lined. The heading may be styled in different ways such as plain, pleated, scalloped or pleated and scalloped.

Tier curtains : Two or more curtains are hung horizontally to overlap with one another. The edges may be ruffled or fringes attached to these. For privacy, the lower tier may be permanently drawn. The upper tier should overlap the lower one by an inch or two.

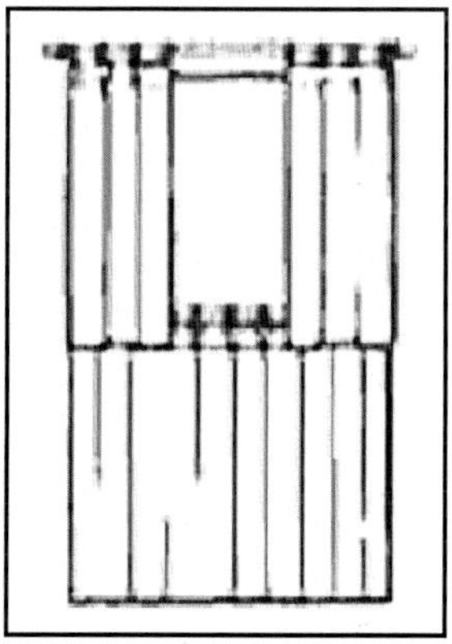

Fig. 7.14. Tier curtains

Draw Curtains : Draperies that can be drawn close to cover the entire window are known as draw draperies. In a formal setting these are designed to ensure privacy in the evenings and are hence more or less opaque. It is generally left open during the day and can be drawn by hand or cord after dark. Pleats are the most effective means of controlling fullness in such curtains.

Ruffled curtains or Priscillas : Priscillas are the ruffled curtains caught up with ruffled tiebacks and are frequently decorated at the top with a ruffled valance. These are

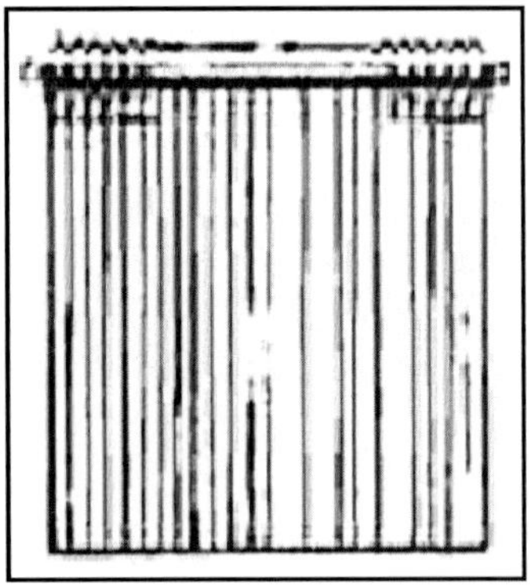

Fig. 7.15. Draw curtains

gathered directly on the curtain rod. Though Priscillas are usually short, just covering the bottom of the window frame, these may be upto floor lengths. Most familiar in white or coloured sheer fabrics, these are often made of semi-sheer muslin and trimmed with decorative binding.

Casement Curtains : These are the curtains used on casement windows that open inwards and on French windows and doors. These are tightly stretched over the glass portion of the window. The fabrics used for the glass curtains may be used for these as well.

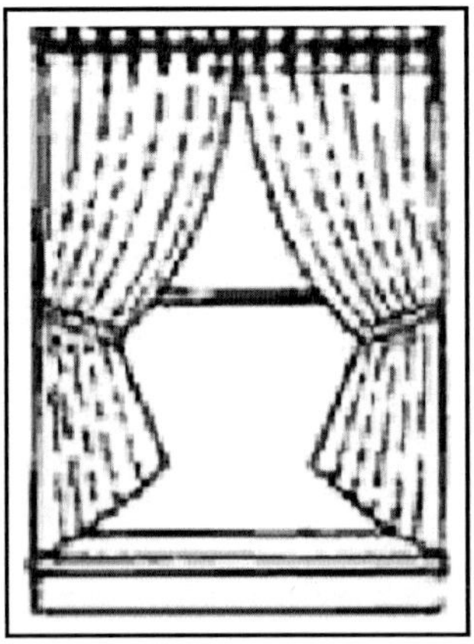

Fig. 7.16. Priscilla curtains

Fig. 7.17. Casement curtains

Swags and Cascades : These are used in very formal settings. Swag is a decorative drapery used at the top of the window. For a large window two or more swags overlapping each other may be used. Cascades are sometimes used at the sides of a swag. The cascade overlaps the swag and is in front by about 6″. The longest part of the cascade is the outside edge and may be about 30″ from top to bottom.

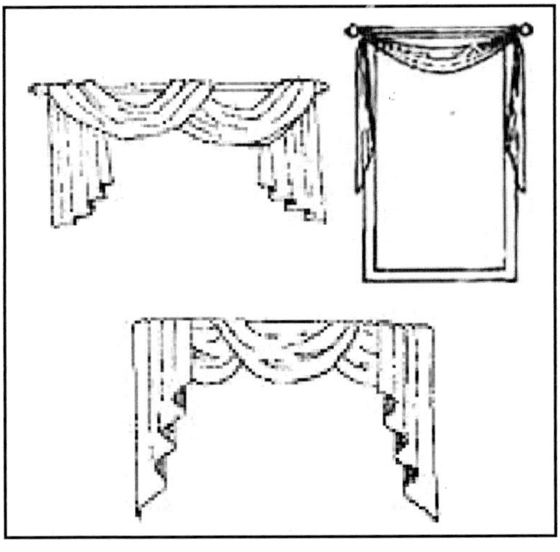

Fig. 7.18. Swags and Cascades

Pelmets : A pelmet is a length of stiffened fabric which is hung above the curtains to conceal the curtain track and help balance the proportions of the window. It can be simply or elaborately shaped and is attached to a pelmet board.

Fig. 7.19. Window treatments can create different moods in interiors. Swags and cascades can be used in formal areas of interiors

Valance : A decorative fabric or board that is installed across the top of a window. A valance is just like a very short curtain and is hung from a pelmet rail with curtain hooks.

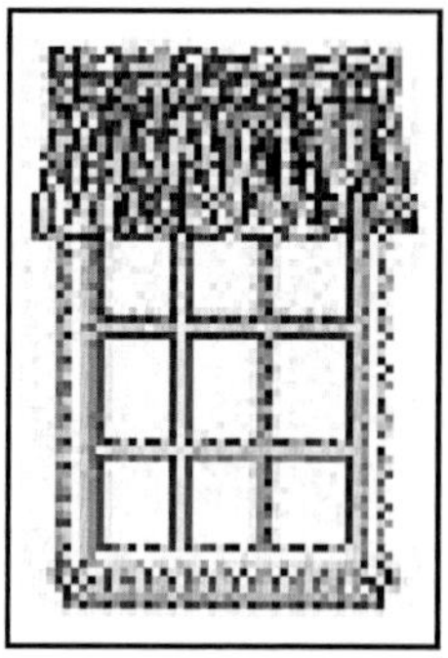

Fig. 7.20. Valance curtains

7.4. *Factors to be considered in the selection of curtains and draperies*

As mentioned earlier, curtains and draperies are used for a number of reasons. Whatever may be the purpose, curtains and draperies should be used in such a way that it allows a window to fulfill its major functions of admitting air, light and view. Since curtains and draperies are used for varied reasons, it is important that they are chosen carefully. By considering the factors that influence their selection, a person is able to make wise purchases, without wasting the valuable resources like time, effort and money.

Style

Initially window hangings were regarded as utilitarian furnishings only. In the last 300 years or so the thinking has changed and gradually they are thought of specifically as decorative items, which has emerged to give more meaning to this kind of window treatments.

During the 10th century, interior decorators started focussing on window as part of their 1professional input. Although decorators of this period preferred pale fabrics, they were usually of rather light weight ones such as satin or tafetta. The drapery itself tended to be extremely ornate replete with overlapping swag, extravagant cascades and elaborate trimmings. In victorian times, the window treatments were considerably simpler. Today's designers still draw heavily on 19th century arrangements of curtains and draperies.

For a formal living or drawing room of whatever style, it is preferable to have full length draperies, probably made of opaque material. In a traditional room, it would look good to use luxurious fabrics, perhaps figured or damask brocade or cut velvet. In modem setting, draperies tend to be somewhat self-effacing. They are generally made of plain coloured, even white fabric, the visual effect being supplied by the fabric texture and the heavy linings. Heavy silk or simple patterns on white jacquard weaves are typical.

For cottage type living rooms, and for family rooms ornamental draperies and opulent fabrics are inappropriately luxurious. Where a real casual requirement is wanted as in kitchens and bathrooms, curtains should be brief, reaching no further than the top of the window sill. This length besides being unpretentious facilitates dusting and protects the curtain from unnecessary soiling. Bright cotton prints are a favourite curtain material in kitchens, but open weaves and printed sheer fabrics are also appropriate especially when good natural sunlight is important.

Pattern

Though plain curtains are common, the patterned ones are more popular as they provide variety and a higher aesthetic value. The patterns can also be overall pattern, Small neat pattern, bold sharp pattern, floral patterns and geometrical patterns.

Texture

One or two different textures do make a room more interesting, and can give a different feeling in the room. When everything in a room has a satin smooth finish, one would feel being in a vacuum. Otherwise if everything has rough hard texture, it would make a person to feel being surrounded by pebbles. So addition of a little textural variation between curtain or upholstery material makes it to look subtle, and at the same time, attractive. Certain textural qualities are generally associated with particular colours, such as dark red, emerald green etc. Bright gold and purple suggest luxury and elegant of textures, when used in correct proportions. Texture has assumed greater importance these days through the use of thicker novelty yarns of various materials.

Delicate rooms require such fabrics like silk, satin, chiffon, taffeta, velvet etc. Sturdy rooms need natural cottons, fish net, casement cloth, voile, gauze, organdy, coloured sheeting, handlooms fabrics etc. Elegant stately rooms require raw silk, satin, damask, brocade, metallic cloth, linen or other high-grade textiles. Modem rooms can use either the new sleek shiny composition fabrics or the boldly textured novelty weaves or polyester blends which can provide contrast for modem smoothness. Other fabrics and weaves are terry, pebble weave, jersey, cheese cloth etc. which are also found in the modem market. Rubber, plastic or cellophane sheets are meant for shower curtains and may also be used for bath and kitchen windows.

Proportion

While deciding window treatments, it is advisable to take into account the line and proportions of the room. For instance, short curtains are more suitable for the lines of a cottage rooms. When additional height is desired in a room, draperies and curtains are hung straight upto floor level. Such curtains create a vertical line effect which gives an illusion of extra height to a room. In this case, the line is formed by the silhouette and the folds of the draperies. Rooms with extra high ceilings are improved by the use of valances or horizontally placed pelmets, which also appear to reduce height. It is advisable to avoid a square line on window treatment. The preferable line and the most pleasing to eye is seen on vertical rectangle, an area that is twice as high as the width of a window.

Another factor for consideration is the number of windows. Whatever treatment is chosen, must be repeated as many times as the number of windows. To avoid the repetition of a striking, bold treatment for too many windows in a room, the drapery may be treated as part of the background and repeat the exact colour of the wall. Another way of handling too many windows is to treat them as a single unit in their curtaining. A single wide venetian blind or a reed roller shade can be made to cover two or more windows. In such a treatment, all the intervening wall space is hung with drapery fabric.

Fashion

Like in other areas, fashion affects window treatments too. To meet the challenge of changing fashions, one should be alert to changes by visiting shops, exhibitions, fairs etc. Acrylic yarns and plain coloured fabrics tend to be fashionable at one time, and patterns are in fashion at other times.

Durability

Ordinary cotton draperies have a tendency to get bleached out by the effect of sunlight, and this in turn may affect the durability of the fabrics. Thicker draperies are preferred as they are more durable than silk or silk cotton fabrics. Acrylic yarns are often introduced for durability in combination with cotton or rayon or silk fibres. Expensive draperies like velvet, jacquard etc. are long lasting and therefore, should be bought with consideration to other upholstery fabrics used in the room. Keeping in mind their respective colour and texture, children rooms should have cheaper fabric that need to be washed very often. Imitation of costly fabrics such as cheap satin, artificial silk and damasks should be avoided; since they prove to be not only uneconomical in the long run, but also spoil the entire look of the furnishings in a room.

Personality and personal preferences

The owner's taste, personality and needs are such important factors in the selection of window treatments that professionals, at times, may not be able to provide such service. Whatever may be the effects of colours, it is important to keep in mind the individual likes and dislikes while choosing the colours for personal rooms.

Colour

Most of the colour interests are generally provided by the furnishing fabrics used in a room. One or two colours are more effective than a larger number of colours. Whatever is the number of colours chosen, subtle and beautiful colours should be sought in them. Finely related colours in drapery, upholstery and rugs are essential for creating harmony and beauty. When different colours are used in a room, some draperies containing all these colours, can help to unify them.

Cost

For most families, the important factor for consideration is the budget allocation for the purchase of household furnishings. Thus the cost of fabrics also influence the choice of furnishings. The cost of fabrics for curtains might be lower as compared to the expenditures for other furnishings, because draperies need to be changed every five years or so.

7.5. Hard window treatments

Blinds and shutters : Curtains are not the only way to cover windows. Shutters, screens and blinds will also ensure privacy. There are many types of blinds, of which roller blinds and roman blinds can be made at home. Most blinds can be fitted either in the window recess, or on the ceiling or wall outside the recess.

Roller blinds: Simple to install and inexpensive to buy in kit form, roller blinds let in plenty of light when drawn up, yet give complete privacy when unrolled. They can be made with material to blend with any colour scheme.

Roman blinds: No special parts are needed to make roman blinds. They are made of fabric attached to cords. When the cords are pulled, the blind rises up in accordion pleats to form a pelmet.

Venetian blinds: These blinds are made of parallel slats of plastic or wood. The slats pivot together to any position from horizontal, which lets in most light, to vertical, which cuts out direct light.

Plastic slats are more suitable for kitchens, wooden ones, which are more expensive, for living-rooms.

Pinoleum blinds: These blinds are an inexpensive covering for large windows. They are made from fine strips of wood, held together by cotton, and let a pleasant, soft light filter through. They may be mounted on a spring operated roller or moved up and down by cords.

Balastore blinds : Another inexpensive blind is the Balastore, which is made of strong paper fibre. It is accordion-pleated to act as a folding blind rather like venetian blinds. Balastores are perforated with small holes to let light through without glare.

Pleatex blinds: Made with a stronger paper than Balastores, pleatex blinds have smaller pleats. The paper gives privacy but lets sunlight through, filtered to the colour of the paper. The four main colours are orange, green, blue and parchment.

Vertical louvre blinds: Most effective on a large floor-ceiling window, these work on the same principles as venetian blinds, except that they close across the window, rather than down. The slats are wider than the venetian type, but less opaque, made from man-made sheer fabric, canvas, silk or thin wood.

Louvre shutters: These shutters are like lightweight doors made or overlapping wooden slats, spaced apart to let light through. For large windows they are made in hinged sections, which fold flat against one another to reveal the window.

Screens: Hardboard panels with cutout patterns of fabric stretched on a frame make the best screens. They are attached to the window frame and so cannot be adjusted to let more or less light through. There are now tracks which allow the screen to be moved to one side when an unrestricted view is desired.

7.6. Summary

Windows are really a decorating opportunity for setting a rooms mood and style. Window treatment can cover faults, create illusions or become focal point. Before deciding on a window treatment several factors need to be considered such as - room size, pattern, texture, durability, personal preferences, cost, colour etc. These factors can be used to select ones choice of window dressing and however there is no hard and fast rule for any window dressing. Hard and soft window treatments can be judiciously combined to achieve the different effects. This chapter gives the reader an idea of the different styles and their applicability in interiors. Several assignments and practical experiences on window dressing can create a professional touch.

Exercise

Student Project / Assignment

1. Suggest a suitable style of window dressing for the following.

   a) Modern house.

   b) Suit in a star hotel.

   c) An adolescent girl's bed room.

   d) Traditional cottage.

2. Calculate the cost of any four types of formal window dressing style. The dimensions of the window are

   1. Casement window of 8′x 4′.

   2. French window 6′x 7′.

Choose the correct answer

1. Windows which project outside the external walls are known as

   a. bay b. sash c. french

2. Windows that extend upto the floor level and often used in the dining rooms are

   a. french b. skylight c. dormer

3. The top of the windows can be treated by

   a. casement curtains b. swags and cascades c. cafe curtains

4. For covering the lower part of the window, the most suitable type of curtain is

   a. cafe b. tie-back c. draw

5. Windows which can be fixed in the sloping surface of the roof is known as

   a. sliding b. pivoted c. sky light

Fill in the blanks

1. ______ is the major criteria for deciding the window dressing (window style/pattern).
2. Illusion of height can be got by use of __________ curtains (vertical line/horizontal line).
3. The most suitable window dressing for a banquet hall is _______ (venetian blind/swags and cascades).
4. Exterior window treatment can be ___________ (soft window treatment/hard window treatment).
5. The main function of window dressing is to provide _____________ (aesthetic appeal/privacy).
6. _____________ windows resemble doors (french/casement).

State True or False

1. The exterior and interior of the windows can be treated with the same style of window dressing.
2. Bay and bow windows add elegance to the elevation of a building.
3. When space is a limitation sliding windows can be used.
4. All window dressings should have a valance at the top of the window.
5. Blinds are more suitable for an office environment rather than a home environment.
6. Shades and shutters can be used to protect windows from extreme weather condition.

Short answers

1. What are hard window treatments?
2. Explain the various methods of soft window treatments.
3. Differentiate a curtain from a drapery.
4. What is a pelmet?
5. Explain a valance.
6. What is a swag and cascade?
7. Write short notes on the following.

   Dormer window

   Skylight

   French window

   Tier curtain

   Cafe curtain

Long answers

1. Explain with illustrations the types of windows.
2. Elaborate on the soft window treatments.
3. Write a short note on the types of hard window treatments.
4. State the factors to be considered while selecting the style of window dressing.
5. Discuss on the different styles of window dressing suitable for a commercial space and justify your choice of the same.

❑❑❑

CHAPTER

8

Accessories

8.1. Introduction

Accessories have an important role in completing the decoration of the room. Accessories are usually acquired slowly over the years. Some of the accessories used in the home includes clocks, pictures, wall hangers, show pieces, calendars, lamps, mirrors, statues, collection of books, curios, murals, handicrafts, artifacts, earthenware, ceramic pots, flower arrangements and indoor plants. All these accessories define the purpose of the room and also exhibit the taste, individuality and personality of the inmates. The right choice of accessories helps to stress the decorative idea of a room. They complete the decorative aspects of the room making the room lively and thus the arrangement can be fully appreciated.

Placement of accessories should be carefully thoughtout and they are placed so that they create focal centres in the rooms. Almost all accessories have some functional as well as aesthetic value, but usually a few articles are chosen which justify their choice by their beauty and mental stimuli. While choosing accessories, it is better to have a collection of accessories which differ in size, height, texture, colour, period and design. Accessories are not items which are bought all together but are usually acquired slowly over the years.

Functions of accessories

1. It adds a personal character and reflects the personality of the homemaker.
2. Used to create a focal centre.
3. Adds beauty to the room.
4. Complete and highlight an aspect of the design.
5. Defines the purpose of the room.

8.2. Classification of accessories

Accessories can be classified into many categories based on

1. Utility 2. Size 3. Area 4. Material

CLASSIFICATION OF ACCESSORIES

Utility	Size	Area	Material
1. Functional accessory - Clocks - Mirrors etc.	1. Major accessory - Large painting - Sculptures - Chandeliers	1. Living room accessory - Clock - Ashtray - Books	1. Metal accessory - Sculptures - Cutlery
2. Decorative accessory - Wall hangers - Pictures - Flower arrangement	2. Minor accessory - Ash tray - Pen holder - Paper weight	2. Dining room accessory - Crockery and cutlery - Towel rack - Spoon stands	2 Glass accessory -Small Sculptures -Flower containers -Ash tray - Chandleirs
3. Functional cum decorative - Ash tray - Mirrors - Clocks		3. Bed room accessory - Night lamps - Photographs / Pictures	3. Plastic accessory - Table mats - Clocks
		4. Bathroom accessory - Towel rack - Soap case	

Functional Accessories

These accessories have specific purpose and are designed to serve the purpose. For example, a simple wall clock, ashtrays, lamps, mirrors, musical instruments, pots are used mainly in interiors because of their utility.

Decorative accessories

These accessories are mainly used in interiors to add beauty to the space, and do not have much of utilitarian value. Examples of such decorative accessories are pictures, sculptures, paintings, flower arrangement etc.

Functional cum decorative accessories

Accessories such as mirrors and lighting are used in interiors to serve the purpose in addition to being beautiful.

Minor accessories

Minor accessories refer to small items that are used in the rooms. For a study room, accessories such as pen holders, paper weights, foot mat, pinholders, mini dustbins etc. are minor accessories.

Major accessories

Major accessories such as chandeliers, show case, indoor plants, painting, help in creating a focal point in addition to identifying the rooms. They are however used in interiors for specific reasons and reflects the personality of the home-makers.

Living room accessories

These are items used in the living area. Functional accessories such as wall clock, ashtrays, books, lamps etc. and decorative accessories like picture, wall hangings, flower arrangements, sculptures, indoor plants and rugs are used in the living room for certain purposes and are helpful in completing the decoration of the room.

Dining room accessories

These are used in dining room and includes a wide variety of crockeries and cutleries, candle stands, napkins, towel rack, soap case, pictures of food stuffs, fruits and vegetables add beauty to the interiors and also help in defining the room.

Bedroom accessories

Functional accessories like ash tray, lampshades, dust bin, wall clock and decorative accessories like night lamps, mirror, sculptures, maps, wall hangers, pictures are used in *bedrooms*. Floor coverings like rugs, carpet, floor mats also find a place in many interiors.

Bathroom accessories

Accessories improve the appearance and increase efficiency of the bathrooms. Some are must and others are optional, make the bathroom more pleasant. Towel rods, soap dishes, toothbrush holder, clothes hooks, razor blade slot, clothes rack drier, hair drier, ash tray, toilet paper holder etc. are some accessories in *bathrooms*.

8.3. Kinds of accessories

Books

Books in open shelves or in built-in shelves are an interesting and decorative accessory. The combination of books and the other objects thoughtfully arranged can be the focal point of a decorative scheme. Books add warmth and character to a room and give a lived-in look and feeling. In any room of any style book shelves and book cases can serve as centers of interest. The shelves should be of adjustable ones to suit a variety of books. Books should be placed with due consideration to their size and colour. The largest books should be on the lower shelves. Bookshelves are also used as room dividers when they extend beyond a certain height. These kind of room dividers are used in modern interiors. Whether the home library is small or big, one can always find ideas for adopting it to one's needs and décor.

It is not surprising that books and fireplaces go together. It is easier to fill in the spaces between the fireplace and the walls with a combination of storage units below and bookshelves above. This will add stature to the fireplace itself and also make the room seem bigger, because the entire wall space is used. Books and fireplace combine to give a home a feeling of warmth and welcome that is hard to duplicate. Bookshelves over the mantel, can, no doubt, provide the ornamentation needed on a fireplace wall.

Small sculptures

Small figures of stone, wood, metal, porcelain, terracotta, plastic, ivory and other materials are suitable for home decoration. Sculptures used in interiors should express to them and also help in identifying the personality of the owners.

Fish

Coloured fishes are praised for their decorative value and pattern and as well as for their graceful movements. Plain glass containers of different shapes are now available in the market which may be used as a fish tank along with small pebbles, plastic foliages and human figures. Fish tanks find a place in majority of the living rooms and in children's room.

Clocks

Clocks are more acceptable one than anything else. A clock is a functional as well as a decorative accessory. Clocks of olden days still serve as antique pieces in many homes and the modern ones are available in different shapes, sizes, materials and colour. Clocks should harmonize with all other materials in the room.

Mirrors

Mirrors produce a feeling of expressiveness and also have a quality of illusion of space. Mirrors work magic, as there are an endless number of visual coups one can pull off in their rooms. When a room is too long and narrow, covering one of the long walls with mirror can widen it. Use of a mirror on a blank wall facing, a landscape or a scenary would bring this visual beauty into the interior of a room in a fascinating way. If a dressing room is tiny, hanging big mirrors on adjacent walls can get a double play of space.

Mirrors have been used in decoration for well over three thousand years. The mirror of the ancient Egyptians, Greek and Romans was a thin disc of metal, usually bronze, slightly convex and polished on one side for viewing. In hand mirrors, the reverse side was often engraved with line drawings, usually of mythological characters. Many of these metal mirrors, can still be seen in museums. It was not until the fourteenth century that the technology was advanced enough to produce glass mirrors in any significant quanitity, but then they were only available to the very rich. It was in Venice in the fifteenth century that the making of a flat glass mirror began on a commercial scale. In France, plate glass was invented in 1691, thereby opening the possibilities of a variety of size and far greater availability. Mirrors are functional and now-a-days beautifully decorated mirrors are available in market. It is advisable to have mirror frames made suitable to the mirrors and frames should not dominate the mirrors.

Birds

Certain type of decoration would seem incomplete without birds to impart a garden feeling. Well designed birds made of wood, or artificial feathers are more suitable when fixed on the walls. These kinds of birds are more suitable in children's room, living hall etc.

Dust bins

These are extremely important accessories from a decorative point as well as functional one. Dust bins find a place in every room in the home. These should be of suitable size, conveniently placed and made of durable material. The colour should blend with the colour of the room and the design should harmonize with other materials in the room.

Ash trays

Unlike dustbins ashtrays also serve as both functional and as decorative accessory. Ash trays are available in a wide range of materials, designs and colours to harmonize with any kind of interiors.

Maps

Maps are generally used as wall decoration material and frequently have a great utility value. Any map used for functional purpose should be accurate and legible. Maps and globes have become a fascinating and an important part of the study room, office room, library and bedroom.

Flower arrangement

Flower arrangement can also be used as accessory to highlight the personality of the individuals living in the home. The containers used for such arrangements also exhibit the taste of the individual. It is discussed in detail in the next chapter.

Lampshades

These are valuable accessories which attract attention of the viewer. Lampshades are used to emit diffused lighting or may be used to focus light to a particular area / point. A variety of materials such as leather, paper, plastic, metal, wood, glass, acrylic, fabric etc. so as to harmonize with the room.

Textile hangings

Textile hangings when used as wall hanging, textile may add an interesting note of colour or pattern to a room. Large textile hangings are particularly suitable for the plain surfaces such as back of sofa, bed etc. Figured textile hangings (eg) batik patterns, embroidered phulkari, and tie and dye are more interesting when placed against a plain background. Textile hangings have naturalistic, stylized and historic designs.

Indian textiles have now captured a world market. The art of fine weaving, varied process of painting and dyeing, hand and loom embroidery have been perfected over the ages. Silks of many kinds ranging from Banaras brocades, Gujarat patolas and Kancheepuram silk are too well-known as textile hangings. Tie and dye techniques are practiced in many states- Saurastra, Jaipur and Madurai being well known for this art. In addition cotton textiles-fine mulmull and cambric, chanderi and kota materials to mention only a few - present an endless variety to choose from.

Hanging shelves

Hanging shelves are mainly used for storage of books or for grouping of decorative objects. Some low hanging shelves are used to display collections having similar objects. Hanging shelves are best suitable over cabinet pieces of furniture which are placed against a wall. However care should be taken to see that the hanging shelves should go very well with the piece of furniture and also the room.

Murals

A mural is a painting or a decorative surface (such as wall paper) applied to a wall. A mural is distinguished from a fresco in that the later is a part of the wall rather than an applied surface.

Murals can be used on walls for colour, glamour, and excitement. Murals are like exclamation points to be used when one has something important to say. They create an intense decorating effect, as large in size, with bold colours and dramatic design. Murals are not for the timid because no other decorating accessory can express so much value for the taste, flair, and creativity one invests in selection and display. One may choose to splash bright colour in bold abstract forms across a dining room wall or paint a whimsical tree, complete with birds and butterflies, on bedroom wall and make obvious that one is approaching decorating with vigour and light heart. On the other hand, if a delicate classic Japanese screen is chosen to cover one wall the entrance foyer, a mood of elegance and quiet restraint is being established, even before guests have entered the living room. As murals are surfaces placed or painted upon walls, murals should be chosen with as much care as painting or paint. Accessories may be placed on a painted wall with adhesive or attach mural-size posters, prints or photostats. Therefore, murals can be devised from almost anything, as long as they are large and effective and choose a mural that complements the room's style.

Artifacts

Artifacts are the relics from the past or products of primitive societies and play a significant role in decorating the home and its immediate surrounding. Among the artifacts more usually found in the home are primitive tools, ancient coins and pottery fragments. These are often displayed in combination, especially as wall decorations. Artifacts – original or reproductions- reflect a time in history, when using these antiquities as accessories, a balance in style may be tried.

Antiques

Antiques include art objects, furniture, porcelain, and commonplace items such as boxes or paper weights that stays around long enough over a period of time. Purists consider items that are made before 1830 as true antiques.

There are many antique items that adapt themselves to be used in living and other common rooms to add a decorative touch in the arrangements. Large ironstone pitchers that, before the days of modern plumbing, stood with the was bowl on top of the wash stand, are good containers for the long - stemmed flowers, or can be wired for lamp bases. Old fashioned washstands can also be refined and re-finished if necessary, to be used as an extra storage space. They can even serve to house stereo components and records. There are a number of antiques like candle stands, bowls, coffee and tea services and many other items in brass, copper, silver or clay that date from earlier times. All these antiques can be put to good use. If they are in need of more than home cleaning or polishing, there are experts who specialize in mending, cleaning and lacquering to restore these decorative treasures to their original beauty and finished form.

Pictures

Pictures are used very commonly as objects of decoration on the walls, tables, mantle pieces and so on. Choosing appropriate and aesthetically sound pictures is rather difficult, but one can learn to do so by study of pictures. Many themes are dealt through various media and styles by artists. One must get familiar with these and learn to appropriate arrange the pictures in order to enjoy them.

Selection of pictures

When selecting pictures as objects of decoration, both aesthetic appeal and subject matter appeal must be considered. Aesthetic appeal is the effect created by colour and form of the picture. A good composition of the picture creates the interest and serves as center of interest. Colour appeal of the picture should be considered in relation to the room where it is to be hung or beautiful colours in a picture may be the basis for the colour scheme of a room.

Subject matter appeal

Pictures should have pleasant subject for the purpose of decoration. Flower paintings, landscapes, portraits, figure paintings and animal pictures are appealing subjects. Pictures drawn with water colours, oil paintings by great artist may be expensive but their reproductions, print in black and white or colour may be possible to use.

Relation of picture of rooms

Suitable pictures for living rooms are landscapes, marines, flower pictures, figure compositions and portrait pictures, for dining room it may be of flowers, landscape and some still life and flower prints in kitchens. Bed rooms may have personal or family photographs. Children's room should have pictures appealing to children, which would also help them to develop aesthetic sense.

Framing of pictures

A frame is used for any picture because it controls the movement in the lines of the picture; also it provides the transmission between the pictures and the wall on which it is hung.

Frames are made of many materials. Improperly framed pictures lose their effectiveness. Many times frames become more prominent than pictures and sometimes they are aesthetically not appealing.

Plain wood frames finished in their natural colours are suitable for nearly all types of pictures. Black, white, grey or dull silver are the usual colours for framing photographs, etchings or black and white prints. Oil paintings require heavy frames, and no glass is used in framing them. Frames for water colours should be of fairly narrow mouldings.

Select frames for pictures by trying different pieces of moldings on the pictures.

Before framing, many pictures need to be provided with a suitable back drop, hence they are mounted on mats before framing. Usually oil paintings are exception to this.

The colour of a mat may be white, a neutral tone lighter than the frame but slightly darker than the light in the picture.

A mat may be of fabric or mounting paper. The size of the mat depends upon the size and type of picture, upon the space where it is to be hung. For the mounting of the pictures 'Law of Margins' is used as follows:

1. In vertical rectangle pictures the bottom of the mat should be widest, the top next width and the sides slightly narrower.
2. In horizontal rectangle pictures the narrowest margin at the top, the medium margin at sides and the widest margin at the bottom.
3. A square picture usually has the same margin at top and sides and a wider one at the bottom.
4. Photographs may be framed with or without mat depending upon the size.

Hanging of pictures in different areas of the house

Pictures should not be hung just anywhere to fill up empty wall spaces but they should be grouped with furniture and wall to give an impression of unity.

a. Pictures should be hung as flat as possible as they will appear to be. The devices used for hanging should not show conspicuously. The hooks and wires should be painted in same colour as wall in order to make them inconspicuous.

b. Pictures should be hung low and not above the eye level of a standing person.

c. Small pictures should be grouped according to a common theme or colour. While grouping the picture, it is desirable to leave less space between the pictures than the pictures themselves.

d. Lower edges of all the pictures in a room should be at the same level from the floor.

e. Pictures should not be hung in a step up fashion because this makes the arrangement more noticeable than the pictures. Odd numbers symmetrically arranged are more desirable than two pictures staggered in height.

8.4. Selection of accessories

Almost all accessories have some functional as well as aesthetic value, but usually a few articles are chosen which justify their existence by their beauty and mental stimuli. Variety is the source of pleasure in accessories. They might differ in height, size, texture, colour, age, period, cost and origin. Following points should be considered while selecting the accessories.

1. Expressiveness

Accessories should be chosen to express the same idea as the home itself. It is more important for accessories to suggest the purpose of the room.

2. Line and form

In line and form the accessories should confirm to the general design of the home. Periodical accessories (or) modern furnishings should include accessories having the same general line and form as the furniture.

3. Colour

An accessory should be carefully related in colour to the furnishing of a room where it is to be placed. If possible it should be tried before being purchased. Although accessories often provide the brilliant colour, it is well to choose some accessories that have less completing colours than others.

8.5. Planning/placement of accessories

In order to obtain maximum service from useful accessories and to enjoy decorative objectives to the fullest extent you should take a great care in their placement and arrangement, (for example) a clock should be placed where you need the time. Vases should be placed where they can be enjoyed by the family.

When a room has the right amount of accessories all of them can be appreciated and enjoyed. If there are too many accessories, a room becomes clustered and disorderly in appearance. If you have a large collection of objects do not try to use all of them but use a few and make changes occasionally to add interest to your room.

Accessories should be placed in a background that is suitable for that. For example, if a room has a simple texture then the finish should be simple while a formal room needs a formal set up. Accessories in a room should show variation for it would be monotonous if they are all made of the same type of material.

8.6. Care of accessories

Brass : Polishing should be done by using brasso. Traditional cleaning was done with tamarind and salt.

Silver : Soap solution should be used for cleaning and polish like silvo can also be used.

Wood : Varnishing and repairing can be done. Polishing gives a new look to the objects.

Glass : Slight warm water with soap (or) with tissue paper dipped in soapy water can be used.

Aluminium : Any detergent can be used for cleaning.

Ceramic : Objects can be cleaned by water and mild detergents.

Cast iron : Rust can be removed, and then synthetic enamel paint can be used.

Fabric : Dusting can be done if it is washable. Dry cleaning can also be done.

Mirror : Tissue paper dipped in water can be used.

Plastics : Cleaned with a soap solution.

Small rugs : Small rugs can be washed if washable.

Porcelain : Cleaned with a soap solution.

8.7. Summary

Accessories are the elements that add charm, individuality and vitality to a room. They play a subtle but a vital role by offering pleasant clues to the personalities of the owners and making the room as unique as the tastes and interests of the people who live there. A house without accessories would look barren and unpleasant. Moreover, accessories reflect a person's personality and quality of the home. An accessory may be a small piece as a curio on the side table or as big as a wall-to-wall carpeting. Therefore it is necessary to analyse the requirements and needs of the home and make wise choices to make the house more attractive and functional.

Exercise

Student Project / Assignment

1. Conduct a market survey to identify the types of accessories for the following interiors and comment on their suitability as accessories.
   a. Study room / class room
   b. Office room located in office premises.
   c. Lounge in a star hotel
2. Make a list of the functional and decorative accessories needed for
   a. Furnishing showroom
   b. Botique
   c. Jewellery showroom

Choose the correct answer

1. Murals are more suitable for
   a. reception area b. private area c. work area.
2. Artifacts refers to
   a. furniture b. products of ancient period c. textiles
3. Handicrafts items can include
   a. glass mirror b. wall picture with light and sound effect c. handmade items
4. Indoor plants are
   a. decorative accessory b. functional accessory c. imitations of original plants
5. Music systems as accessory can be more suitable for
   a. living room b. kitchen c. study room
6. Fish tanks used as accessories have – – – – effects
   a. therapeutic b. decorative c. functional

Fill in the blanks

1. Accessories which are used only for decorative purpose is known as ______________ (functional/ decorative).
2. ______________ define the purpose of the room (accessories/lighting).
3. Mirror is a ______accessory (functional/drawing room).
4. Accessories that are used mainly for its utility is referred as ___________ (living room/functional accessory).
5. A clock is a ________________________ accessory (functional/functional and decorative).
6. Books as indoors are _____________ accessories (decorative/functional).
7. Murals are made of ________________ materials (ceramic/glass).

State true or false

1. Accessories should always coincide with the colour scheme.
2. Accessories can be made as center of interest.
3. Artifacts reflect the personality of the individuals.
4. In recent years fish tanks and indoor plants have gained momentum in office premises.
5. Living room and dining room accessories define the characteristics of a room.
6. Towel rods are merely decorative accessories in the kitchen.
7. Flower arrangements can find a place in any part of the room.

8. Figuratives can only be used in a child's room.
9. A hand fan is a decorative accessory.
10. Curios can be used as functional accessories.

Short answers and Long answers

1. What is an accessory and give the classification?
2. Name few educational accessories used in a child's room.
3. Differentiate a functional and a decorative accessory.
4. What are the factors to be considered while selecting accessories for a home?
5. Write a short note on the care of accessories.
6. "Pictures are an important accessories in interiors" discuss.
7. Elaborate on the use of accessories in defining a room.
8. Define accessory. Discuss about the livingroom, dining room and bedroom accessories. Add a short note on their placements.

❐❐❐

CHAPTER

9

Flower Arrangement

The familiar phrase- "Say it with flower" is meaningful because flowers do say special things for which it's difficult, perhaps impossible, to find the right words.

9.1. Introduction

Interior Decoration cannot be complete without the presence of flowers. Flowers suit any room in the house and give tremendous variety and interest. They add glamour and charm to one's residential life, apart from enlivening the appearance of a well kept room. In former times flowers were stuffed into a vase. Today arranging flowers has become the fascinating hobby of many houses and a specialized art. We use this art not only in homes but also in our temples, at the festivals and auspicious occasions by making decorations in the form of garlands, wall hangings, floor decorations etc., by using flowers and foliages. Also these days, we see many displays of this art in the competitions and exhibitions of flower and garden shows.

Flower arrangements are used at various locations such as on tables, window sills and corners to suit the occasion and space. The colour of the arrangement should be in harmony with the colours in the rooms. Flowers show off better against plain backgrounds and curtains than against patterned ones.

9.2. Definition

Flower arrangement may be defined as "the art of organizing flowers, other plant materials and receptacles into compositions having harmony of form, texture and colour" (Rutt, 1973). Its purpose is to add cheer, life and beauty to the surroundings. It gives us aesthetic experience and an expression of appreciation of beauty and love of the home.

9.3. History of flower arrangement

It existed in the sixth century when Chinese, Buddhist priest taught scholars how to arrange the plant material with reverence before the shrines in the temple. The Japanese have developed the art to a high degree through their many different schools of flower arrangement. In Europe and United States, people themselves are developing it. Art teachers and garden clubs have contributed greatly to the growth of this cultural interest but flower arrangement is comparatively a recent origin in our country.

9.4. Materials required for flower arrangement

There are four basic materials that are needed for making flower arrangement. They are

- Flowers and foliages
- Containers / flower vases
- Aids / tools
- Accessories

9.4.1. Flowers and foliages

Successful flower arrangement depends on the selection of flowers and foliages. The flowers should be collected either early in the morning or late in the evening.

i.e. in the dawn or in the dusk but never when the sun is burning hot. Place the flowers immediately after cutting in a bucket of water exposing only the petals. Leaves, buds and half-open or full bloom blossoms should be cut with a very sharp knife and the use of scissors is not advisable as it compresses the stem cells. If the cut end of the stem exudes latex, it should be singed over a lighted candle for a few minutes. Woody stems should be slit at the bottom or it should be crushed with a mallet so as to absorb water. Cutting and splitting exposes the inner tissues of the stems to water and speeds the flow of water to the leaves and petals before they wilt. Woody plants can also be treated by standing the stems in hot water. This treatment is good for roses and other plants which are slow to take up water. Place the ends in a bucket containing 50 ml of very hot water and leave for one minute. Then fill the bucket with tepid water and allow the stems to stand in it for several hours. Cover the heads of delicate flowers with newspaper or tissue paper to protect the petals from steam. Punch holes in a tissue paper, insert the stems through the punched holes, and then fold over the paper to cover the heads of the flowers. Fresh flowers brought from market should be carried in a wet newspaper, covering their heads. Stems of these plants should be re-cut again at home and immersed in a bucket of water for few hours before using them in flower arrangements.

It is possible to increase the life span of cut flowers by adding certain materials to the water. Most designers have special "home" remedies which are supposed to have special virtues in prolonging the life of cut flowers. A small amount of sugar will help to increase the life span of many flowers; vinegar or other acids added to the water will help to improve keeping quality. A few drops of bactericide may also be effective.

Leaves as foliages play an important role in flower arrangement. It is not necessary to use the foliages of the same plant but other foliages, which will harmonise with the arrangement can be used. Foliages are used to prepare harmonious transitional lines in the arrangement. Preserved flowers and foliages make attractive long-lasting arrangements on their own or they can be used as part of a fresh display.

9.4.2. Containers / Vases

Selection of the correct container is a significant part of any flower arrangement. It plays an important part in any design and is considered sub-ordinate only to the flowers inserted into it. A container may be defined as "Anything that will hold flowers". It may be a discarded tin, can or a fine piece of porcelain, or silver. Containers may be classified as bowls, vases, pedestals, baskets and miscellaneous types. Bowls are generally considered as those containers where width exceeds height. It may be rectangular, round, oval or irregular in shape, made of various materials and can be plain or highly decorative.

If the height exceeds width, the container is usually referred to as a vase. Vases may be cylindrical, triangular or rectangular. They may have small or wide openings. These are used for arrangements where height predominates.

The pedestal container is one of the more popular types and includes urns and compote. These containers have fixed base. The urn is distinguished from the compote by having a shorter pedestal and usually a greater water holding capacity.

Baskets are available in a variety of sizes and shapes, some made of water proof material, some provided with liners to hold bowl. Baskets come with and without handles. The novelty or miscellaneous containers include teapots and pitchers. Care must be taken that these odd shaped items do not detract from, but add to the overall arrangement and setting.

Containers can be made of any material. Pottery, metal, wood, plastic, paper and glass are satisfactory. The colour of a container must be in harmony with its surroundings. Neutral colours are generally best, but there are times when strong contrasting colours may be used. White, black and pastels most often will complement or harmonize with the plant material.

Bases, blocks or stands are often used in conjunction with a flower arrangement. They are placed under vases and become an integral part of the container. Not all arrangements need some type of bases or stands but many times a stand will help to give necessary height or to present a stabilizing force to help balance the design. Bases or stands should be selected carefully and be of correct colour, size and texture to harmonize with the rest of the composition.

Fig. 9.1. Types of flower containers

9.4.3. Aids / Tools

A plastic bucket is much more of practical use when collecting flowers from the garden. It can be partially filled with water into which the freshly cut stems may be immersed. A pair of scissors and knives are useful for cutting the stalks of the flowers and foliages. Specimen tubes may be used to lift short stemmed materials to a higher level. Other materials such as cello tape, small twigs and rods, marbles, pebbles, shells and granite pieces may be used in glass containers to camouflage ungraceful stalks.

Pin holders consists of a series of metal points, placed close together, which project upwards from a heavy metal base. The shapes and sizes of the bases vary. The most useful base is round and about 75 mm (3") in diameter. The pin holders are best suited for use in low or shallow containers. To prevent pin holders from moving around in the containers, they should be secured with florist clay.

One-inch mesh chicken will make a satisfactory flower holder for tall or medium height containers. It can be crumbled to fit any containers. When using the chicken wire, it is important that the proper amount be used for the specific container. If too little is used, the wire will tend to move, spaces will be large and the flowers will not be held securely.

Water retaining plastic foam such as Oasis, is sold by florists. It holds most stems easily in any position, but it is not suitable for very soft stems. It is particularly useful for holding flowers in shallow saucers and vases. Before putting the foam into the flower container, soak it in a bowl of cold water. If the plastic foam is used in a shallow container without water make sure it is kept moist by pouring in a little water everyday or two.

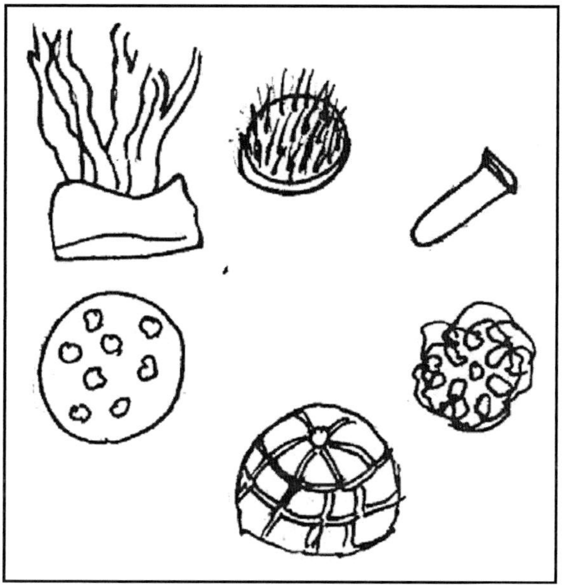

Fig 9.2. Types of stem holders

9.4.4. Accessories

Accessories are objects or materials added to an arrangement, either within the container of a plant material or separate from it, which will contribute to the overall theme of the composition. All accessories should be in scale with other parts of the composition. They include items such as figurines, ceramic figures, fruits, beads, candle stands, covers of containers etc. Placing accessories forward or toward the rear can be effective in helping to create depth.

9.5. Steps in making a flower arrangement

Whatever may be the types of arrangements the following simple rules or guidelines will help to arrange the flowers.

1. Make a definite plan of the arrangement (i.e.) whether mass, line or modern based on the occasion and the availability of the area.

2. Select suitable containers, flowers and foliages for making the selected arrangement.
3. Select flowers with varied stem lengths.
4. Arrange the tallest flower first and then others according to your choice of arrangement.
5. Large flowers with bright colours can be used in short numbers and at the centre in tall vases.
6. Arrange the foliages after the flowers so as to serve as a background for flowers.
7. Do not mix up fresh flowers and artificial flowers.
8. Cover up the stem holders.
9. Pour enough water in the vases.
10. Change water everyday.

9.6. Styles in arrangement

There are three main styles in arranging flowers namely:-

a. Traditional
b. Oriental /Japanese
c. Modern

a. Traditional style is a form of arrangement of mass of flowers of all kinds, colours and sizes and are used together in a decorative container. The arranged flowers present a multi-coloured effect.

b. The oriental style is in fact the Japanese mode of arrangement. The most striking characteristics is that it gives the impression of natural growth. The basis of all Japanese art is symbolic of nature. In its three main lines it represents Heaven, Man, and Earth. These are called respectively Shin, Soe and Hikae. The ancient schools of Japanese flower arrangement were very strict regarding the choice and amount of materials used. The modern school, which is the one imitated by the west, allows considerably more freedom. One important rule, however is that the plant materials used must be those which are natural associates in nature. In other words, flowers, trees and shrubs which grow in a similar environment.

• Shin representing Heaven is always the longest and most important line, wherever it may happen to be placed. It generally takes the form of a carefully pruned branch. Shin is placed at an angle of 10° off vertical. Shin should slope slightly forward and be impaled on the back of a pin holder, which is set to one side or the other of the container but never in the centre.

• Soe, representing Mankind is also chosen for a lovely curve. It is cut to three quarters of the length of the shin and placed at an angle of 45° off vertical and set, so to speak in the middle distance.

• Hikae representing the Earth, is the shortest line. It is cut to three quarters the length of soe and is placed

Fig. 9.3. Japanese Flower arrangement

at an angle of 75° off vertical. It should be tilted forward and outwards again utilizing graceful curves, all of which should have preferably an upward tilting tip. This upward tilt suggests happiness, the curve of smiling lips.

c. The modern arrangement, the most recently developed of the three styles, owes more to oriental than traditional in its fascination with line. Modern arrangers pay small attention to mathematical recipes for the right proportions and thus it concentrates much on line designs.

9.7. *Types of flower arrangement*

Flower arrangement can be classified into

a. Line arrangement

b. Mass arrangement and

c. Combination of line and mass arrangement.

9.7.1. Line arrangement

Compositions in which the elements of line is of first importance is known as line arrangement. Only a relatively small amount of plant material is used in order that the beautiful and characteristics lines of plant growth will show clearly. A favourite line arrangement consists of 3 sprays of different lengths that go in the same direction or suggest a triangle.

9.7.2. Mass arrangement

Full bodied compositions in which a comparatively large amount of plant material is employed is known as a mass arrangement. The grouping as a whole and the colours are more important than line. Mass arrangements may be compact, semi-compact and airy. These may be natural or stylized. Natural effects are suitable in informal rooms, stylized ones have a centre of interest, segregated colours and linear patterns.

9.7.3. Combination of line and mass arrangement

This popular type of arranging is contemporary American in origin. This composition combines the best features of line and mass type arrangements. Design is

Fig. 9.4. Basic shapes in arrangement

emphasized in these arrangements, they are usually stylized. Some popular shapes are the triangle, pyramid, circle, upright, semicircle, crescent and 'S' curve.

The basic line is the main line or backbone of the arrangement. It is the foundation upon which the whole arrangement is built. There are six basic lines in flower arrangements. They are the vertical, horizontal, inverted 'T' and 'L', crescent and Hogarth curve.

The vertical line is perhaps the easiest of all to make. It is a line that possess the qualities of strength and balance and can best be accomplished by the use of rather bold, spiky-type flowers such as gladioli, snapdragons or stocks. The gladiolus with its fully opened flowers at the base of the stem, flowers in the various stages of maturity in the middle, and buds at the top, makes an ideal flower to use, to establish this line. Selection of tall, narrow container will help to accentuate the line. There are many places in the home where vertical arrangements can be used. They may be placed at either ends of a mantel, in a narrow wall space between two doors or windows or in a small wall area in a small hall.

The horizontal line is used for low arrangements when length is needed in preference to height. An arrangement for a mantel, a coffee table or a dinner table might fit into this category. The overall shape using this line may be a symmetrical or asymmetrical triangle, an oval or a rectangle.

An inverted 'T' is a combination of a vertical and a horizontal line and is the basis for the overall shape of a symmetrical triangle. Arrangements using the line of the inverted 'T' can be used in many locations. They are commonly seen as table decorations where a triangular or cone shape is desired. They are often seen at flower show, and they find many uses throughout the home.

Fig. 9.5. Modern arrangement

An 'L' line is also a combination of vertical and horizontal lines and is the basic line for the asymmetrical triangle. The crescent line is one of the more interesting lines in flower arranging. It is characterized by a slow, smooth, rhythmic movement which extends from the high point through the centre to the low point of the area.

Hogarth curve, which derives its name from the English artist William Hogarth, is one of the most interesting and difficult lines in flower arrangement. It is referred to as the "line of beauty" of lazy 'S' and is characterized by its graceful rhythmic motion throughout the arrangement. Basically, the line consists of parts of two crescent lines or two half circles or ovals joining at or near the focal point and flowers in opposite directions to form an overall 'S' or reverse 'S'. The curves may be of equal size one may be larger than the other depending upon the design. If arranged vertically, the lower half of the 'S' is usually smaller than the top and flows across the front of the container. One of the prime requisites of the Hogarth curve is proper balance. This can be achieved by having the ends of the lines at equidistant from the centre line and concentrating the weight of the arrangements at or near the rear of the container.

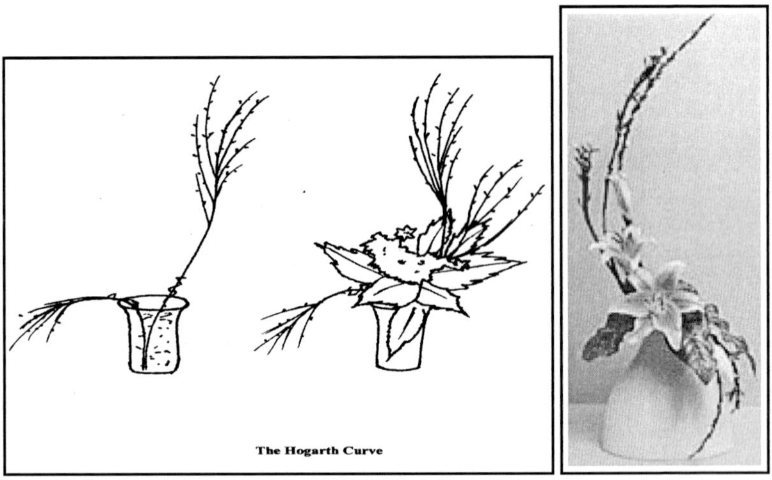

Fig. 9.6. The Hogarth Curve

9.7.4. Miniature arrangement

Small arrangements may be used on food trays at individual placement, at a dining table, in a small end table or in children's play houses. All diminutive arrangements depend largely upon proper scale for success. The size of the flowers, leaves and containers must be consistent. Dolls dishes, lipsticks tubes, perfume vials, thimbles, buttons, bottle caps, egg cup, seashells, ash trays etc., may serve as containers.

A miniature arrangement according to certain garden club classification is the one that does not exceed 6 inches in any dimensions. The arrangement should reproduce in miniature the effect of a large flower arrangement. Small arrangements are those with minimum dimensions of 8 inches. Small zinniah, marigolds, button chrysanthemum work well.

9.7.5. Floating arrangement

Flowers can also be attractively arranged in a different fashion drawing ones' inspirations from such flowers as the lotus and water lilly. One can arrange them in such a way that they seem to be floating in a pond or a tank. The floating arrangements can be made in shallow bowls and trays with flowers whose stems are short. The largest and most attractive flower can be grouped around. The flower should not completely cover up the water and flowers of different colours are used in this type of arrangements.

9.7.6. Dry arrangement

During those months when little or no flowers are available in the garden an arrangement of the dried flowers and foliage is extremely useful from a florist. From a florist or one can obtain a great variety of dried materials. Wood roses, wood berries, poppy heads, cones, eucalyptus, ferns, multitudes of grams and reeds provide suitable materials for flower arrangements. Some may have original lengthy stems but other flowers have to be made lengthier by use of a wire etc. Flowers and foliages can be dried naturally or drying agents can be used.

9.8. Principles of design

Balance

Balance is the visual stability of the arrangements and may be considered in a number of ways. The arrangement should appear to be stable in the container for the sake of balance, the heaviest mass of the plant material the largest flower and the longest stem should be usually be close to a line extending upward from the centre of the container. In symmetrical or formal balance the plant material on one side of the container is approximately equal to the other side. In asymmetrical balance, a heavy weight near the centre is balanced by the lighter weight further away from the centre.

Rhythm

Radiating rhythm occurs in most flower arrangement but particularly in round or triangle compositions where the lines radiate from one place. By proper manipulation of flower sizes and placement – small or partially opened flowers at the extremities and fully opened flowers at or near the focal point and the blending of colours from lighter to darker ones within and toward the base, the feeling of rhythm can be created.

Proportion

The arrangement of the plant material should be in proportion to its setting. As a general rule, the arrangement should be one and one half to two times the height or length of the container whichever is greater.

Emphasis

It is usually drawn to the centre or focal point when the flowers are the largest, most numerous, and brilliant in colour. For the sake of stability the focal point belongs to the centre of the container. In triangular compositions the focal point occurs naturally at the point where the lines converge in the containers. This point must never be left open or weak.

Harmony

Unity is the sense of togetherness, all parts of the composition, including flowers, foliage, container, background and setting should fit together in such a way that there is no discord or conflict among them.

9.9. Summary

Flower arrangement plays a significant role in the interiors and is widely used in all walks of life. The basic styles of flower arrangement includes traditional, oriental and modern. However, most people prefer modern arrangement due to its versatility. The tools and accessories used in the flower arrangement depend on the taste of the individual and is available in wide range in the market. The application of principle of design is also discussed in detail. The taste of the individual is evident in their choosing of tools and accessories.

Exercise

Student Project / Assignment

1. Prepare a teaching module for making dry flowers.

Choose the correct answer

1. Flowers for flower arrangement should be cut

   a. early in the morning b. in the afternoon

   c. in the forenoon d. none of the above

2. When the height exceeds width, the container is usually referred as a

   a. bottle b. bowl

   c. vase d. cup

3. Japanese mode of flower arrangement gives the impression of
   a. fast growth — b. artificial growth
   c. slow growth — d. natural growth

4. One of the prime requisites of the Hogarth curve is
   a. proportion — b. proper balance
   c. rhythm — d. all the above

5. The most suitable arrangement for a dining table is.
   a. vertical arrangement — b. mass arrangement
   c. dry arrangement — d. shallow arrangement

6. The brightest and the largest flower should be placed at the ______ of the arrangement.
   a. lowest — b. top
   c. middle — d. none of the above

7. Wood roses, wood berries and cones are more suitable for
   a. foliage arrangement — b. mass arrangement
   c. dry arrangement — d. floating arrangement

8. The most suitable type of arrangement which can be kept for few month is
   a. foliage arrangement — b. dry arrangement
   c. floating arrangement — d. mass arrangement

9. Standard height rule for arrangement is that in low containers, the tallest stem should be
   a. 1 to 1 ½ times the length of the container
   b. 1 ½ to 2 times the length of the container
   c. 2 times the length of the container
   d. 2 ½ to 4 times the length of the container

10. Modern style of arrangement owes more to
    a. Oriental — b. Traditional
    c. Both traditional and oriental — d. None of the above

Fill in the blanks

1. ______________ may be used for cutting foliages and flowers for flower arrangement (scissors /knives).
2. ___________________includes urns and compote (pedestal, baskets).
3. __________________is suitable for food serving tray (miniature/diminutive).
4. ___________________is also referred to as line of beauty (hogarth curve/circular arrangement).
5. __________________can be made in shallow bowls and trays (floating arrangement/tall arrangement).
6. The size of the __________ arrangement should not exceed 6 inches (miniature/diminutive).
7. ____________is also termed as oasis (florist foam/ pin holders).
8. Flower arrangements should be placed against _________ background (plain/patterned).
9. The stalks of the flowers should be cut in__________. (slanting/horizontal).
10. _____________ should not be combined with fresh flowers while making a flower arrangements (artificial/dry flowers).

Short answers

1. Define miniature arrangement.
2. Differentiate diminutive arrangement from miniature arrangement.
3. Explain the three levels in Japanese arrangement.
4. List the accessories used in flower arrangement.
5. Which arrangement is more suitable for

a. Conference Hall b. Dining table

6. What is florist foam?
7. Name arrangements that can be kept for more than a month?
8. Enlist the special features of a 'Hogarth curve'.
9. List the different types of flower holders used in flower arrangement.
10. What does singeing in flower arrangement refer to?
11. How can the life span / shelf life of flowers be extended?
12. What is the purpose of flower arrangement?
13. How should the woody plants be treated when they are cut for flower arrangement?
14. Give two tips for prolonging the life span of cut flowers.
15. What does shin, soe and hikae in Japanese flower arrangement refer to?
16. Suggest few examples for containers which can be used for miniature arrangement.
17. List out the materials required for dry arrangement.
18. Explain the relevant features of diminutive arrangement.
19. Illustrate any two basic flower arrangements.

Long Answers

1. Discuss the steps in making a flower arrangement.
2. List out the factors to be considered in the selection of containers for flower arrangement.

3. How do accessories enrich/highlight a flower arrangement. Discuss.
4. Explain the role of principles of design in flower arrangement.
5. Bring out the importance of flower arrangement in interiors.
6. Explain with illustration the Japanese flower arrangement.

❏❏❏

CHAPTER 10

Floor and Wall Finishes

10.1. Introduction

Floors are important areas which are readily noticed on entering a room or particular area and they may be both functional and decorative. They cover a tremendous area and are subjected to a great deal of wear and tear. In order that floors should remain in an hygienic condition, and retain as good an appearance for as long as possible, some knowledge of the various types of floor finishes, their advantages, disadvantages and maintenance is necessary. It is essential that the floor finish chosen for any particular place should be suited to the purpose of the room. There may be places where durability and hygiene are of more importance than appearance, for instance in the kitchen, however, appearance is of prime importance in the entrance and living hall where an impression of comfort and quietness is expected; there is no ideal floor surface common for all areas.

10.2. Factors considered while choosing flooring

Appearance

Appearance is usually the first consideration when choosing flooring. It is mainly a matter of personal taste, but there are some guidelines which may help in making a choice. Pale colours, especially blues and greens, as well as shiny colours give a cool appearance, while intense colours and matt surfaces give an impression of warmth. Patterned surfaces tend to make a large room appear smaller, but plain colours make a small room appear larger.

Comfort

Warmth, quietness and softness of floor surfaces are the factors to consider when assessing comfort. People who like to walk about the house in bare feet may regard warmth as a vital factor. To old and disabled people, a non slippery surface is of primary importance and could be a matter of life and death, since more than 50% of the accidents at home are caused by falls.

Durability

Resistance to wear has to be considered in relation to the kind of use the floor has. For example, a living room will need a more hard wearing flooring than a bedroom, a kitchen will need a tougher one than any rooms. Spillages of water, grease and food acids are more likely in some places and will harm certain floorings.

Safety

Safety is of great importance to all occupants of the building. Surfaces should have non-slip qualities when wet and dry and over polishing may cause slipperiness.

Ease of cleaning / maintenance

The floor chosen should lend itself for easy cleaning and should remain so even at the end of the day. Floorings cannot be constantly cleaned, however easy they may be to clean, so for a well maintained flooring, the flooring material, colour and pattern must be carefully selected.

Cost

Cost often limits the choice of flooring. The true cost of a flooring is the initial cost, including laying, plus estimated maintenance cost. Hence care should be taken to choose a flooring that suits the family budget.

Resiliency

Resiliency refers to the ability to minimize sound either by absorbing it or by other means. The floor finishes selected should have this quality, but due consideration is given to this factor while selecting for office premises.

10.3. Classification of floor finishes

Floor finishes may be classified according to their hardness, porosity or the material from which they are made. None is ideal and here they will be classified as hard, semi-hard or soft. A choice may be made from those given in the table.

Table 10.1. Classification of floor finishes

Hard finishes	Semi-hard finishes	Soft floor coverings
Cementious - Terrazzo, granolithic, concrete tiles	Thermoplastic tiles	Carpets-woven and tufted
Stone – marble, slate, quartzite, sandstone, limestone	Vinyl in tile or sheet form	
Ceramic tiles – quarry tiles, brick, mosaic, clay floor tiles	Rubber in tile or sheet form	
Wood- hard woods laid as strip, block or parquet	Linoleum in tile or sheet form	
	Cork in tile or sheet form	

10.3.1. Hard floor finishes

Concrete flooring

Many types of concrete are used for indoor and outdoor areas in the home. Terrazo consists of marble and other decorative chips set in cement and is machine ground to produce a smooth surface. This is harmed by strong alkalis and acids. Wide variety of colours and patterns are available. Granolithic consists of granite chips set in cement. It is a heavy duty flooring and used for basement corridors, store rooms, hallways etc. Concrete tiles are hardwearing aggregate surfaces applied to concrete backing. They have good wearing properties and are available in different sizes.

Qualities of concrete

Concrete is good for areas, which take hard wear, as it is highly resistant to chipping and cracking, scratching, indentation, heat, insects and rot. All types of concrete flooring are easy to clean. Structural concrete flooring and concrete and granolithic paving stones are relatively cheap, while concrete tiles and terrazzo are of medium to high cost.

Stone Flooring

For a natural appearance and an almost indefinite life, stone floors are a good choice. All types of stones are very heavy and must be laid on a solid sub-floor. A variety of marble from the continent provides a wide range of colours including white, green, grey, pink, brown and black.

Marble makes beautiful surround to recessed carpet and can run through from hall to living room. Marble is available in tiles ranging in size from 305 mm (12 inch) upto 450 mm (18 in.) square, but special slabs upto 1.5 m x 900 mm (5 x 3 ft.) can be obtained.

Quartzite is a crystalline rock with a matt finish, the quartz grains give it a slight sparkle. Colours range from silver grey to olive, yellow and gold. Very hardwearing, non slip finish suitable for inside or outside. The thickness of the quartzite depends on the rock formation. Slate is a hard impervious stone obtainable with a polished, sawn or riven surface. Riven slate is split, and the natural undulations give it a rippled surface which is less slippery when wet than a smooth surface. Colours include the blue grey and green. Interior slate slabs are in standard sizes of 457 x 229 mm. (18 x 9 in.), but larger slabs are available upto 2 m x 900 mm (6 ft. 6 in x 3 ft.). Slate makes an excellent kitchen floor and is particularly suitable where the same type of flooring is needed to extend from the house to form a patio or terrace. Sandstones, limestone and granite all make good flooring materials. A popular sand stone is York Stone. Colours include various shades of grey, beige and brown. Sizes vary according to quarry and types - upto 2 x 12 m (6 ft 6 in x 3 ft. 3 in.) although paving stones are usually in smaller random sizes.

Qualities of stone

Stone floors are resistant to wear, water and indentation and to most household chemicals. But marble stains easily from ferrous metals and oils, and limestone and sandstone are stained by oils and fats and are affected by weak acids and alkalis. Slate and quartzite floors have good resistance to stains, when very dirty from spilt oils or fats, they can be easily secured clean. Granite is the most costly form of flooring, with other stone floors varying in price from marble down to local stone. Stone flooring is not expensive if a life of 100 years is required, but it is expensive in circumstances where only a short life is needed. Looking after stone floors in the home is comparatively easy. They can be swept, washed and mopped. For highly resistant stains a scouring powder may be needed. Soap should not be used on marble as it tends to make the floor slippery, detergent is preferable. If a marble floor should become badly stained it can be machine ground by specialists to remove the surface and restore the original colour and texture of the natural stone.

Ceramic flooring

For a long lasting, hardwearing floor that is easy to clean, ceramics are an ideal solution provided warmth and quietness are not important factors of choice. Clay tiles are made from refined natural clays fired at high temperatures and glazed, some are specially made for external use. There is a variety of sizes, shapes, textures, colours and patterns. Some of the commonly well known ones are Vitrified tiles, Eurocon, Johnson etc. Special brick paving stones (pavers) are available which are hard, well fired brick and are available in colours such as red, brown, blue, purple and yellow providing a wide choice suitable for inside or outside. Quarry tiles are made from unrefined clays, hard burnt, and only those of the first quality can be used outdoors. The standard size of 6 inches square and 15mm thick is readily available. Mosaic is of three types -clay, glass and marble. They are made in small squares and other shapes which are assembled into larger areas. Fully vitrified mosaic is made especially for outdoor use. Ideally, mosaic tiles need a solid floor, but they can be laid on a suspended floor over a small area like a shower compartment in a special construction.

Qualities of ceramics

Ceramics are hardwearing, resistant to chipping and cracking, scratching, indentation, heat and fire, acids, water, oils, fats, alkalis, insect and fungal attack. They may crack or break with heavy weights and marks can be difficult to remove if left. All types of ceramic flooring retain their appearance. Quarry tiles and brick mellow with increasing age. Maintenance is comparatively easy, and quarry tiles may be lightly polished occasionally but washing with soap and water is usually sufficient.

Timber Flooring

This flooring, which are mainly uncovered, subjected to a good deal of wear, must be of hard woods which come from broad-leafed trees such as oak, teak, maple, walnut, etc., Any subfloor is suitable for timber, except in the case of hardwood block which requires a solid construction. In all cases the sub floor must be level and damp proof.

Plywood tiles are made to look like wood parquet. Various patterns in herringbone, basket weave or strip are available. Plywood parquet can give a smart appearance initially, but is unsatisfactory in areas of heavy wear. It can be pinned to any timber flooring, but requires plywood underlay when used over floorboards. It is supplied in various squares from 228 mm (9 in.) to 914 mm (3 ft.). Wood mosaic are hardwood fingers arranged in a basket weave pattern are stuck to a sheet of backing material to form panels 457 mm (189 in.) square and 10 mm thick. Very good wearing characteristics and a medium price range have greatly increased the use of wood mosaic.

Floors made of hardwood strip and block are of high quality floor. Woods used include oak, maple, teak and beech. A well maintained hard wood floor improves with age. Hard wood blocks vary in thickness from 19 mm to 31 mm (1 ¼ in.) in sizes upto 305 x 75 mm (12 x 3 in.) Strip is used upto 100 mm (4 in.) wide, and is tongued and grooved to allow concealed nailing. Hardwood block must be laid on a dry solid sub-floor. Blocks are laid with cold bituminous adhesives. A high quality hardwood floor in which special decorative hardwoods are cut into blocks and formed into panels, permitting elaborate geometric designs are called as wood parquet. The panels vary from 25-32 mm (1-11/2 in.) thick in squares from 305 mm (12 in.) to 610 mm (2 ft.). Parquet may be laid over any rigid wooden subfloor. It is rarely used because of its cost and is not to be confused with plywood parquet.

Qualities of Wood

The durability of timber floor depends on good maintenance and on the quality of the timber. Hardwoods are resistant to abrasion and indentation, but they should not be used in wet areas, whether the damp is from above or below. Plywood floors are only as good as the thickness of the decorative surface, and will not withstand heavy wear. Cigarette marks can be removed easily from hardwood floors.

Softwood timber boarding looks good when it has just been sanded and sealed, but does not wear well under heavy use. It is best used as a surround for other flooring, such as carpet. Timber floor are warm to the touch and reasonably resilient. They tend to be noisy, but are not slippery unless too much polish is used. Plywood parquet is the cheapest of timber floors. Wood mosaic and hardwood block and strip come in the medium price range, and wood parquet is in the high cost bracket. A good quality timber floor will repay itself in excellent wear and appearance over the years. There are three methods of maintaining a timber floor - a spirit based wax polish (this is hard work but the appearance will improve with age), an oil resin seal which can be retouched annually, and a hard polyurethane seal which needs to be sanded off and replaced every three or four years. Sealed floors are improved by polish and, as timber is susceptible to water, wax, emulsion polish (which is water based) can only be used when the floor has been sealed. The floor needs a daily sweeping to remove grit and dirt and an occasional light coat of polish.

10.3.2. Semi-Resilient floor finishes

Plastic Flooring

A wide range of colours, designs, textures and prices makes plastic flooring very versatile. Any sub floor is suitable, except for thermoplastic and vinylised thermoplastic tiles, which need a solid construction. But floor boards should first be covered with hardboard or plywood.

Thermoplastic and vinylised thermoplastic tiles

The original thermoplastic tiles have except, for dark colours, been replaced by the vinylised version. Vinylsed tiles are more pliable, less likely to crack and are available in more colours. Sizes are 250 mm (10 in.) and 300 mm (12 in.) square in thicknesses of 2.5 mm and 3mm. As these tiles are fairly rigid they should be laid on a concrete sub-floor. Vinyl asbestos tiles are a development from thermoplastic tiles. The binder is mainly PVC and the tiles are more flexible and durable. Available with textured or embossed finishes which imitate natural materials. Sizes are 225 mm (10 in.) and 300 mm (12 in.) square, and they are in thicknesses of 1.5, 2, 2.5 and 3 mm. Flexible PVC sheet and tiles are plain surfaced or with an embossed or textured finish in the form of tiles or as sheets. Expensive special quality tiles give the appearance of natural stone such as travertine or brick, ceramic tiles or timber. These tiles have an authentic look, but they do not feel like the genuine product underfoot. A high grade material is also available, consisting of coloured PVC chips set in a matrix of clear PVC.

The material is available in tiles or sheet, and sheets may be welded by the installer to avoid open joints. Sheets come in widths of 1.2 m (4 ft.), 1.5 m (5 ft.) and 2 m (6 ft 6 in.). Tiles are squares of 225 mm (9 in.), 250 mm (10 in.) and 300 mm (12 in.) and thicknesses of 2, 2.5 and 3 mm. Large tiles in 500 mm squares are also available in special ranges. Reverse printed PVC are ones in which a pattern is printed on the reverse side of a clear PVC sheet which is in turn bonded to a PVC backing or it may be printed directly on to the backing. This process allows any type of pattern – imitating cork, timber, ceramic floors or others – but its durability is only that of the clear PVC layer which protects the pattern.

Qualities of Plastics

The hardest wear is obtained from those floor which contain a high PVC content in the surface, for example, flexible PVC tiles and sheet and PVC with various backings. These are all resistant to wear, water, indentation and to most household chemicals. Minor bumbs can be removed by rubbing the surface carefully with wire wool. Thermoplastic and vinyl asbestos tiles last well, but thermoplastic tiles are softened by grease and are not ideal for kitchens. Reverse printed PVC is not as durable as some other types and there is no easy method of removing burn marks.

Comfort PVC floors with various forms of backing are thicker and therefore more comfortable to walk on. They are also warmer and quieter than the thin reverse printed PVC and thermoplastic tiles. Plastic floors range from the cheapest reverse printed PVC to the expensive ranges of special PVC tiles with embossed finishes. These can cost as much as the tiles or bricks they imitate. The more expensive the floor, the longer its appearance will be maintained.

Rubber floorings

These are obtainable in tile and sheet form. During manufacture, rubber with filling materials and pigments is vulcanized to give a hard finish and the resulting tiles or sheets may be of many colours. They should be laid in a suitable adhesive on a smooth subfloor, and may be left unprtotected or polished with a water based polish. Rubber flooring is soft, quiet, resilient and comfortable to walk on.

Qualities of rubber flooring

It is extremely durable if properly maintained and a life of twenty to thirty years is not uncommon. It is non-absorbent and resists water. It is harmed by spirit, grease, sunlight, alkalis and coarse abrasives and it marks badly, especially with rubber heels. Oil and grease resistant rubber tiles are now available but the colour ranges are limited.

Linoleum

This consists of a mixture of powdered cork, resin, linseed oil and pigments, put on a foundation of jute canvas and subjected to heat and pressure. The product is passed through polishing rollers and further treatment is given to harden it. In good quality linoleum the colour and pattern are inlaid, ie. right through the backing, whereas in cheap qualities they may only be printed on the surface and so wear off. Linoleum may be bought in rolls, usually 182cm wide or in tiles.

Qualities of linoleum

It is extremely hard wearing but subject to denting and scratching, but there are special toughened form available which does not dent or scratch easily. Linoleum is harmed by coarse abrasives and alkalis, and becomes slippery if over polished. It is marked by cigarette ends and rubber heels, but the marks may be removed by light rubbing with fine steel wool, fine scouring powder or a paraffined rag.

Cork flooring

These are made from granulated cork, moulded into blocks which are subjected to pressure and high temperature. During this process the natural resins bind the granules, and the blocks are then, cut into tiles of the required size and the required thickness usually 0.5 to 1 cm.

Qualities of Cork

Good wear, but has low resistance to indentation. Avoid furniture with highly pointed legs. Untreated cork should not be used in rooms where the floor is likely to get wet, but the PVC faced cork gives protection against splashing. Direct sunlight on cork will bleach out the natural colouring. Cork is warm, quite and resistant, and therefore makes a good flooring for upper corridors, children's rooms and bedrooms. PVC faced cork is slippery when wet, and can be dangerous for flooring bathrooms and kitchens, especially for elderly and infirm people. Clean with a damp mop and polish waxed or untreated tiles occasionally. Sealed tiles and PVC faced tiles should not be polished.

10.4. Wall finishes

Walls are virtually essential for a dwelling; they give protection and privacy, affecting light, heat and sound. Modern concept of interior design has broadened ideas about what walls and ceilings should and should not do.

Wall coverings and finishes

Wall coverings come under three main groups - paint, wall paper and wood paneling. Less frequently used coverings are linoleum, textiles, tiles, and simulated tile.

The structural finish of the wall may be plaster, concrete block, brick, glass brick, tile, wood or wall board. At present wide variety of wall finishes are available in different colours, textures, and pattern.

Wall covering

Plaster and stucco

Plaster is a thick, pasty mixture of treated gypsum and water, combined with such materials as sand and lime.

Stucco refers to weather–resistant plaster most often on exteriors. Like concrete, plaster and stucco will hold any shape given to them before they harden. They can smoothly cover simple or complex surfaces with no visible joints. Under some conditions both plaster and stucco create maintenance problems. Cracks or chips are common unless precautions are taken. Although not expensive, the original cost of plaster is higher than for many of the hard boards, which provide insulation against heat, cold and noise. It often cracks or chips.

Laminates

A popular process of binding together layers of various materials with resins and plastic has resulted in a variety of novel, extremely useful wall covering. Laminated sheets are durable and resistant to heat. They are easily cleaned with a damp cloth. Marble effects and beautiful natural effects can be obtained in laminated sheets. Laminates are available in different patterns and textures. Wood laminates are very popular.

Laminated wood is a type of plywood in which the grain of successive layers goes in the same direction. Factory - built wall panels of plywood have been used both as structure and as surface, interior and exterior, of a house. Made of synthetic resin, fabric, and paper laminated plastics are used in kitchens and bathrooms as wainscoting or as an entire wall finish.

Glass

Clear glass may be used as an entire window wall, while patterned glass is usually used for a divider wall. Patterned glass walls let in more light than opaque walls, but they are translucent enough to give privacy, clear glass improves indoor and outdoor relationships and gives spacious effect. If tinted glass is used, privacy is obtained. Glass needs frequent cleaning. It is a poor insulator for heat and cold. It is easily breakable.

Mirror tiles

Mirror tiles are current favourite on walls because they create an illusion of spaciousness. Many metals can be given reflecting finishes, but mirrors as we usually think of them consist of glass with a metallic backing that provides make walls seem warmer. However they are difficult to clean and tend to be expensive and in most cases, joints show prominently.

Wood paneling

During the gothic period wood paneling was the principal wall finish. Wood finishes have a reassuring air of permanency. Precut and prefinished paneling comes in natural wood finishes nearly walnut, birch, mahogany, pine, fruitwood, maple and oak. These panels are usually upto 2400 by 1200 mm (approximately 8 by 4 ft) and made to interlock. They give a handsome finish to living, dining, recreation and family rooms and to the library. The wood panels fixed horizontally at top and bottom of wall and vertically correspond with width of the board or they can be stuck direct to plaster, brick, concrete or wood using a new gap filling wall board adhesive that is sold in cartridges by builders merchant. Often a wood finish is used only on one or two walls, with an interesting wall paper on the other walls. True wood paneling is much more expensive then plywood paneling.

Tongued and grooved boarding

It is popular, especially as a reasonably quick and long lasting covering for walls in bad condition in older properties. It is very simple and handy for a person to use. Each board has a tongue running along its length one side and a groove along its length on the other. The tongue from one board fits into the groove of the next, and so on. We must treat the boarding with 2 coats of polyurethane varnish (or glass) for a dirt - resistant finish. Alternately painting it, or use a colour wood stain plus varnish.

Glass brick

With the development of modern architecture, glass brick is sometimes used as a wall finish. Glass bricks are distortion free reflections of whatever in front of them. They can be applied effectively to an area, but care should be taken since mirrors multiply images and overall effect may be cluttered. Mirrors should not be placed opposite to seating areas, as they tend to make people self conscious.

Ceramic tiles

Ceramic glazed or unglazed tiles are highly desirable wall coverings especially for kitchen, bathroom and other utility areas.

Tiles come in standard sizes, many ranges are sold in packs, small square tiles are 108 by 108 mm (4 ¼ by 4 ¼″), those look particularly neat in small rooms. The large size of tile available measures 152 by 152 mm (6 by 6″) looking perhaps slightly more old fashioned. Rectangle tiles (sometimes called border tiles) are available in 216 by 108 mm (8 ½ by 4 ¼″) .

In addition to standard square and rectangle special tile effects are also available. Hexagonal wall tiles are also available; they fit together like a patch work. There is also wall mosaic, tiny ceramic tiles in various shapes, including rounds and hexagons, which come in sheets about 300 mm (6″) square. Patterned tiles are usually more expensive especially hand printed tiles.

Mosaic tiles are very attractive. Because of its durability and easy maintenance, ceramic tile is a favourable finish for certain wall areas. True ceramic tile is expensive and somewhat difficult to apply. Tiles are available in many delightful colours and designs and are relatively easy to fix.

Linoleum

Linoleum is a mixture of wood flour, ground cork, gum, linseed oil and pigments, though mainly used as a floor covering, its use as a wall covering is becoming popular for certain sections of interior walls. It is available in sheets. As a wainscot finish with a border, a linoleum is some times used on walls in nurseries, playrooms, kitchens and bathrooms.

Cork tiles

Cork tiles made specifically for walls are now widely available, they are sold in packs in various sizes. Used for a smaller area, they make an attractive pin up board. Used over a larger area, they will deaden noise and improve insulation. Thinner types (3 mm - 1/8″ thick) are available plain or mottled. Thicker types (13 mm - 1 1/2″) are sold specifically for insulating purposes and have an attractive dark brown colour and a rough granular texture.

Adhesive cork tiles are stuck up with contact adhesive. You will need to apply adhesive both to the wall and to the back of the tiles, waiting for a few minutes until both are touch dry before pressing into place. Be sure to coat tile edges to prevent shrinkage and ensure satisfaction of joints.

Cork tiles can be bought with a bonded vinyl finish that requires no treatment, or they can be treated with a wax polish or clear polyurethane varnish. Cork wall coverings improve insulation against heat loss. Naturally, the thicker panels provide more insulation against noise transmission and heat loss; they also make better pin boards.

Asbestos

New colours and textures make asbestos an interesting material. It may resemble wood if painted. It costs less and upkeep is easy. It has high resistance to fire; weather and insect.

Wall fabrics

Fabric wall coverings are very appealing; they add a touch of softness to any room, and thicker types will also strong and provide heat insulation. Bricks used as walls are translucent, thus admitting some light but ensuring privacy within the area closed. Other bricks which are transparent are often etched or painted and used purely as decoration.

Vinyl

Most vinyls are patterned to resemble wall papers, although they are far more resistant to wear and easier to clean than ordinary papers. Colours tend to be brighter. Some vinyl's are plain coloured, but textured to imitate fabrics. Using this type of textured vinyl, we can achieve the look of a fabric, at a cost considerably lower than the real things. Fabric-look vinyls wear well and can be cleaned easily. The new metallic vinyls are also worth mentioning as the designs look spectacular upon the wall, although they are not cheap to buy.

Wall paper

Wall papers present a real challenge to the interior decorators imagination. This is the most popular of all wall coverings, as it has an extensive range in colour and design as well as price. Its history is interesting. The first papers were imported from abroad, chiefly from China. They were used like tapestries, mounted and hung, but not stuck, on the walls. It is the cheapest and commonest form of wall covering. The main types of wall paper are:

Ordinary surface printed papers

Spongeable papers, specially treated during manufacture to withstand water.

Anaglypta, which has an embossed or raised pattern. It is white and normally painted over except when used as a ceiling paper.

Wood chip papers, which have interlayered chips of wood, are usually cream in colour and are normally painted over.

Oatmeal papers, where texture is produced by the interlayering of wood dust, chopped straw or similar material during manufacture.

Flock papers, which are treated with adhesive to which silk, wool, cotton or synthetic fibres stick to give a raised pile.

Wood grain papers, photographic reproductions of various wood grains, waxed during manufacture.

Metallic papers, printed with metallic powders and paper backed felts.

Advantages

1. It can be used in any room in the home.
2. It is available in many colours, pattern and textures and in varying degrees of durability.
3. It is a quick and easy way to remodel with or self adhesive tapes.
4. It makes a room seem to become large or small, gain height or reduce height, become more active or passive.
5. It minimizes architectural defects.
6. It hides disfigured walls.
7. It makes rooms with little furniture seems furnished. It distracts attention from miscellaneous furniture.

Disadvantages

After two or three layers have been applied to wall they must be removed before a new finish is applied. Soaking the paper with hot water, scraping it off is a common method applied. There are some varieties that can be stripped off and used again. But with a wrong choice of wall, changing every time is more difficult than repainting.

Choice of wall paper

In choosing wall paper, patterns, colours and texture are important. The patterns should be in accordance with the purpose and size of the room. Vertical lines lend height, horizontal lines minimize height and are restful. Small patterns look better in small rooms, and large patters in large rooms. Texture is also an important consideration in selecting wall paper. Overly rough and overly shiny texture should be avoided.

Principles of design must be applied in selecting figured wall paper – proportion, balance, and harmony of shapes and sizes. For bedrooms, - papers with restful designs and in light colours are advisable. Steam proof or washable papers, which have a thin coating of plastic, are ideal for bathroom and kitchen which are subjected to heavy condensation.

A much stronger, really washable paper is made of vinyl. It will withstand practically every form of stain and has flame resistant outer coating. A ready pasted vinyl paper is also available which just has to be dipped in a trough of water and then hung. Thin wall paper is inclined to tear when pasted and handled and may be difficult to hang.

Avoid putting wall paper on to damp walls as this may cause the growth of moulds and discolor the paper. Newly plastered walls should not be papered until they are perfectly dry which takes 6-9 months.

Paint

Almost any interior walls can be painted in any colour. It is quick and easy to apply and it is relatively inexpensive.

Essentially paint is a mixture of three basic ingredients, pigment, solvent and binder. Pigment determines colour, solvent a volatile substance that carries pigment and binder acts as a fixer.

Some important paints are

1. *Sealer and primary paint :* A sealer and primary paint is necessary on any new surface – wood or plaster to fill in the pores and give a good painting base.
2. *Undercoat:* On non-porous surfaces, an in expansible undercoat gives a good base for the final coat of paint or enamel.
3. *Oil base paints :* These come in flat, semi gloss and gloss finishes, and they are usually thinned with mineral spirits or paint thinner. Two coats of oil base paints are needed – three coats if a very light colour is painted over a dark colour. Flat oil paints give an attractive finish for all rooms except the kitchen and bathroom, but it is somewhat difficult to wash as it absorbs grease and oil.
4. *Enamel :* It comes as high gloss, semi gloss and low gloss. It dries with a very smooth hard finish. Before applying enamel, rub the surface lightly with fine sand paper and wipe with a cloth slightly dampened with turpentine.
5. *Alkyd :* These paints are thinned with mineral sprits and an undercoat is necessary. This type paint comes in flat, semi gloss and gloss finishes. Alkyd paint is durable, washable and transparent to light, brush marks do not show.
6. *Latex:* This is some times referred to as rubber base paint, but true rubber-base paint requires a strong volatile solvent. Latex paint is thinned with water. This paint is less expensive than oil base paint, is easy

to use, and dries with a durable finish. It has little odour, does not show brush marks, covers well and dries in about 30 minutes.

7. *Vinyl:* Vinyl paint is thinned with water. It is washable, easy to apply, dries fast, covers well and has very little odour.

8. *Calcimine:* This is a water soluble paint made of uniting glue, water and colour pigment. It cannot be washed.

9. *Varnish :* Varnish is a colourless liquid which gives a firm hard surface. Varnish comes in dull, semi gloss and high gloss finishes. A special finish must be used for out side surfaces. Varnish should be applied only in dry weather and only when there is ventilation. It takes atleast 24 hours to dry. There are clear streakless varnishes that may be applied to wall paper to make it washable.

10.5. Summary / Exercises

Student project / Assignment

1. Prepare a project report on choice for floor and wall finishes for different interiors. Analyse their suitability to the interiors.
   a. Office room and corridor
   b. Classroom
   c. A road side restaurant (Motel)
   d. Shopping centres
   e. Furnishing showroom
   f. Interior designers/architects consulting room

Choose the correct answer

1. The most commonly used wall finishes by a middle income group is

   a. paint b. tiles c. wall papers

2. A kitchen counter top material should be

   a. resistant to any kind of stain

   b. resistant to action of acids and alkalies

   c. colour scheme

3. Use of ________________ as wall finishes tends to create illusion of space in interiors.

   a. mirrors b. wall papers c. murals

4. Granolite is a ________________.

   a. floor finish b. paint c. cork tile

5. Wood panelling is more suited for ___________.

   a.warm environment b.cold environment c. desert region

Fill in the blanks

1. ____________ is one of the constituents of a paint (binder/asbestos).
2. Self sticking adhesive coating is given for ________________ (tiles/wall papers).
3. Additional ceiling can also be called as ________________ (false ceiling/elevated ceiling).
4. The most widely used floor materials by a low income group is ________________ (cement flooring/mosaic flooring).
5. ____________________ tiles have the quality of transparency (glass/ceramic).

State true or false

1. Wall papers can only be used in hotels and hospitals.
2. The quality of a paint is determined by the rate of drying.

3. Murals can be used only as wall decorations.
4. Wooden flooring is more suitable for hilly areas.
5. Stone flooring is hot during summer seasons.

Questions

1. What are the factors to be considered while choosing a floor covering?
2. Explain the term hard floor finishes.
3. Write short notes on
   - Concrete flooring
   - Ceramic flooring
   - Timber flooring
4. What are resilient floor finishes?
5. State the characteristics of Vinyl and Linoleum.
6. Give an account of various wall finishes used in interiors.
7. What is wood panelling?
8. State the advantages and disadvantages of wall papers.
9. Explain the types of wall papers.
10. Discuss paints as a wall finish for modern interiors.

❑❑❑

REFERENCES

Borkar, S., 'A text book of applied art', Himalaya publishing house, Mumbai, 2003.

Branson, J. C., Lennox, M. 'Hotel, Hostel and Hospital Housekeeping', ELBs, Hodder and Stonghton Limited, Britain. 1996.

Bridger, R. S. 'Introduction to ergonomics', Taylor and Francis, London. 2003.

Deutch, Y. (Ed.). 'Curtains and cushions – Exciting ways to beautify your home', Marshall Cavendish Publications Limited, London, 1976.

Driscoll, M., and Skolnik, L., 'Lampshades and Lighting – The project and decorative source book', Rockport Publishers, Massachusetts, 2002.

Goldlstein, H. and Goldstein, V. 'Art in Every day Life', Fourth Edition, The MacMillan Company, New York. 1958.

Grandjean, E, 'Fitting the task to the Man – An ergonomic approach', Taylor and Francis, London, 1985.

Hess, K. P. 'Textile fibres and their use', Oxford and IBH publishing company, New Delhi.

Indian Standards Institutions, New Delhi, IS: 3634 (Part I) – 1966.

Mann, M. K. 'Home Management for Indian families' 4th revised edition, Kalyani publishers, Delhi, 1984.

Peet, L. J., Picklett, M. S., and Aronold, M. G. 'Household Equipment' – Eighth Edition, John Wiley and Sons, New York, 1979.

Philips, B. (Ed), 'Readers Digest Household Manual', The Readers Digest Association Limited, London.

Rao, M. R. 'Interior design – Principles and practice', Standard Publishers Distributors, Delhi, 1998

Raul, J. 'Dictionary of Textiles', Anmol publications Pvt. Ltd., New Delhi, 1998.

Rutt, A. H., 'Home furnishing', Second Edition, Wiley Eastern Private Ltd., New Delhi, 1961.

Seetharaman, P. and Pannu, P. 'Interior design and decoration', CBS publishers and distributors, New Delhi, 2005

Sundarraj, S. 'A text book of Household Arts' Orient Longman Ltd., Madras, 1991.

Varghese, M. A., Ogale, N. N., and Srinivasan, K. 'Home Management' Wiley Eastern Limited, New Delhi, 2001.

Wingate, B. 'Textile fabrics and their selection', Prentice Hall of India. Private Limited, New Delhi, 1995.

Yates, M. Fabrics – 'A guide for interior designers and architects'. W. W. Norton and Company, New York. 2002.

❑❑❑

Conversion Formula

Non - Metric to Metric

Linear

To convert	Multiply by
inches into millimeters	2.54
inches into centrimeters	2.540
inches into metres	2.540 x 10
feet into centimeters	30.48
feet into metres	0.3048
yards into metres	0.9144
miles into metres	1609.344
miles into kilometers	1.609344

Area

To convert	Multiply by
sq. inches into sq.centrimetres	6.4516
sq. feet into sq. centimeters	929.03
sq. feet into sq. metres	0.092903
sq. yards into sq. metres	0.8361
sq. miles into sq. kilometers	2.58999

sq. miles into hectares	258.999
acres into sq. metres	4046.856
acres into hectares	0.40469

Metric to non Metric

Linear

To convert	Multiply by
millimetres into inches	0.03937
millimetres into feet	3.281 x 10
centimetres into inches	0.3937
metres into feet	3.281
metres into yards	1.09361
kilometres into yards	1093.61
kilometres into miles	0.62137

Area

To convert	Multiply by
sq. millimeters into sq. inches	1.550 x 10
sq. centimeters into sq. inches	0.1550
sq. meters into sq. feet	10.7639
sq. metres into sq. yards	1.19599
sq. metres into acres	2.47105 x 10
sq. kilometers into sq. miles	0.3861
sq. kilometers into acres	247.105
hectares into acres	2.47105

ABOUT THE AUTHORS

Dr. (Mrs.) P. Parimalam, Associate Professor is in the Department of Family Resource Management in Home Science College and Research Institute, Tamil Nadu Agricultural University, Madurai. She is involved in teaching, research and extension activities in the area of resource management. She has carried out research projects funded by agencies such as ICAR, DST and UGC. She has published several articles in the National and International journals.

Dr. (Mrs.) A. Andal, is the Dean, Home Science College and Research Institute, Tamil Nadu Agricultural University, Madurai. She is involved in teaching and research for more than three decades. She has guided several Masters' researchers and has carried out several research projects in various fields of Home Science. In recognition of her teaching, she has been awarded with "Best Teacher Award" by Tamil Nadu Agricultural University in 2001. She has been instrumental in the development of different faculties in Home Science. She has authored two books and has presented several research papers in National and International Conferences.

Dr.(Mrs.) M. R. Premalatha, is Professor and Head, Department of Family Resource Management, Home Science College and Research Institute, Tamil Nadu Agricultural University, Madurai. She is the Academic Co-ordinator of the College. She is involved in teaching for more than 29 years and has guided several Masters' and Doctoral researchers. She has authored two books and has presented several research papers in National and International conferences. She has undergone six months of training in Canada.